Motivated Learning

Originally published in 1966, Dr Hebron provides a comprehensive account in this book of the main theories of motivation and learning as applicable to each phase of the human life cycle at the time. She synthesises current theories by placing each within the context of the developmental phase for which it has the greatest significance; and she provides 350 supporting references.

Each stage of human development is discussed separately, through infancy, early childhood, the transitional intuitive phase, middle childhood, and adolescence, to maturity and senility. Two chapters are devoted to adolescence, and there is interesting material on the gifted adolescent. The chapter on physiology describes with clarity the changes in physical structure and function which ensue as children enter into their cultural heritage, as adults become socially involved, and as the elderly undergo gradual disengagement.

The book was addressed to the more advanced student preparing for the newly instituted degrees in education, to post-graduates in education, and to students in their third year of degree courses in psychology and sociology. Today it can be read in its historical context.

Motivated Learning

A Developmental Study from Birth to the Senium

Miriam E. Hebron

Routledge
Taylor & Francis Group
LONDON AND NEW YORK

First published in 1966
by Methuen & Co Ltd

This edition first published in 2026 by Routledge
4 Park Square, Milton Park, Abingdon, Oxon, OX14 4RN

and by Routledge
605 Third Avenue, New York, NY 10158

Routledge is an imprint of the Taylor & Francis Group, an informa business

A Library of Congress record exists under LCCN: 66070974

ISBN: 978-1-041-23395-4 (hbk)
ISBN: 978-1-003-73690-5 (ebk)
ISBN: 978-1-041-23401-2 (pbk)

Book DOI 10.4324/9781003736905

Motivated Learning

A DEVELOPMENTAL STUDY
FROM BIRTH TO THE SENIUM

BY

MIRIAM E. HEBRON
Senior Lecturer
in the
Department of Psychology
University of Hull

METHUEN & CO LTD
11 NEW FETTER LANE LONDON EC4

First published 1966

Printed in Great Britain by
Butler & Tanner Ltd, Frome and London

Foreword

In this book I have attempted to show the relevance of the various theories of motivation and learning as applicable to the seven ages of man. Both physiological and psychological components have been considered, and at each developmental phase emphasis has been placed on those most relevant. Supporting references have been included which may be helpful to a reader wishing to gather further information concerning the methodology of research or further knowledge of the literature in a particular field.

The book is addressed to students in psychology and in the fields of child and adult education. Since it is concerned with the complete life cycle, those interested in a particular phase of development may find the whole of significance for the antecedents and outcomes of its characteristic behaviours. Moreover, as no motivational or learning pattern ever falls into complete desuetude, the macro- viewpoint should contribute to an understanding of specific learning at later ages. The learning of infancy is sometimes experienced in maturity, as any student knows who has attempted to learn a new and hitherto unpractised technique.

The age span covered by each chapter increases from two years at infancy to thirty in maturity. Adolescence, however, has received attention in two chapters, one of which has been devoted to the development of the gifted adolescent. I have begun with a chapter on the physiology underlying the psychological processes, because it is particularly helpful to an understanding of motivation in infancy, early childhood, and the senium. Even a general idea of what may be happening in the 'black-box' of the soma can illuminate theories of behaviour.

I am grateful to my colleagues Professor A. D. B. Clarke and Professor C. I. Howarth for reading some of the chapters and for their helpful comments. My thanks are due to Professor D. B. Lindsley for permission to use a combination of two of his diagrams of the nervous system for the figure on page 22.

M.E.H.

June 1965

Contents

Introduction

The purpose of this book is to consider current theories of motivation and to suggest how each is particularly applicable to a certain phase in the human developmental cycle from birth to senility. This does not imply that each is relevant only to a particular stage of development, for motivation is a global aspect of the personality and its several major dimensions are continually operative. It should be possible, however, if the thesis of this book is correct, for a profile of the various dimensions of motivation, which is characteristic of each developmental phase, to be constructed. Such profiles would indicate that some dimensions contribute more than others to the process of maturation, because of their primacy in pacing the experiential front.

1 *The interaction between nature and nurture*

An organism is motivated to behave as it does because it is constructed to operate in a characteristic manner. Structure and process are thus essential built-in aspects of motivation. On the other hand, the change of structure and process which occurs on account of motivational urge is termed learning. Therefore any learning alters to some extent the motivational pattern. For this reason the environment cannot be ignored as a source of motivation. Yet it is the environment as perceived by the individual organism which is significant, and responses can be understood fully only in terms of this subjective determination. Mace (1946) includes both the idiosyncratic and the cultural stereotype in his threefold summary of the reasons why a man works. First he may want to, when in his perception the response appears as pleasurable; secondly he may accede to the expectations of others that he should do so, because he perceives it as an act of social adaption; thirdly he feels he must, because desisting from work may be disadvantageous. These categories imply systems of motives and it is the task of this book to discuss the psycho-genesis of these phenomena.

2 *Theories stem from techniques of research*

Research into motivation is peculiarly difficult because the methodology of observation must take account of the whole self in action. Moreover, such studies of spontaneous behaviour are limited by the environmental setting of observation. For this reason theories of the essential aspects of personality and motivation tend to stem as much from the observational opportunity afforded by the environment as from the continuing nature of the organism. For example the professional interests and circumstance of the observer limit his viewpoint although he may observe his subjects in the round, as it were. This may be seen in Rogers' (1951) client centred therapy which resulted in the formulation of numerous 'laws' governing the maturation of the self; Horney (1937) and Fromm (1941) emphasised the importance of the culture pattern in personality development because of their professional observations in two cultures in one of which they were regarded as neurotics and out-groupers, in the other as welcome aliens; Hull's (1952) concept of man as a creature of drive and habit would tend to occur to someone working among the lower mammals. Thus psychologists have formulated a variety of theoretical viewpoints concerning the nature of motivation and each might be regarded as the rationalisation of a technique. Yet all are valid methods of approach to an exceedingly complex problem and it is to be expected that there will ensue eventually a gradual integration of the viewpoints into a single schema. Meanwhile, the diversity is wholesome, for there are as many facets to the personality as there are situations common to humanity. From this it follows that either a change in the organism (through pervasive mutation), or in the institutions in which it inheres, would result in the production of a new personality type. The aim of the psychologist, however, is to discover general laws both genetic and environmental which will explain how such motivational changes are brought about.

3 *Freud's theory of stratification*

Freud was a pioneer in this field of psycho-genetics and his theories burst upon the western civilised world with far-reaching effects. His discoveries were the outcome of his background, both professional and personal, but in his case their confluence was particularly auspicious for an understanding of child development. The three aspects of his environment which contributed richly to his thinking were his training in physiology, his observation of his patients with cultural and socio-economic trends held constant, and his intense interest in the familial reactions of his own children. His inspired guesses concerning the relationship between these three sets of phenomena led to the first coherent system of stratification of personality, extending from birth to maturity, which attempted to explain both child and abnormal behaviour in a developmental sequence. Mental disorder was seen by him as a partial arrest of development, and the earlier in life this occurred the more severe and fundamental the subsequent deviation from normal. Although Freud's work has been pruned considerably by experimental enquiry, much of it has been confirmed and there is no doubt that many of the traits commonly selected for observation derive from his writings. His theory is usually associated with abnormal psychology, but in actual fact he always regarded the neurotic as a special case of the normal. He wrote " – neuroses have no peculiar psychic content of their own which is not also found in healthy people. Or as Jung has expressed it neurotics fall ill of the same complexes against which we healthy people struggle" (Freud 1910).

The value of Freud's work stems from its seminal quality. It gave a great fillip to research in providing an abundance of hypotheses for investigation. For example his theory of projection may be contrasted with the approach to developmental changes in perception of William Stern. The former implied that perception is a selective process determined by a person's needs and that it is not merely recognitory. Stern's viewpoint was confined to a study of recognitory norms. There is no doubt that Freud's viewpoint has had the more revolutionary effect in our understanding of perception. Studies of projection seek explanations in terms of antecedent states and thus have special relevance for a psycho-genetic study of motivation. It is true that facility in the perceptual act is a matter of habit rather than drive, but past drives lie behind this facility. The emotive factor is thus psycho-genetically prior to the skill.

4 *Methods of research*

Experimental verification of hypotheses in the field of child development is fraught with methodological difficulties. To observe the growth of a group of human beings in their natural environments of family, neighbourhood and nation in an effort to establish the antecedents of more mature manifestations is a slow process enduring for many years. A recent survey of the major longitudinal studies at present operating in America (Kagan 1964) reveals that the subjects of the most long-standing project are now forty-four years old. The most recent was started in 1956. One of medium length is that of the Fels institute (Kagan and Moss 1962). Its subjects have now reached maturity and it has been possible to examine the relationship between caretaking style and practice, and adult attitudes in society and marriage. Such results are less ambiguous because of the maintenance of the identity of the subject as he develops in the view of the observers. This makes possible an observation of sequential changes in caretaking styles and of the ages at which they occur. Such sequences appear to be crucial and it is clear that longitudinal studies are an essential type of research for this reason alone.

It would seem a short cut to the same end, if representative cross-sections of society were studied for each age group, yet such studies have produced an abundance of conflicting results. There are two reasons for this. In the first place it is difficult to ensure the reliability of sampling, especially in the study of young children, and in the second, age groups may have been differentially affected by socio-economic conditions, changes in educational opportunity, wars, and developments in techniques of communication. The dynamic state of social life in a technological age militates constantly against valid interpretation of developmental norms by means of cross-sectional studies. This criticism applies less to longitudinal studies for all significant changes tend to affect all the subjects contemporaneously, and these pervasive influences are thus held constant for the group (Laslett 1962).

A similar vagueness attaches to the results of comparative studies in which different socio-economic groups are measured for incidence, say, of corporal punishment as a technique of child rearing. From counting the incidence and assessing intensity in working-class and middle-class groups, the conclusion may be drawn that there is a tendency for working-class mothers to punish corporally. An examination of the data usually reveals, however, a very great resemblance between the two groups with a very small difference of from 5 to 10 per cent. This difference may be statistically significant for the group, but it is not present in 90 per cent of it. Group differences of this order are virtually useless as a means of establishing antecedents to mature behaviour patterns and are probably not directly related to the differentiating criterion of socio-economic class. It is more probable that there is some genetic factor which is both the cause of economic decline and a tendency to become severely exacerbated by child behaviour. Conversely a common cause may facilitate both a rise in the economic scale and a tolerance of children's nuisance value. Similar difficulties of interpretation are present when heads are counted in inter-cultural studies. Young (1946) presents a comparative table in an attempt to equate child-rearing practices with tribal characteristics, but it is highly dubious whether child-rearing practice would lead to such end results unless there was continual cultural reinforcement after early childhood. For this reason, perhaps, the anthropologist today is tending to report observations of cultural practices and stereotypes using a standard cross-sectional method of observation (Whiting 1963), rather than attempting to relate caretaking practices to the national character and mores. Here as elsewhere, cross-sectional studies can lead to the establishment of facts from which antecedents cannot be reliably deduced.

Multifactorial analysis of data in a cross-sectional study is of value in demonstrating which are the most pervasive influences among the population observed. For example, permissiveness-strictness appears to be the most general differentiating trait among parents (Sears et al. 1957). The effectiveness of this approach, however, is dependent entirely upon the acumen with which the variables are selected, for the factors depend on the kinds of traits assembled. But choice of areas for measurement may be justified in terms of previous research and by other criteria, and there is no doubt that well-designed factorial analyses can provoke further research through the hypothetical interpretation of factors. The greatest value of the technique lies in its demonstration of variables relevant for longitudinal studies and other experimental approaches. Conclusions drawn from all studies based on correlation can never be more than hypothetical regarding causation, but concomitant variation implies usually some relationship which other research methods can elucidate.

Longitudinal studies of deprivation would appear to be a ready made experimental approach, with a dependent variable built into the situation. When the development of the deprived baby is compared with the normally situated infant, inferences may be drawn that the missing antecedents are the cause of any positive qualities which the deprived personality comes to lack. One of the difficulties in such studies, however, lies in establishing controls which are precisely the same except for the area of deprivation. It is necessary to establish that the control groups have the same genetic endowment and are subjected to the same caretaking as the deprived group, both before and after the period of deprivation. It is virtually impossible to achieve this. Neonate groups can be equated for normality of birth, freedom from birth-injury and health of mother, but attempts to establish adequate controls for deprived groups at later ages have failed dismally, and antecedents in caretaking have been confused with genetic endowment or the effects of ill-health or a weak constitution in the experimental group. Where there has been no previous caretaking as in the neonate and where physiological normality can be established, there is more chance of a longitudinal study proving reliable in a comparison of deprived and normally situated babies. It is disconcerting, however, when the effects of deprivation appear to be dissipated by subsequent environmental amelioration. This negates the conclusion that the missing element was an antecedent determiner. It is possible, however, that this recovery of lost ground may conceal some continuing effects of privation. In a careful follow-up of institution babies for five years after their adoption, Provence and Lipton (1962) concluded that their dramatic gains obscured developmental defects to the casual view.

To sum up it might be said that the only reliable technique which can lead to information concerning the early origins of behavioural structure and process is the longitudinal one. All others should be ancillary to this. In relation to them such terms as 'tends to' and 'is suggestive of' are necessary qualifiers, but in the longitudinal study facts rather than guesses may be asserted about the antecedents of mature behaviour patterns.

5 *Learning and motivation*

Increasing attention is being given in longitudinal studies to motivational patterns, i.e. acquiring the capacity to set about the business of learning. Motivation in this sense is a more subtle concept and less amenable to observation than the end results of such activity. For this reason the growth of skills has been studied more extensively than the development of a 'learning to learn' facility. This aptitude is exemplified in such traits as capacity for forming emotional relationships, for defensive and adaptive approaches, for enjoyment and for imaginative initiative (Provence and Lipton 1962). These dynamic motivators are more in the nature of habits of orientation rather than the actual mental process itself. They are the prerequisites of mental processes which lend relevance to the mental processes which follow. The end result is learning of some kind, but its flexibility, comprehensiveness and areas of peak clarity are largely dependent on the motivational dynamics of the organism when stimulated. It is not outside the bounds of possibility that 'learning to learn' in infancy and early childhood is the most basic determiner of intelligence. The differences which exist between individuals in capacity to learn may derive not from a better 'brain' but from some system which activates the brain prior to its mental operations. This postulates an elemental orientation of the whole organism which has become habitual to the merest stimulus and which was acquired basically in infancy and early childhood. Such a concept is nearer to motivation than to thinking.

A basic capacity for learning to learn appears to be acquired at a time when motivation is mainly autistic, and it is consequently based in spontaneous desire and impulse. For this reason a happy confluence between environmental opportunity and spontaneity of behaviour is desirable. In later years, even in old age, the same principle may be observed. There is less unlearning and decline of potency in new learning where this confluence between enjoyed activities and environmental opportunity is maintained. It is a more specific phenomenon in maturity affecting behaviour in specialised areas, but it is the same motivational phenomenon. Learning to learn declines as well as learning, and it is possible that the former is psychologically prior in pacing the onset of the senium.

6 *Plan of the book*

Since motivation and learning are so closely integrated in a continuous process the two concepts must be considered together. It is obvious that the learning of today enters into the motivation of tomorrow. This continuous process of re-structuring calls for a cybernetic explanation, and for this reason the first chapter will be concerned with the physiology of motivation. This is an aid in subsequent discussion of each stage of development when considering the interplay of genetic factors and environmental influences. In addition, it seemed helpful to delineate developmental phases according to the postulations and techniques of Freud and Piaget. Both imply the same sequence of development and similar emergent characteristics. Freud's has the advantage of leaning towards the bio-social, while Piaget contributes empirically derived age norms and a study of mental processes in greater detail. A consideration of the processes of maturation in thinking would seem desirable since motivational levels appear to be geared to a large extent to cognitive efficiency, through the individual's perceptual impact on the environment (Granger 1953). Freudian and Piaget type theory lend themselves to a discussion of both the emotive and the cognitive aspects of motivation, and both sources are drawn on in planning each chapter. Information contributed by other types of research is introduced where relevant, and the discussion above of the reliability of conclusions which can be drawn from these various approaches should obviate the necessity of hedging statements about with precautionary qualification.

CHAPTER I

The physiology of motivation and learning

I. THE MECHANISMS OF ATTENTION

1 *Arousal and activation*

Although much remains obscure concerning the relationship between physiological and psychological functions, it is perhaps true to say that the major organs of motivation have been identified. These are concerned mostly with the mechanisms which underlie attention on the one hand and maturational levels of functioning on the other.

Attention is a key concept in the phenomenon of motivated learning and the correlative term in physiological psychology is 'arousal'. Arousal is a term which has reference to changes in the chemico-electrical aspects of the nervous system. For example, the electro-encephalogram indicates graphically whether the wave pattern of the brain is slow or fast, deeply undulating or shallow. The pre-arousal or resting state exhibits the slow, deep and regular waves designated Alpha. These succeed one another at the rate of 8 to 12 per second. When arousal occurs and the organism is attentive, the shallower, faster and irregular waves of the Beta type are recorded. This suggests that the sense of tension and activity within the skull at moments of excited attention can be accounted for by an increase in electrical discharge or innervation. Other electro-chemical changes which accompany arousal are measured by means of the electrical conductivity of the sweat glands of the palms, in blood pressure and heart rate. Where a state of shock is present, such changes are proportionately violent, but for the most part the organism oscillates gently from one side to the other of a steady characteristic potential.

This total picture is more comprehensively termed 'activation', and arousal may be defined as an increase in activation. States of low activation have received less experimental attention, except through an interest shown in normal sleep and hibernation and analogous abnormal states such as those of torpor, depression and cataleptic trance. The degree of activation most common to any individual is usually termed his 'resting level'. Presumably this could be expressed as the average of all his non-arousal states throughout any time-sampled period and it would be to this level that he would tend to return after periods of arousal. This tendency of the organism to return to a customary resting level of activation was termed by the French physiologist Claude Bernard 'homeostasis'. Homeostatic level may be disturbed by stimuli from both inside and outside the organism and usually both are operative at the same time. Attention operates best when both are harmoniously and mutually supplementary, with stimuli from within being muted when the situation demands an externalised vigilance. Should threat cause too strong an arousal from internal sources the two sets of stimuli would tend to compete for the attentional field which is limited in size by the individual's span of attention. Such competitive overcrowding among stimuli often results in a lessening of mental acuity in relation to those from external sources. The competition of stimuli for brain space is particularly important under conditions which arouse anxiety, and it is of obvious significance in any consideration of motivation and learning.

2 *Regulation of activation*

Activation is maintained and arousal generated from external sources through the mediation of the distance receptor nerve endings in eyes, ears, nose, skin and tongue. Arousal from these sources may result in reactions as complex as aesthetic judgments or it may serve merely as a simple topping up of activation to a level which does not emerge in the form of conscious mental activity. These numerous minute stimuli which may go unobserved are an essential element in the maintenance of the organism's equilibrium, and have an important role in preserving normal mental functioning. Problems of modern space travel and underwater exploration have led to experimental studies of sensory deprivation and it is clear from these (Solomon et al. 1961) that hallucination and disorientation result when the usual external sources of sensory arousal are removed for several days. Other sources of sensation, deriving from the interior of the body, are the sensory nerve endings situated in the striped muscles which effect voluntary movement, and those in the inner ear which convey a sense of balance and position in space. Weightlessness is a condition in which these two sources of stimuli can no longer interact in their customary fashion, and it is conceivable that four days or so in extra-terrestrial space could also result in some form of deprivation. Paradoxically enough, however, too concentrated and prolonged a stimulation of any one neural area results in unpleasant disequilibrium also. Nerve cells become fatigued and reactive inhibition builds up. It would appear that the topping up of activation must be well distributed and random. The organism endeavours to effect this when too concentratedly and uniformly stimulated, by fidgeting, chattering, daydreaming and in other forms of distractible behaviour. The extent to which sameness can be endured, however, can be increased by experience to some degree, but in the main inattention is a randomised form of restoring equilibrium. It provides rest pauses for overworked cells. Thus, the brain is kept in a state of rhythmic readiness by chemical changes in the nerve endings remote from it. Many of the electrical impulses generated discharge into a neural channel which has been identified as RAS (the reticular activating system). See Fig. 1 (Lindsley 1951). Electrical stimulation of this pathway results in a change of brain rhythm (Magoun 1954). RAS collects its impulses from all sources of activation both within and without the organism and it might be regarded as the central regulator of activation. While sensory input is operative RAS maintains the vigilance of the organism. In sleep, however, other centres in the brain inhibit the role of cortical discharge into RAS, acting as servo-mechanisms which switch off the part of the brain subserving conscious awareness (Ranson 1939, Nauta 1946). Mental activity persists, however, because RAS continues its lessened discharge into the cortex, and at peak periods of activation, perhaps when sleep is threatened by some stimulus, the dream image may occur. Sometimes such dreams have disguised relevance for the sleeper's waking preoccupations which suggest that brain activation during sleep is an assimilatory mechanism. Should stimuli discharge strongly into RAS the organism must be very exhausted in order to sleep at all. Indigestion or a state of anxiety can cause sufficient activation of RAS to keep the organism in a state of wakeful readiness. Tossing restlessness adds a further source of stimulation from muscular nerve endings, and the greatest chance of sleep is to abate the action of RAS by supinely daydreaming into the night. It is doubtful whether the directed attentional effort at counting imaginary sheep would lull by its monotony for it is an activity which tends to arouse the cortex. The sheep farmer might succeed without an undue amount of cerebration, if he was accustomed to seeing sheep pass before him in single file, and had an easily available imaginal representation of such a happening.

3 *The growth of attentional patterns*

These internal and external sources of activation build up in the course of experience both tolerances and intolerances for stimuli. For example,

FIGURE I. *Schema of Activation System*

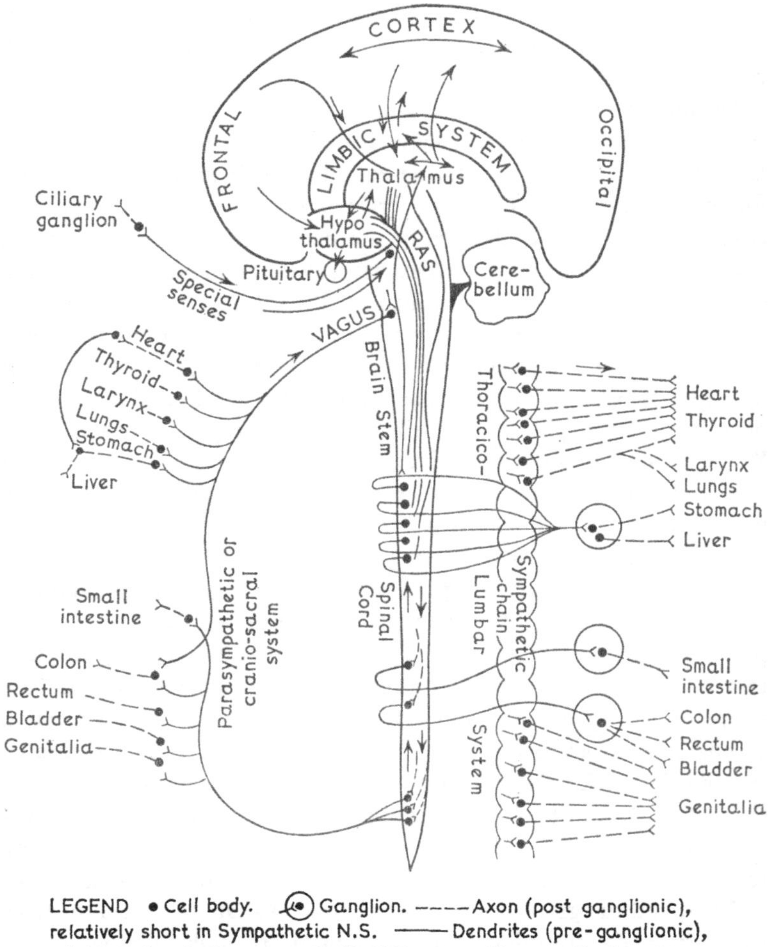

LEGEND • Cell body. (•) Ganglion. ---- Axon (post ganglionic), relatively short in Sympathetic N.S. —— Dendrites (pre-ganglionic), relatively long in Parasympathetic N.S. ⟷ Transcortical and intrathalamic connections. ↑↓ Ascending and descending corticospinal pathways

[*After Lindsley* (1951) *with modifications*]

intolerance of sound in an adult suddenly restored to hearing and of light in the animal reared in darkness can reach painful levels. In fact, kittens reared from infancy in unpatterned diffuse light play normally until the hood obscuring their vision is removed. This causes acute distress and the animal may languish and die if such exposure is continued (Solomon et al. 1961). These facts suggest that the brain activation necessary for optimal attention is subject to an interoceptive and exteroceptive calibration through the mediation of RAS. This becomes established in early growth as a more or less permanent pattern, characteristic of the individual. It is a highly complex pattern, for the entire input summates in the diencephalon and the brain stem (Fig. 1) and it is considered that reverberating circuits maintain association between this lower part of the brain and its upper sections (Penfield and Jasper 1954). The higher levels subserve the processes of perception and thought and are responsible for the direction of attention. Thus the more primitive parts of the nervous system, although of importance as prime movers in the early part of the life cycle, become integrated with those aspects which are phylogenetically more recent and which subserve more adaptable behaviour.

4 *Arousal and temperament*

There are widely spread individual differences regarding arousal patterns. Some people are so constituted as to experience rapid and intense arousal from a resting state which is already comparatively high, and some return more quickly to their pre-activation level because their resting state of activation is comparatively low. Thus each individual has his peculiar activation potential seen in dynamic patterns of the speed and intensity of arousal and subsidiation (Lindsley 1961). This determines the 'temper' of his dynamic states and constitutes his temperament. Pavlov observed such individual differences in temperament among his dogs (Frolov 1937). Some were more responsive than others and acquired conditioned reflexes more quickly. He described this temperament trait as one of cortical excitation-inhibition. Arousal states would be manifest sooner in those whose resting level of excitation was already high, while those at the inhibited end of the continuum would appear to be more phlegmatic under arousal conditions.

The upper brain or cortex or cerebral spheres or neo-pallium, to give it its several names, acquires a dominant controlling function in relation to the lower brain. This means that individual differences in cortical excitation-inhibition will affect the pattern of control exerted by the dominant higher centres over the arousal impulses discharging into the lower centres, such as the hypothalamus, the limbic system and the thalamus. Eysenck has postulated that the well-known temperamental dimension of introversion-extraversion has close affinity with Pavlov's dimension of cortical excitation-inhibition. He holds that the resting level of extraverts occurs towards the inhibited end of Pavlov's dimension while introverts have relatively excited cortices. This is a confusing idea for it is well known that extraverts tend to be uninhibited and introverts inhibited in external behaviour. This confusion is dispelled, however, if it is remembered that an excited cortex can the more easily maintain its control over the emotional uprush from the lower activating centres, while an inhibited cortex will exercise a less ready suzerainty over free expression. Thus the uninhibited and vigilant cortex holds arousal in check. The importance of the E–I (extraversion-introversion) dimension for developmental psychology is threefold. As young children, extraverts are less easily trained by reward and punishment techniques; as pupils in schools they tend to be less error avoidant than introverts and in contrast they tend to be synthetic rather than analytic in the critical stages of meeting with a new experience. These tendencies will be discussed later in the book, but they are mentioned here to assert a relationship between physiology and behaviour which has significance for motivation in learning situations. It is intended to show that each pattern has its advantages and disadvantages, according to whether the situation calls for caution or free-flowing self expression.

Another aspect of arousal which is of particular interest is Berlyne's (1960) concept of 'arousal jag'. According to this hypothesis small spurts (jags) of arousal are pleasant and large ones unpleasant. What is felt to be a small or large jag will depend on the resting level of the cortex at the moment of stimulation. For example, the extreme introvert with his comparatively excited cortex experiences a considerable 'jag' from a relatively small amount of arousal. The reverse is true of the extravert, who would tend to experience pleasurable arousal only when the stimuli were rather stronger. For him the experience would have to be rather more intense if he is to have 'kicks'.

These individual differences have been experimentally investigated by means of drugs (Eysenck 1963). Alcohol is a means of chemically lowering the inhibitive power of the cortex over the lower centres for it is a depressant drug. This accounts for the fact that it increases extraverted behaviour at a cocktail party. It is a pleasant way of making one person more socially available to another. At the first glass, the extreme extravert would be affected, but several more might be required by an introvert if his cortical vigilance is to be similarly reduced. For this reason it is not surprising that Parnell (1955) should find that introverts are more partaking of alcohol, for it brings relief from error avoidance and preoccupation with anxieties at a slower rate. Other experimental approaches of the same kind, using various depressant and stimulant drugs, suggest the presence of individual differences in the resting states of cortical excitation-inhibition. This E–I dimension represents a constitutional unity imposed from within the organism by hereditary and physiological factors and it manifests itself in affecting all kinds of dynamic and ability traits (Cattell 1946).

Introversion–extraversion is easily recognised as a factor in behaviour, for when teacher's estimates of children according to a definition of the factor are correlated with the actual factor measurements, correlations as high as 0·967 are found (Burt 1939). Thus this dimension of temperament arising from the superordinate action of the cortex in relation to the subcortical structures is not only a fertile and seminal source of predictive hypotheses but is also amenable to reliable observation. In a study of motivation it cannot be ignored, for it creates a disposition to enter the perceptual field in certain ways and to experience different after-effects of response, which will make for success or failure, ease or difficulty in problem solution and in learning.

5 *The autonomic and central nervous systems*

Some temperamental trends associated with arousal concern the muscular response systems, blood pressure, heart rate and other responses suggestive of somatic preparedness to take action of an assertive or withdrawing kind. In moments of stress these internal forms of arousal create sensations which compete in the attentional field with the input from exteroceptive sources and are thus important in explaining the behaviour of a person under stress. Such internal sources of arousal stem from in what is called the autonomic nervous system (ANS). This section of the total nervous system is to be distinguished from the central nervous system (CNS) which mediates voluntary action and sensory reception. The two systems, however, are functionally integrated at all levels in the mature organism, and they must be regarded as constituting a functional unity.

Several analogies might be drawn between the ANS and the CNS (see Fig. 1). Each has a 'head ganglion' which exerts a controlling and co-ordinating effect. This is the hypothalamus in the ANS and the cerebral cortex in the CNS. Each has a synaptic or relay system at the spinal and diencephalic levels and each could be regarded as having an afferent (sensory arousal) system and an efferent (response) aspect. The main distinctions between the two systems are that the ANS does not mediate consciousness, and that although the ANS is the dominant system in infancy the CNS is paramount in maturity. Any awareness of what is happening in the ANS such as emotional tension is made possible by synaptic relays into the CNS, and until these are established the infant lives without perception of sensation or emotion out of his brain stem. To the observer the neonate appears to experience the extremes of rage, but it is also clear that the behaviour is convulsive rather than patterned. He may be regarded as a puppet under the influence of his ANS which galvanates his reflexes even as the puppeteer pulls strings.

Although eventually the ANS becomes subordinate to the CNS, it has its own system of push and pull regulation, and at any time in later stages of maturity this system may become superordinate. This is particularly so when the cortical patterning provides no ready-made template for responding to a situation or stimulus. For example, a person who is expected to meet new conditions of living must be carefully prepared over a long period if they are not to be rendered 'childish' and impotent by them on first impact. Astronauts are carefully educated in spacecraft, and children in schools are educated into the skills of a technological society. Without these periods of preparation there would be no pattern in the CNS which would direct and harness the uprush of arousal from the ANS brought about by everyday stimulus situations. Should the individual not be so prepared panic could ensue, and in that event he would be 'lived-by' the impulses of the ANS and display in his behaviour many characteristic infantile reactions to pain and discomfort. In the experienced person, however, sensory input is matched by a neural representation of response, and no disintegrating autonomic effect occurs. It is in the orienting or initial phases of novel experience, or when an expected sequence in a familiar situation fails to materialise, that the large regular alpha waves in the brain indicate that autonomic effectors of activation have taken precedence over cortical ones. It is as though a rudimentary and unstructured 'error awareness' stems from the phylogenetically and psychologically more primitive part of the nervous system, while the more recently evolved and structured cortex is dominant when exteroceptive impulses find well-worn paths to consummation. It is not difficult to identify the ANS with unconscious sources of behaviour and the CNS with the conscious mind. In behavioural terms it might be said that the UCS 'mind' may lead the CS into 'error awareness' during the initial attentional phase. It cannot, of course, define the error. Definition of the error will result from cortical processing of these autonomic signals together with a continued sensory input arising from the phase of secondary attention. This secondary phase is exploratory in intent and mediated cortically, though maintained by autonomic activation (Sokolov 1960). Thus it is important for smooth mental functioning that the alarm note of error awareness should not be so strong as to disrupt and foil this searching after a remedy or solution to a problem.

II. THE PHYSIOLOGY OF LEARNING

1 *The nervous systems and learning*

It is an interesting thought to realise that whenever a person meets a new situation, i.e. something which must be learned, the same law of assimilation is followed in the current learning sequence as has been followed in the life history of the organism, but of course more rapidly because of all the ready-made mental aids he can draw on. For example, the expediting factor in understanding the statement 'aeroplanes fly' in a society which has never seen a plane would be the spontaneous question 'Like birds?' Moreover, when an attempt is made to recall something from past experience the mature organism may retrace the neural sequences of past assimilation. For example, should the name or title of a past event be forgotten, while all else associated with it is well remembered, it is an interesting experience to observe closely the stages passed through in restoring such a noun to available recall. Theoretically speaking the first established neural traces should be re-energised first, and the recall stages should match in order of occurrence those of the assimilation process. This was evident when the writer wished to recall the title of a propaganda film directed against the Nazis' treatment of the Jews, seen in the 1930's. She had been much moved by it and remembered it in considerable detail, but the second word in the title eluded her. The first word was 'Professor –'. Regarding the second word, the initial blankness was replaced by a vague 'feeling' that it was there ready for recall. This was recognitory yet quite unstructured perceptually. Then followed a shadowy awareness of the length of the word, rather like a mottled shadow on a lighter background. At the third stage certain specific though tentatively held details began to emerge namely that it began with an M and had a Russian ending. Then hypotheses concerning the second letter were posed and an 'a' seemed most correct of the possible vowels. Finally there jumped into consciousness the fully fledged word 'Mamlok', and it was seen that the ending was not quite Russian (Lov), but it was remembered that the film was Russian. These five stages in recall, introspectively observed, correlate very well with probable stages of assimilation beginning with the most rudimentary and ending with the most structured. These could be designated thus: (1) Negative awareness – a blank in response to an attempt to recall. (2) A feeling it is not lost and can be recalled – positive awareness on a feeling plane. (3) Perceptual awareness of tone stemming largely from thalamic processing with the most rudimentary figure-ground patterning contributed by the cortex. (4) Cortical mediation of letters contributing detail to the vague whole. (5) Cortical mediation of general principles, e.g. if M comes first it ought to be followed by a vowel. (6) The emergence into consciousness of the whole, with the firm conviction of its authenticity and the realisation of how an association had transmuted 'lok' into 'lov'. These stages in recall are an example both of the stages passed through in learning the name, and in learning to learn in childhood. Each stage represents an increase of integration among the various strata of the nervous system. For example, stage 2 might be aligned with learning at the rudimentary hypothalamic level; at stage 3 thalamic processing is added to this; at stage 4 the specific projection paths of ear, tongue and larynx introduce cortical processing of the input; at stage 5 the association areas further integrate the mental schemata; at stage 6 neural firing into the ideational speech centres evokes integrative comment, which feeds back into the complex mental structure differentiating it further.

The term 'serendipity' is usually applied to this sixth stage. It is a non-intentional, fringe learning by means of which new lines of thought and fact are discovered. The conclusion that 'lok' had been thought of as 'lov', because of the forgotten Russian origin of the film, was the kind of observation which led Freud to formulate his theory of 'condensation' in the work of the unconscious. It resulted from a generalisation of numerous incidental observations of his patients' dreams and slips of the tongue, in which two meanings were telescoped into a symbol transmuted to fit both. Serendipity then may be the seminal point of a new theory although originally it was tangential to the observer's line of thought. In neurological terms it implies that electrical impulses in the nervous system radiate in all directions with apparent redundancy. Yet this overflow beyond what is necessary 'accidentally' enlarges schemata to include new material.

Thus discharge through reverberating circuits between upper and lower ganglia ensures that the organism functions with continuity and unity in all its parts. Discharge across the cortex, however, increases complexity in those schemata which mediate conscious awareness. But any increase in complexity through trans-cortical patterning is also conveyed centrecephalically to the lower ganglia with consequent restructuring of them. The extent to which this occurs may be regulated by the extent to which the experience is affectively significant, and arousal correspondingly vigorous.

2 *Experiential structuring*

An important concept which explains growth in schemata is that of 'feed-back'. This implies that response and the observation of its effects are fed back into the receptor cells which triggered off the trend of behaviour. For example, a small child experiencing a scratch wound from a pet cat will know that the pain is a sequence from the picking up of the cat, because the neural excitation set up by the pain stimulus will discharge from the cortex and basal ganglia into the still excited cells by means of which he perceived the cat and reached out to grip it. Thousands of neural elements would be involved probably in this behavioural sequence and all constitute a sequential schemata whole and entire with dynamic unity between its phase sequences. The later run phase sequences are fed back into the earlier and thus the relationship between antecedent and consequent becomes reversible. In future, the sight of the cat is not merely recognitory of purring and soft fur but also of the pain dealt by hidden claws. In a similar way praise or blame as a consequent of an antecedent is fed back into the original percept. The greater the pleasure or pain involved, the greater the participation of the ANS, and any action of the CNS which perpetuates or ameliorates the condition should contribute to a highly dynamic circuit of feed-back.

Feed-back and reverberating circuits are thus both vertical (or centrencephalic) and also horizontal, i.e. between and across the major ganglia. RAS as an essential aspect of these interconnections becomes structured too and may be modified in its functioning to 'lock-in' with the sensory receptor organs involved (Lindsley 1961). Such locking-in tendencies influence attention by setting up predispositions to attend in certain ways. Individual differences exist in these predispositions but they are a matter of style rather than of the content of perception and thought. One of the main differentiating criteria appears to stem from whether wholes are seen prior to parts or vice versa. But whichever takes precedence in the perceptual act, the same perceptual object is appraised. Yet entering situations with a tendency to appraise the whole in a vague way before filling out the detail could conceivably affect motivation in a significant way in certain situations. These would be presumably where a quick hunch concerning the significance of the whole was particularly relevant for action. The same remarks apply to prior perception of details with subsequent appraisal of the whole. The passage from the initial impact to the fuller cognisance of a situation is so rapid as to pass undetected in ordinary experience. But it is during the initial phase that orientation of response occurs, and this perhaps is the reason why synthetic and analytic types of perception are significant for an understanding of cognitive and emotive responses. Reference was made earlier to synthetic (seeing wholes prior to parts) and analytic (seeing details prior to wholes) styles as being characteristic of extraverts and introverts respectively. This could result from the structuring of RAS in so far as it is activiated by temperamental arousal patterns, genetically determined. The significance of these cognitive styles will be further considered when the motivational significance of special abilities and disabilities is discussed.

The structuring of RAS is important not only in the processing of sensory input. It is also of vital importance for maintaining a course of behaviour in action. Should an injury or lesion disrupt the reticular activating system, the patient cannot 'set' himself to reach a desired end. This is particularly so if there is injury in the limbic system into which RAS discharges. This failure of 'set' results in a forgetting of intention in mid sequence (Pribram 1961). The importance of 'set' in learning is obvious, and in unimpaired organisms it can be weak under conditions of fatigue, somnolence and boredom, when the activation system lacks impetus from either cortical or ANS sources. Learning is expedited when the system of activation is normal or perhaps slightly aroused above resting level.

From these remarks it can be concluded that mental events are as much dependent upon the dynamics of the nervous system as upon its physical structure, and that it is in all probability its activation and systems of arousal which give rise to individual characteristics of behaviour. This can be analysed down to individual differences in the biochemistry of organisms which may be genetically determined. The passage of biochemically generated electricity along conduction paths constitutes an activation system which concentrates mainly in RAS. This vast dendritic network, however, is subject to modification through its functioning. From the evidence of individual differences measured by the electro-encephalogram it is suggested that RAS may become conditioned to a characteristic pattern of regulation imposed on it by its habitual excitation, adaptation and learning. This would be manifest in fast or slow reactions, attentiveness or inattentiveness, susceptibility to arousal or lack of it, stability or instability. These are usually regarded as arising from temperament but RAS as a self-regulatory mechanism, holding the organism to a constant homeostatic rhythm, may have its neural and hormonal elements patterned by both innate and learned effect (Lindsley 1961). For this reason it is possible that only marked genetic factors remain amenable to inspection despite the structuring of experience. Where temperamental disposition is not extreme it is conceivable that any characteristic pattern may be wrought by experience, and since most organisms conform to an average, experiential structuring is usually responsible for style in behaving. Punishment and reward in various forms can turn slightly extraverted children into introverts and vice versa. Where, however, a child with a strong extraverted innate disposition is forced into an introvert pattern it may result in a weakly structured personality liable to breakdown. Conversely, a child who has been led to adopt a socially conforming style of behaviour which harmonises with his temperamental style should do so at less cost and thus have more available nervous energy for advance on a wider experiential front. Some evidence concerning what a person's temperamental disposition was at birth is afforded by body build, on the theory that this too is genetically determined. But as with temperament pure types are rare and most people present a mixture of each bodily component. Where it is clear that temperament type differs from what one would expect to find having regard to an unambiguous somatotype, it may be inferred that caretakers were adamant in the face of the child's natural propensities, thus occasioning more than the usual amount of stress and trauma. Sheldon and Stevens (1940), in their close observation of a male undergraduate population, suggested that such a marked discrepancy between body build and behavioural style was prognostic of maladjustment. This seems plausible, but it would need to be confirmed by longitudinal research, if it were possible to find children of clearly defined genetic constitution and parents with caretaking expectations not conducive to a behavioural style suited to the child's temperament.

3 *Psycho-somatic dimensions*

Whatever the cause psychogenetically, it is clear that in any human trait there are proportionately a few deviant persons with the majority less distinguishable from one another. The nature-nurture controversy may be settled only when suitable tests are devised revealing the characteristic state of a baby's activation system prior to the structuring effects of an experimentally observed upbringing and education. At present, hypotheses exist which may lead the way to this delectable state of affairs, and the most valuable of these is the fact that behavioural styles in both normals and neurotics appear to be correlated to some extent with what are regarded as temperament types (Eysenck 1964). In addition, the development of instruments for the measurement of neural activation patterns is progressing.

Psychology and physiology are disciplines each providing hypotheses for the other to investigate. For example, Wenger (1941) experimentally investigated the behaviour traits associated with autonomic arousal. He based his hypothesis on the physiological concept of the ANS as having an arousing function in its sympathetic section, and a subsidiation effect on its parasympathetic side. To test this he measured the level of arousal and speed of recovery from startle response to a loud noise. Where arousal was high and prolonged and recovery slow he postulated dominance of the sympathetic section of the ANS, where recovery was rapid, parasympathetic dominance. The ready discharge of tension in the parasympathetic cases and the prolonged feeling-disturbance of the sympathetic would seem to be the extravert and introvert patterns respectively. In fact the theory of dominance in one or other section of the ANS would appear to be the E–I theory of Eysenck regarded from the viewpoint of arousal, rather than from that of cortical super-ordinacy.

The structure of the ANS suggests that it has both a function of arousal and subsidiation. The sympathetic ganglia of the ANS innervates RAS and thus brings about a state of general arousal. Its neural elements are so constructed (with short dendrites) to bring about communication with other cell-bodies in the shortest possible time. The cell-bodies of the parasympathetic system lie, in contrast, at the end of long dendrites, and its fibres transmit electrical discharge more slowly than those of the sympathetic. Also in contrast is the fact that it is more specific and local in its effects because the cell-bodies connect to the effector organs with short axons. These two sections of the ANS present an impression of a servo-mechanistic push and pull system, regulated to act synchronously, yet the one more slowly than the other – i.e. a general arousal state is effected before the specific check system can complete operations. In a state of rapid change requiring continuous adjustment in the interests of safety (e.g. when astride a bolting horse) this oscillation between arousal and subsidiation will be rapid and at a high level, maintaining a vigilance and degree of responsiveness necessary for 'riding out' the situation. In more simple behaviour such as startle at a loud noise, arousal and subsidiation are more discernible as first and second phases of reaction.

These functional characteristics of sympathetic generality and parasympathetic specificity are further supported by the bio-chemistry of the body. The hormones secreted by the ductless glands produce an adrenergic compound, which facilitates the operations of the sympathetic system in parts of the soma at a distance from the centre of arousal. The contrary is true of the cholinergic products of the parasympathetic section which is destroyed in the blood and tissues by the enzyme cholinesterase before it can become widespread in its effects (Dempsey 1951). Thus each organ of behaviour is both generally aroused and specifically regulated by the incoming fibres of the two sub-systems of the ANS. This gives rise to both emotional sensation and alerted attention, the interplay between the two having an optimal balance for clear thinking and co-ordinated behaviour. A rapid action on the part of the parasympathetic section is more likely to convert emotion into attention and to bring about subsidiation before a disruptive level of arousal has been reached. Those in whom sympathetic arousal tends to be intense display a behaviour pattern suggestive of stress expressed in heightened blood pressure, increased heart rate, increased blood supply to the striated muscles (which subserve voluntary action), and an inhibition of peristaltic rhythm which has repercussions in the digestive tracts. From these characteristics it is not difficult to deduce that the chronically anxious person is too frequently in an aroused state of emergency, ready for fight or flight. Milder and less frequent reactions of this kind to stress situations serve a useful purpose by alerting the organism in preparation for some clearly perceived course of action. Parasympathetic dominance would seem to be aligned with extraverted behaviour and sympathetic with introverted. In these types, sensory processing tends to differ in ways one would expect having regard to the generalised and specific effects of the two sections of the ANS. For example perceptual after-effects are more prolonged in introverts and tend to influence similar subsequent perceptions. In extraverts the converse is more apparent. Such type differences would be mediated by RAS in a two-fold way, one affective and the other cognitive. In processing sensory data, emotionally toned cues should bring about autonomic arousal of RAS through circuits inclusive of the limbic system. On the other hand, appraisal of form and colour, wholes and parts are contributed by cortical habitude. But this habitude has by definition been established in the course of experience and includes an element of temperamental preference for this style or that when processing sensory data into response channels.

Intensity of arousal varies along a continuum with faintly increased alertness at one end and extreme emotional response at the other (Sheer 1961). Alerted attention and emotional response are thus the two extremes of a scale of arousal to which any individual is subjected. Where sympathetic arousal is predominant there will be a tendency for arousal to be at the emotional extreme and Eysenck (1953) has noted this to be characteristic of neurotic introverts. His term 'dysthmic' refers to 'disturbances of feeling'. The parasympathetic strength of individuals has been experimentally defined as speed of recovery from stress, measured in physiological terms (Freeman and Katzoff 1942), and is exemplified in quick recovery from startle effects. What might be termed a reactive inhibition builds up rapidly and this is more characteristic of extraverts. In introverts, the resting level of cortical excitation is more intense, and they are therefore more quickly roused sympathetically and less readily subsidiated parasympathetically. It would seem the introvert is more frequently in a state of tension which fails to discharge itself readily in action.

Temporary predominance of one or other section of the autonomic nervous system may be seen in neonates before and after feeding (Ting-Chuan 1949). Autonomic arousal before feeding and in other states of need bring about diffuse and generalised movements, which, after the need is satisfied, become sectionalised. After feeding, tongue, head, eyes, fingers and the smaller segments of the body are moved specifically. This satisfied condition presents a picture of parasympathetic innervation. These are the only two activation trends observable in the neonate, and at this stage functioning of the autonomic nervous system is seen in its pristine condition. It is the instrument of instinctual motivation not yet subjected to the restructuring of cortical feedback. As experience increases the selective potentiality of thalamus and cortex, motivation becomes associated at all levels with cues afforded by the distance receptors in eyes, nose, skin and ears. Through these structuring agents the first bodily states of satisfaction and need are differentiated into feelings associated with perceptual cues. The cortex increasingly becomes the head ganglion, and the original push and pull system is incorporated into the new system of regulation. The originally prior system may continue to take the physiological lead in all new situations; but the autonomic patterns of behaviour such as the emotional responses specifically related to vocalisation, attack and defence, become subordinate largely to the acquired reward and punishment points of the brain (Miller 1961). Thus although the CNS contributes both cue and drive properties of a motivating kind, the neural substrata of autonomic activity remain important as sustainers of these central directors of behaviour. In this way, experience gives direction and form to responses grounded in innate reflexology. This patterning does not commence with the birth trauma but with foetal sensori-motor activity. For example the 'following' response, in which a neonate moves the face to confront a touch on the cheek or lips, is present in contralateral form in the 8½-week-old foetus (Blauvelt and McKenna 1962). In the course of experience there is a change in emphasis from interoceptive excitation to an ever-increasing responsiveness to exteroceptive stimuli, and from relatively simple reflex motor responses to complex patterns of simultaneous inhibition and facilitation within motor and symbolic neural schemata. Accordingly motivation moves its main seat of operation from the spine and brain stem towards the cortex without shedding any of its more primitive aspects.

4 *The dynamic and directional aspects of motivation*

Most controversies as to whether the motivational aspect of behaviour is dynamic or directional spring from a failure to realise that it is both, but that there is a change of emphasis during progress towards maturity. Where the child or person is inexperienced regarding any type of situation it follows there will be no neural effector system correlated with the stimuli. The individual will thus be at a loss about what to do. Where, however, the experienced person has a cortical structure to match the environmental stimulus, there ensues the shallow rapid waves of the beta type. These indicate the activation which aligns response with stimulus, and the initial large alpha waves of the questing organism are replaced. In other words, a shift has occurred from a precedence of brain-stem arousal to a cortically led activation (Sokolov 1960). This brings about a second system of arousal which takes precedence over the first as exploration and trial after error results in habituation. Thus from being lived by his ANS, the child comes to live through his CNS, yet at no stage can the developing voluntary and conscious powers negate entirely the involuntary and unconscious ones if a maximally efficient organism is to result. All later physiological developments integrate more or less harmoniously with those established earlier, thus causing their continued elaboration. This increase in complexity is made possible because of the enormous potentiality of the two to three billion cell bodies of the cortex which provide an infinity of possible associations. Some of these cell bodies are specifically tied to axons and dendrites connecting the brain with parts of the body and these are situated in much the same area of the cortex in most mammals. A larger proportion of them in man are free of this specificity and have only an associative function. The proportion of freely associating cell bodies to the specifically geared ones is termed the association-specificity ratio or the A/S ratio. In man this is at its largest and decreases as the phylogenetic status of the organism decreases. A large amount of associative potential makes possible a bringing together of the six specific senses into an amalgam of meaning in which sound can be thought of in terms of colour, and scents in terms of the twilight and warmth of a summer evening. The possible associative synaptic pathways between the various areas of the brain are infinite and result in a unique product in each individual constituting his 'personality'. Yet each stage of structuring is in a certain sense limiting, for once a phase sequence is fired between associative areas, it is more probable that this synaptic pathway will form a vector for subsequent electrical discharge. This means that every phase sequence which occurs results in a loss of some degree of freedom to associate. The cerebral mantle has lost so many degrees of freedom by the tenth year that the association areas of the cortex are less free to undertake new learning should injury oblate the effects of past learning. This is most marked where the associations are built up on one side of the brain only. Where there is an area in both hemispheres subserving the same kind of function re-learning may be affected by transferring the operation to the opposite sphere. For example, the sensori-motor organs of speech which are subserved by the specific bi-lateral speech centres (Broca's area) can substitute for one another in re-learning where there has been injury to one of them. Such aphasic patients can re-learn to speak intelligibly within a year. Should the injury be in an association area subserving the meaning of words, the loss is total, for the ideational speech centres are unilateral. Before the age of ten, however, this function can be relearnt through the mediation of the same area (in the parieto-occipital lobe) on the other side. This area is normally concerned with spatial awareness but there is apparently sufficient room and scope enough to subserve both speech ideation and spatial awareness. After ten years of experience such transfer is less possible (Penfield and Roberts 1959).

This suggests that learning is to a large extent physiologically paced and that the first ten years may have a different significance than subsequent phases. Piaget has demonstrated that all the concrete (as distinct from abstract) operations needed for a successful management of everyday affairs are mature by the mental age of ten years, and traditionally a mental age of ten years has been regarded as the level below which a person is considered to be mentally handicapped and in need of statutory supervision. Moreover, school learning appears to be paced by intelligence prior to ten, but subsequently by skills learned during that period (Burt 1943, Brennan 1962). This could be explained by a greater freedom to establish neural connections prior to this age in accordance with the individual's capacity for forming neural schemata. Subsequent to this, learning would seem to depend on the background thus established providing educational opportunity is held constant. It may well be that the schemata established during this relatively unstructured period set the limits to future advance. This is further supported by the findings of Zazzo (1960) that among mentally handicapped people who are older than nine years of age, the weakest and most retarded areas of skill are of a basic sensori-motor nature. This evidence cumulatively suggests that the ground work of sensori-motor experience is the necessary precursor of more abstract and symbolic forms of thinking. Underlying this fact is perhaps one simple law namely, that where there is competition between neural pathways for the reception of innervation the older trend claims priority. This law, adumbrated by Jost in 1897, suggests that the individual who established several adequate responses to the same stimulus early in life is in a better position to try out solutions to new problems than someone who at the same age established fewer. Jost's law applies at any age but is most crucial, perhaps, during the phase of basic cortical structuring. It is perhaps during these early years in the life cycle that the whole nervous system is subjected to its most fundamental patterning through the reverberating circuits of centrencephalic functioning. RAS would be a prime mover in this flux.

5 *The directional properties of speech*

The hierarchical system of neural controls established during the first years of life in humans is not unlike that found in other mammals on a simpler basis. The other primates tend to reach maturity in cortical superordinate functioning by the age of two years. If man's skeletal and muscular system matured as rapidly as the chimpanzees, the average two-year-old child would be capable of much the same skills as that animal in its maturity. The practised chimpanzee at a tea party handles his cup with much the same insouciance regarding tilt as the young child. The two-year-old in the climbing frame acquires considerable dexterity comparable to that of simians. Yet the human child develops not only in stature and strength but also to a level of mental dexterity far beyond the best of other well-trained mammals. This may be due to the complexity of his physiology of vocalisation and hearing. These neural structures have a capacity for differentiation which is absent in the other higher primates. The language of communication among simian communities is confined, in all probability to the necessary minimum for survival, in signalling emergency, vegetative and sexual situations. The human child, however, learns to name every object and action to which he is exposed and also to attribute value to them. In this way a substitute structure for stimulus-response behaviour is established at every point. This facilitates the rehearsal of behaviour in speech, both silent and overt, and reduces the cumbersomeness of trying things out in practice. Moreover, the benefits of such explorations and rehearsals can be conveyed to others and their responses in speech observed. New words or signs or symbols can be invented to designate new strategies thus envisaged. This makes possible the transmission from generation to generation not only of personal wisdom, but also of cultural tradition in ethics, art and science. Thus, the ideational speech area of the cortex in each individual might be regarded as a cultural storehouse closely packed by the age of thirty with a wealth of meaning derived from words spoken and heard. This part of the cortex which subserves meaning integrates the elements of speech into communicable units ranging from exclamations to sentences comprised of twenty or more words. The sensori-motor speech mechanisms of ears, mouth and larynx can operate independently of the ideational speech area, because they are activated from different neural centres. They speak gibberish, however, if they are not subordinate to its patterned direction. The fitful mutterings of sleep and the ravings of fevered delirium imply that the various neural centres subserving language are not in full association.

During the first two years of life words tend to be simple pointers to objects, but these named things become endowed with value in the child's perception, in that they seem good or bad, nice or nasty. These feelings about individual objects in daily experience constitute in all probability their first nexus of meaning. The primal attitude to things as good or bad provides a basic element of meaning to their names. In later life when language is highly developed, the good-bad semantic dimension is still to be found in the majority of words as an element of meaning (Osgood 1957). Thus the fragmentary world experienced through his senses and muscular responses becomes bonded by his own feeling evaluations of it. This is sufficient understanding to permit him to imitate models in his environment. A chimpanzee reared as a human infant in every respect (Hayes 1950) can reach this level but not surpass it. To do so requires more than an affectively toned observation of another's behaviour. This in man is provided by what Pavlov called his secondary system of signals, i.e. language.

A psychological account of how this is brought about will be given in subsequent chapters. The present discussion is concerned with the physiology of motivation, and it is sufficient to say here that there are two ways in which the cortex is involved in speech. One is with its sensori-motor aspects, i.e. speaking behaviour, and the other with the meaning and significance of the activity. The former is a primary system and the second a superordinate one. These two neural systems are usually supplementary and complementary but it is possible for each to act independently. This is apparent in everyday living. When intensely preoccupied with the content of thought one can speak mechanically – the words seem to be spoken spontaneously, without effort. On the other hand if one is very preoccupied with the business of correct phrasing and enunciation it is possible to read or recite long passages without any clear cognisance of their meaning. The former state was exemplified when Spearman (1927), introspecting on his own abstract thought sequences, described the images of words, i.e. the sensori-motor components, as 'twittering sentience' – an unnecessary or redundant accompaniment of his ideational processes.

Recent research, particularly that of Penfield and Roberts, has identified more accurately the area of the brain which subserves verbal meaning. They have located it in the parieto-occipital lobe on the dominant side of the brain. The sensori-motor areas have long been recognised. The areas of the cortex normally devoted to ideational elaboration of speech are mapped and described by Penfield and Roberts (1959), and their last two chapters provide a fascinating summary of their findings and their implications for education should the reader wish for more detailed information.

This secondary system of signalisation in man, because it is aligned at all points with his sensori-motor behaviour, constitutes a duplicate directive system for his responses. Because of its capacity to 'think things out on its own' it can comment on the efficacy of what is done and the significance of what is perceived in the subjective and private world of the individual. But it has been acquired through social communication, and for this reason, within the confines of culturally homogeneous groups, it remains a vehicle for the refinement of one person's perception through the comments of another on his performance. This applies as much to the young child learning to eat and drink 'correctly' as to the techniques of a potential opera or ballet prima donna. It is thus the chief mediator of culture in national and international spheres. With regards to international culture one might say that a naïve tourist experiences the habits and customs and attitudes of a country at a sensori-motor level if he cannot speak its language but this insight is refined and rendered more subtle and complex if he takes the trouble to learn the language and thus comprehend better the emotive significance of gesture and sentiment. There is little doubt that language of some kind is a necessary vehicle for the cultural development of a child beyond the age of two years. The fact that language can be acquired through sensori-motor systems other than the larynx and ear suggests that the one requisite is the existence in the cortex of large areas which may be structured by any overflow from the specific sensori-motor areas. It may be, of course, that this greater potentiality for elaboration exists in man not only in the association areas but also in all the sensori-motor modalities, but the greater significance is usually attached to the A/S ratio.

6 *A cognitive theory of motivation*

This elaborate system of linguistic signs is one of the most stable features of human learning. For example, the vocabulary test is not only the best criterion of mental status in an individual but also the one which remains unchanged through such vicissitudes as ageing and mental illness. Rabin and Guertin (1951) conducted an extensive enquiry using the Wechsler-Bellevue Scale and found that among mental patients the test-retest reliability for vocabulary was as high as 0·94. All other sub-tests were considerably less reliable (0·56–0·79). A similar distribution of reliability was found among the sub-tests in an ageing professional population. Moreover, an assault of any kind to the brain, whether by accident or surgery, results in less loss of verbal skills than in the capacity to organise in the practical sensori-motor field (assuming the injury not to be located in the speech centres of the cortex) (Wechsler 1958). In many cases of brain injury regressive changes in behaviour patterns are observed which have significance for motivation. These are indicated by such appellations as 'not trying so hard', 'indifferent and casual', 'flighty and irresponsible'. Such characterological traits would be regarded as normal in less mature people whose neural structures though intact are less integrated through experience. It can be taken then that reduction of cortical area through injury is correlated with loss of capacity to initiate and sustain integrated effort. Lashley's study (1929) of learning in brain-injured rats supports this hypothesis of a relationship between the number of associated neurones and the efficacy of the organism's responses. This integration is not that of processing the primary sensory input for this is carried out at the thalamic level (Fig. 1). The failure occurs in the organisation of these sensory impressions into more elaborate patterns at a cortical level. For example, in the object assembly test of the Wechsler scale, a brain-injured patient may recognise that the pieces are those of a face, yet succeed in placing only two of the pieces in correct juxtaposition. This is probably because he fails to bear in mind for long enough the total image of a face in relation to its parts, and so does not understand the incongruity of his placements. Similarly in the processing of an auditory pattern, his capacity to change a stimulus in accordance with some rule is defective. This may be seen in his incapacity to repeat digits backwards while retaining an unimpaired capacity for rote repetition of digits as spoken by the tester. The former feat calls for more elaborate cortical processing while the latter will occur largely at a thalamic level with more simple cortical adjuncts (Neff 1962).

Among the well-known projective techniques the Rorschach is the only one which derives its diagnostic significance from style in perceptual processing rather than from emotive content. This test is scored according to the formal properties of the subject's thought processes and takes no account of the emotive content of responses. It is necessary for the tester to ascertain from the subject being tested what element in the ink blot caused him to make his interpretation. The three main categories of cues are colour, form and apparent movement, e.g. 'the red made me think of blood', 'the shape of this part reminds me of two witches who look as though they are flying on broomsticks'. When colour responsive groups are compared with others they tend to be rather more extraverted, emotionally labile and perceptually passive. Groups selected because of their greater tendency to produce interpretations of movement tend to have higher mean scores for introversion. They are as inhibited as the colour-prone interpreters are facilitated (Ovsiankina 1960). This typing in terms of perceptual predilection bears an obvious relationship with the temperamental dimension of cortical excitation-inhibition. The inhibited cortex of the extravert causes perceptual passivity, hence the colour preference, while the cortical excitation of the introvert makes for a more perceptually active and detailed approach to the non-structured stimulus. With regards to the behaviour traits characteristic of those with colour preference, the relatively inhibited cortex exerts a feebler suzerainty over the autonomic processes which results in emotional lability. The suppression of spontaneity in the behaviour of those with more movement preferences arises from inhibition of the autonomic activation system by a cortical excitation which is above average. Colour and movement preference would seem then to have a temperamental or genetic basis. The greatest number of responses in most subjects, however, are those suggested by the form of the ink blot and these are taken to be an indication of ego-control. This suggests an acquired rather than a temperamental dimension, and it should arise from an harmonious integration of central and autonomic processing. Perception of form, when justified by the clues inherent in the blot, is regarded as depending upon the highest levels of cerebral organisation (Beck's Z score).

Rorschach research has thrown up suggestive relationships between constitutionally induced behaviour patterns, both normal and abnormal, and preferences for cognitive modes of operation. This is true also of the cognitive Wechsler-Bellevue Tests. There is a tendency here for individual test profiles to be correlated with constitutional types. For example, the schizophrenic tends to have a relatively wide span of attention as measured by the test of digit span, while the person suffering from anxiety neurosis does less well in this subtest than is to be expected from his average level. The former is characterised by low drive and the latter by high reactivity. This would cause too great an arousal for clear perception in the anxiety neurotic but reduce the degree of interference in the schizophrenic who would thus retain the sensory impression long enough to repeat the digits correctly (Highfield 1945). Recent experimental work in motivation (Eysenck 1964) has been pursued through studies of changes in cognitive processes rather than with the use of concepts relating to the content of the personal psyche. This relates therapy to learning, and symptoms to acquired structure. Such an hypothesis is that of Easterbrook 'the number of cues utilized in any situation tends to become smaller with increase in motivation'.

This suggests that the attentional field becomes relatively narrow, and exclusive of the peripheral. On the other hand, Feldman (1964) observes after considering the work of Eysenck and Berlyne that it is during rest pauses that incidental or peripheral learning occurs. These two hypotheses are perhaps of importance for a developmental study of motivation. Narrowed attentional fields should accompany the higher levels of excitation experienced by introverts, while the greater degree of reactive inhibition experienced by extraverts would make for more frequent rest pauses. These observations have relevance for an explanation of the cognitive styles of the two types. The introvert tends to note details, to be error avoidant and to think covergently rather than divergently. The reverse picture is presented by the extravert. These characteristics will be considered more fully in the chapter on adolescence, but it is appropriate here to discuss their possible physiological basis.

It is conceivable then, that conventional and unconventional motivation may arise largely from this physiological source where there is more extreme temperamental disposition along the E–I dimension. In fact, Feldman concludes as a result of surveying the literature on motivation and task performance that 'motivation may eventually prove to be a superfluous concept with motivational phenomena accountable in terms of associative theories'. From the foregoing remarks it could be postulated that drive energises associations of two kinds, according to whether brain cells are inhibited or excited.

It is clear from these considerations that fruitful research in motivation is moving away from the examination of thought content to a study of the dynamics of thought processes. The latter are already represented in techniques of measurement with crude beginnings in Wechsler profiles and Rorschach analyses but almost any perceptual test serves to throw up group differences between types (Granger, Brengelmann 1957, Hamilton 1964). Thus motivational levels are to a large extent geared to cognitive efficiency through the individual's perceptual impact on the environment (Granger 1953). In fact, Allport's definition of motivation might be extended by the writer's italics to include this element thus – "any internal condition *or preferential style in the processing of sensory data* that induces action or thought".

CHAPTER II

Motivation during the sensori-motor stage of the first two years

I. THE EFFECTS OF CARETAKING

1 *The first responses*

An account of developmental trends in motivation from birth to the end of the second year can be based profitably on the hypothesis that RAS receives a primary imprint of structure and function during this period. This is effected by an increasing maturation of central processes, inaugurated largely from autonomic sources, at a time during which the myelinisation of motor nerve axons is completed. Since growth in complexity of behaviour becomes increasingly paced by response potential, the maturation of neural paths conducting efferent discharge is of special significance for the relationship between structure and function. The hypothesis that growth tends to follow the direction of innervation would ensure a built-in pattern associated with its own dynamic style. The general result of such an interaction between structure and function could be a style of perception and response unique to the individual yet more or less like that of others of similar genetic constitution, and of similar cultural placement. Of these two influences during the first two years, the former is likely to be of greater importance. Subsequently, the latter becomes increasingly dominant as a structuring influence.

Since the advent of Freudian theory and the study of neurosis in World War One which it informed, there has been a move towards greater tolerance of childish ways. This might be described as a re-evaluation of the ANS as a profitable source of activation. The typical American mother of today regards her new-born baby as 'a potential', and there is a relatively good agreement in the community on how it should be developed. It is commonly held that parental restraint should not retard development and that the child should not be pushed into the acceptance of adult requirements. Parents derive comfort from the ideas of stages, norms and the inheritance of characteristics as explanations of the behaviour of the child (Fischer 1963). This implies a profound revolution in the social aspects of the western cultural pattern over the last hundred years which crystallised into applicable principles with the writings of Freud in the middle of this era. Today, the products of psychological and educational research percolate rapidly into most households through the media of mass communication, and the new term of the campus soon becomes the popular jargon of the nursery or of the pop singer. The terms cognitive dissonance and arousal jag are reflected in the adolescent's explanation that he does things for 'kicks'.

Recent emphasis has been on the effects of stimulation during the first year and the arousal for which it is responsible. The most fascinating work in this field has been done with babies privated of normal family stimulation in caretaking. The studies of Spitz (1946), Provence and Lipton (1962) and others have demonstrated the function of early stimulation on behaviour responses during the first two years and after. Studies of this kind allied to longitudinal research with normally placed children such as that of Wolff (1963) are elucidating the problem both of norms and of their optimal and critical antecedents. In the longitudinal study of Provence and Lipton, group differences between their matched samples of institution and home-reared infants began to appear after four weeks. They report that by this age the home-reared infants adapted themselves readily to the arms of the adult while the institution babies felt more like saw-dust dolls. They were less cuddly and seemed to lack pliability. At the later age of four to five months the home-reared babies had acquired head control when pulled from supine to sitting position. This structuring was delayed in the institution babies, but they could be 'taught' this skill within a single session by playfully pulling the child to sit upright. After some repetition the head was raised in anticipation of the pull on the shoulders. This was evidence of a maturational readiness which was not exploited. Doubtless the handling of the institution, though less frequent, would have resulted eventually in head control; but it is an example of the necessity for the child to learn through adult stimulation where there is no innate reflex pattern for the skill.

The only kind of motor activity that was increased in the institution babies was rocking, which was universal by eight months of age. If Luria's (1949) hypothesis is correct this is caused by a readiness for more complex behaviour, but a delay in making the transition on account of an absence of external pressures on the relevant skeletal and muscular areas. Rocking is perhaps the most rudimentary form of self stimulation and one which simulates the rhythmic activities experienced in utero.

In the institution babies it served the basic need for arousal, utilising those neural pathways which were sufficiently mature. By the end of the first year maturational pressures and chance stimulation caused the children to advance from frequent rocking on all fours to pulling themselves into upright positions in their cots. The home-reared infants had been prepared for this much earlier by frequent experience of pressure of feet against the mother's body, before there was sufficient strength for them to support body weight. This earlier preparation means a more gradual integration of developing bodily skills along a multiple front, and it is to be supposed that this would result in refinement of all the postural requirements for walking. Privation of opportunity for such comprehensive integration could account for the observation that, at the age of five years after adoption during the second year, the institution children lacked grace of movement. After adoption there had been an acceleration in the growth of purposive motor activity but it was gawkily executed. It might be postulated from this evidence that the handling of the first year can provide opportunity for optimal learning in walking but that opportunity to rock and facilities for pulling the body into an upright position are the critical or necessary aspects.

2 *The body image*

The comparative study of Provence and Lipton undoubtedly throws considerable light on the way in which the body image is formed. During the first two years the integration of action units into a perceptual schema normally achieves its primary unity, for by the end of this period the child is mobile and manipulative, and able to adapt himself and his environment to his wishful or autistic urges. Since it is clear that this sensori-motor structuring underlies self-awareness, it may be regarded as the foundation of self-hood, both as a concept expressed in verbal terms and also as a state of continuous awareness of the self as distinct from the non-self. The sense of the non-self is conveyed by the handling of others which is distinguished from customary self stimulation in various bodily areas. Schilder (1956) remarks "there is no question that our own activity is insufficient to build up the image of our own body. The touches of others, the interest of others in different parts of our body will be of enormous importance in the development of the postural model of the body."

There is ignorance, however, about what are the minimum requirements of mothering for the body schema. It is suggested that too much stimulation during these years could give rise to an unstable body image especially if it was expressive of the adult's libidinous and aggressive impulses. Under such conditions, in Ritvo's longitudinal case study reported by Provence and Lipton (1962), there was good development of skills but collapse and regression, and heedlessness concerning safety, when scolded or punished. Provence and Lipton deduce from these observations that there are two requirements for the establishment of an adequate body image: firstly physical handling and opportunity to use emerging motor skills, and secondly a modicum of control in the caretaker of impulses and feelings conveyed through touching and handling. The disintegrating effect of punishment on motor co-ordination in those who have been over stimulated in infancy would appear to be due to an uprush of anxiety. This would bring about over-arousal in a child whose infancy had been subjected to decremental conditioning by apparent withdrawal of affection and support in moments of parental anxiety. Moreover, the child's distress signals would be reinforced by the return of comfort and support when the parent experiences remorse. For all practical purposes this conditioning results in an unstable body image under stress, an accident proneness which has been reinforced by its power to win back adult support. It is therefore as much a learned response as the harmoniously integrated schema acquired under the influence of normal handling. The over-anxious parent is more likely to lose an objective view of her infant and to convey anxiety to him abruptly in a manner which interrupts his normal exploratory and manipulative activities. His subsequent 'collapse' pattern under stress is thus as learned in all probability as those skills which emerge from normal opportunity.

The genetic motor passivity of the schizophrenic baby should lead to an inadequate body image because of lack of experience. His failure to explore his own body and discouragement of the approaches of others brought about by his chronic lack of responsiveness result in privation of the usual infantile sensori-motor learning. Weckowicz and Sommer (1960) regard the loose and blurred boundaries of the social ego as based upon a similar body schema. The adult schizophrenic may report that parts of the body do not belong to him or that he is part of other creatures or the whole of mankind or of the whole universe. They also underestimate the size of the distal parts of their body when compared with non-schizophrenic controls. Such observations of adults afford hypotheses which call for verification in longitudinal studies. It seems reasonable, however, to suggest that both the sense of merging with one's environment and that of separateness is a normal outcome of experience during the first two years reinforced at later ages by poetic and religious metaphorical reference. The main difficulty in longitudinal studies of the effects of privation would appear to be control of the genetic factor. This is a covert cause of the extent to which the child is a stimulus to the adult in handling, and may be both a-normally positive and subnormally negative in reinforcing caretaker responses (Vernon 1964, Clarke 1965). For example, favourite babies in institutions tend to be placed nearer the caretaking table and are in consequence stimulated more, and show the effects of privation less. But it is likely that these favoured children are those who are more responsive for genetic reasons (Provence and Lipton 1962).

Pathological privation of sensori-motor experience may be studied in children who have become paralysed by contracting poliomyelitis. Morgoulis and Tournay (1963) using such tests as the imitation of the gestures of a mannikin and Goodenough's Draw-a-man test concluded that an early onset of the disease before the age of three was more crippling than a later assault to the brain. They concluded that the handicap was global rather than specific in its effect on perceptual structure and that this stemmed from an inadequate body image. Wallon and Lurçat (1962) postulate three levels of movement in relation to surrounding space. The first is non-purposive, habitual and automatic with subsequent awareness. The second is externally motivated to adapt to space and the third a spontaneous anticipation of an object in space. These three types of movement were certainly present during the first six months of life in the study of Provence and Lipton and it seemed clear that handling facilitated the second and third levels, for the movement of the lower limbs in particular. Movement of the upper parts of the body was less impeded in the prone position.

3 *The body image and emotions*

For Wallon (1962) postural space contained the psycho-genetic ingredients of social attitudes in the sense that it referred not only to perception of shape but also to 'affective space' seen in a feeling for withdrawal or approach. Approach and withdrawal tendencies are first evident in the massive patterns associated with satisfaction and dissatisfaction, and later with smiling and crying in response to gross bodily comfort or its absence. These primary motivational systems become differentiated through conditioning into dependence and aversion, constituting secondary motivational systems. They may derive from the resolution of conflict when incompatible expectancies arise, regarding the rewarding and punishing of what appear to be the same actions in the perception of the child. The discovery of the action which mollifies the caretaker results in incremental conditioning through anxiety drive reduction (Mowrer 1939, 1960). This tendency to positive conditioning by drive reduction results in what is termed dependency behaviour because the mother is the chief arbiter of anxiety drive reduction as she is of its arousal. Whiting (et al. 1953) remarks on a small positive correlation between nursery school dependency and infant feeding frustration, and it appeared to these workers as a central aspect of the dependency drive, whereas toilet training factors were unrelated to dependency. These observations applied in particular to girls which suggests some additional cultural reinforcement is operative in their case. Wallon's affective space is seen here as growing out of the early sensori-motor systems of aversion and receptivity in relation to the reduction of pain and its psychological derivative, anxiety. The built-in autonomic reflexes subserving flexor and extensor movements are patterned differently for reaction to states of satisfaction and dissatisfaction, and they are probably the foundation systems of all approach and withdrawal tendencies at subsequent stages of maturity. It is to be expected then that there will be a body image gestalt comprehending all forms of approach and retreat and also conflict between these tendencies.

4 *Early social responses*

Two extremely important sensori-motor experiences, which in all probability are the first to be conditioned by arousal from parental interest, are eye convergence which emerges in the fourth week and the smiling grimace. Wolff (1963) reports that whereas the drowsy 'drunken' smile of the second week was a source of amusement to parents the eye-to-eye contact of the fourth week was taken as 'really being seen' and 'fun to play with'. By this time, too, smiling in his babies had become a predictable and repeatable response to a number of specific stimuli in wakefulness. Two months later the babies were spontaneously 'practising' smiling and gurgling, and the activity was less stimulus-bound. Moreover, they were capable of ignoring the usual stimuli to which they smiled when engaged on some other activity originated by themselves.

The morphological smile of the first week became fully recognitory in the ninth month in Ambrose's (1962) study when the child sobered at people perceived to be strangers. In a later article Ambrose (1963) suggests that the level of responsiveness to people other than the mother is related to the level of responsiveness achieved earlier to the mother. Such transfer is to be expected because of the common sensori-motor components of the mother-derived experience and the components of the strange situation. The greater the complexity of the former the more probable it is that a similar cue significance will arise in contacts with other persons. Such complexity is not necessarily dependent on the level of mothering but may be a function of the child's capacity for response. As Ambrose points out, there is only slight evidence to suggest that this is more related to quality of mothering than to genetic factors. This statement refers of course to individual differences among children in normal family circumstances and not to the grossly privated. Providing the child has a normal constitution and is normally mothered from the psychological angle it would appear that the effect of much apparent cultural privation can be reversed. This is exemplified perhaps in Davis's (1947) Isabella, who was incarcerated with her deaf-mute mother in an attic until she was six. From being a severely rachitic mute imbecile she was restored to normality within two years. This suggests that she had been subjected to appropriate handling in infancy and to gesture language in early childhood, and that her defects were in the main cultural and skeletal. Within the private world peopled by herself and her mother, she had experienced no privation of basic sensori-motor structuring.

5 *The organisation of behaviour patterns*

The evidence so far supports a gestalt rather than a connectionist view of learning and suggests that a dynamic postural schema of approach and retreat is the crucial forerunner of later growth complexities. This would not seem congruent with the view that conditioning is an appropriate theory to explain learning in infancy, because of its specificity. Conditioned reflexes, however, would imply holism if it was assumed that reflexes are activated by a general push and pull system such as the ANS. Conditioning could then be regarded as a re-organisation of this autonomic neural field. In this way the primary gestalt would be provided by the autonomic nervous system, and reinforcement of one mode of behaviour rather than another through drive potential would entail the restructuring of the vegetative and emergency systems in the first place. Conditioning through more socialised drives again would constitute a total modification of such earlier established gestalten. The perception of the caretaker in all her guises would emerge as part of the whole and constitute the origins of the social self, integrated with structuring from the vegetative and emergency functions. Such considerations suggest that it was the neurologist in Freud that led him to make the mystical statement that the mother imago is 'incorporated'. Thus the largest and most comprehensive schema is inclusive of all others which become intrinsically integrated with it. Yet as Allport insists each stratum can re-assert its autonomy by abandoning the later stages of re-organisation. When this occurs regressive behaviour results. Interesting examples of this occurring under the influence of hypnosis have been cited by Reiff and Scheerer (1959). In one of these, the production of the physical stigmata of injury received in childhood demonstrated that the body schema is conserved by 'memory' of function. Those nerves which mediated subcutaneous bleeding responses were reactivated and the earlier weals were reproduced in the hypnotic state.

Regressive behaviour in childhood is more frequently in evidence than at later stages of maturity. It implies a reassertion of autonomy in more primary schemata because they are the best match in the child's repertoire for the situation as perceived by him. In fact, regression may be called an adaptable device used *faute de mieux* to meet a problem situation. It is a strategy which has succeeded in the past. It is unsuitable and 'regressive' only to the observer. For example, if at the age of nine months a child sobers at a stranger, behaviour is at a normal maturational level. If the stranger persists in making advances the child may cry. This response may be a regression to an earlier form of behaviour which has been positively conditioned by his mother's comforting. If, however, the comforting had been supplemented in the past by distracting conversation and play, the child's expectancies concerning reassurance would be more complex and he would tend to be the more readily mollified if similar comforting advances were made by the stranger.

Such regressions and returns to more recently acquired responses are implied perhaps in the Freudian concept of introjection and projection. Introjection involved an attempt at appraisal of the present situation, and projection the production of a neural template of response to match it. During the first year caretaking compensates for the paucity of projected know-how and facilitates introjection of new modes of response. Caretakers, however, are dependent on their perception of the child's needs and proclivities, and the more overtly they are expressed the better the quality of the caretaking. The responsive child who is apparently recognitory in his glances and appears to enjoy the caretaker's advances will provide entertainment and a growing awareness in the mother of her unique role in relation to her offspring. Bowlby's (1958) view that mothering is a conditioned response to built-in releasing stimuli presented by the child such as sucking, clinging, smiling and crying is of central importance in the structuring of personality. Moreover, the child's position on the major temperamental continua should affect his general behaviour in terms of speed, duration and intensity. These dynamic aspects of his responses tend to become regulators of the approaches of caretakers. In Wolff's (1963) study one baby responded in sleep or drowsiness to a stimulus within two seconds of its onset, some needed six to eight minutes, and some failed to respond at all. His experimental interest in arousal states should reveal the importance of these individual differences when similar cross-sectional studies are made. His categories of arousal states were regular deep sleep, irregular light sleep, drowsiness, alert inactivity, waking activity, waking alertness (after the third week) and crying. It is clear that individual differences will exist in the relative proportions of these states, conveying to the caretaker impressions of indifference or affection on the part of the child as maturation proceeds. The child who is frequently unresponsive tends to be at a disadvantage in releasing caretaking tenderness. Further differential structuring arising from the same source would be contributed by the extent to which parent-child reinforcement is regular or intermittent. Where the child is of a strongly extraverted disposition, the freer discharge of autonomic arousal should facilitate reinforcement of his own actions. Such ready release of impulse, however, would render reinforcement from caretaking more intermittent. He would thus be more difficult to 'train'. A strongly introverted baby, with his cortical liveliness, should by the same theory be more observant of his environment and at an advantage in instrumentally conditioning both himself and his caretaker. Vernon (1964) criticises the Eysenckian hypothesis that 'condition-ability' is a unitary trait while considering it reasonable to suppose that there may be some linkage between extraversion-introversion and attitudes to authority. This problem could be resolved by relevant longitudinal observation of learning patterns in babies, where it might be found that the child's temperament largely controlled the reinforcement interval and also the appraisal of the cues in the conditioning situation.

II. THE COGNITIVE FUNCTIONS

1 *The structuring of perceptual-response mechanisms*

The dynamics of the relationship between cortex and subcortical systems could possibly be at the crux of most temperamental differences in learning. The view may be taken that the reflex groundwork of behaviour is the mediator of its total integration, while the acquired cortical structure is the main source of differentiation within this total gestalt. This is seen in its simplest perhaps through experimentation in the psycho-physiology of learning (Morgan 1951). It is helpful in this to consider the contribution of a subcortical ganglion such as the thalamus and its relation to the cortex. The thalamus mediates an awareness of simple differences in intensity of say light flux or sound or tactual awareness. This appears to be largely undifferentiated. The patterning of these simple schemata is brought about by cortical processing. This adds detail to the simple differences of intensity. For example without the posterior parietal lobe of the cortex chimpanzees cannot be trained to distinguish between wedges and pyramids, but prolonged training enables them to distinguish between cones and pyramids, the latter distinction being more crude and simple. It would seem then that some learning occurs sub-cortically prior to the contribution made subsequently by cortical structuring.

This process of differentiation within the total sub-cortical gestalt may be deduced from Ambrose's (1962) delineation of the way a baby comes to demand more and more detail in a face as a stimulus to the smiling response. In the first stage of discrimination the eyes of the facial stimulus elicit a smile, but gradually other details such as mouth, nose and hair come to be regarded as essential aspects of an acceptable percept, if smiling is to ensue. Thus at first there is a simple perception of differences in intensity of light in the eye-ball with the high light moving against the dark background of the pupil. This might be regarded as very close to a thalamic level of sensory processing. At this stage the child is indifferent to other facial details and is no way perturbed when they are masked out. As every painter of portraits knows the greatest contrast in tone in a human face is that between the high light of the eye and its pupil and it is therefore the simplest difference in that it is the most extreme. Between these two extremes of dark and light all other grades of tone that make up the pattern of the face must be fitted on a grey white continuum. It is probable that no colour is seen in the earliest stages because the retinal rods mature prior to the cones.

By the ninth month, however, recognitory criteria are so advanced that there is a sobering at all people seen as strangers. This progressive patterning mediated by cortico-thalamic circuits is so closely geared to the biological needs of the infant that it may be regarded as an integral aspect of biological inheritance. The absence of the true mother and the frequent contacts it implies merely retards these emergent characteristics by three weeks or so. If the drowsy smiling grimace of the first fortnight is taken as the starting point it would seem that a change in sensory thresholds is the first stimulus to the smile (Wolff 1963). By the fifth week, however, this change has become a gestalt perceived in a waking state, a simply structured juxtaposition of dark and light tones. The drowsy smile of the first fortnight suggests the operation of a servo-mechanism activated by a gross occlusion of light through the slow drooping of the eyelids. Within a few weeks, the simultaneous presence of contrasting extremes is realised, through familiarity with a caretaker's eyes, after convergent occulo-motor control is in evidence.

2 *The origins of attention*

The emergence of the recognitory face in stimulating approach or withdrawal is a clear example of differentiations occurring within a vaguely structured total field as a result of the dynamics of response. At the outset of this chapter it was suggested that the structuring of RAS during the first two years of neural maturation was a highly significant determinant of future motivation patterns. Such structuring implies the locking-in of the requisite circuits of response to match the pattern of stimuli and also the modulation of the dynamic intensity of arousal. These preparatory activities of the organism have been studied, mainly by the Russian psychologists, under the heading of 'orienting responses'. Pavlov invented this term to cover the minute twitches and tensions manifested by his dogs as they stood harnessed and awaiting the appearance of the experimental stimulus. He noticed individual differences among his subjects in this behaviour, which caused him to postulate a temperamental dimension of cortical excitation-inhibition (identified by Eysenck as the neural counterpart of Jung's temperamental dimension of Introversion-extraversion). If this is so, orienting responses will tend to differ according to whether the human baby is introverted and has an excited cortex or extraverted with a relatively depressed cortex – taken by and large. Moreover, if RAS becomes structured in a way which will never be completely revised at later ages, the baby may receive during the first two years a strong slant in perceptual style.

It is probable that all orienting patterns originate through sub-cortical conditioning in the earliest stages of their formation. Presumably the reinforcing element would be need-reduction. An even more organismic concept to explain primary orienting would be that of homeostasis. This would be more by way of a servo-mechanism in which the firing of neural sequences occurred along optimal paths, these being constitutionally determined. The nearer to conception one traces the origin of orienting responses, the more likely they are to appear as mechanistic. The more mature they are, the more they will appear as purposive and volitional. The broad constitutional primary pattern becomes highly differentiated into the power to initiate strategies leading to decision and choice. Since elaboration is a cortical function, the operations of RAS could be regarded as a structured lead into action provided by the lower centres to the higher, each centrencephalically differentiating the other. During the first two years elaboration of this kind will tend to become built into the organism's physiology through its material effect on the physical structure of the motor axons. This means that in a very general sense a built-in disposition is acquired post-natally.

An orienting reflex which can be more easily observed during its primary developmental phases is that basic to language. Speech is a sound-articulation complex but the ear is the receptor organ for the sound that coincides with awareness of the articulatory movements which produced the sound stimulus. Wolff's (1963) exceedingly detailed study revealed some of the stages in the early development of this skill. Before discussing them in detail it is necessary to point out that his eight babies were subjected to more than the usual amount of stimulation, for as he remarks the parents competed with him to elicit the child's responses. Thus although the stages he noted may present a normal sequence the ages may be precocious. During the first week smiling responses could be elicited during sleep to a variety of aural stimuli including bells, whistles and high-pitched voices. This is perhaps the initial stage in which the lips and larynx convey kinaesthetic sensation associated with sound. Wolff noticed a vestigial 'cocking' of the ears which preceded the mouth stretching and which was not a mechanical consequence of this movement. The term vestigial seems an appropriate descriptive term, for in animals when eating the auditory sense is enhanced whereas a man munching celery is less likely to hear his neighbour at dinner. This observation has relevance if the morphological smile is regarded as a generic grimace resulting from all forms of arousal.

During the second week this grimace becomes patterned by the addition of wrinkling at the corners of the eyes and by contraction of the superficial muscles of the cheek, and there is an increase in response to a high-pitched voice. The activation of the muscles which will be involved in speech has spread from lips to cheeks and possibly tongue while a degree of selectivity concerning sound has appeared. This can be expected from more frequent aural experience of the mother's voice and from the varied experience of the face in contact with the breast and in the course of washing and drying.

By the nineteenth day all eight babies had responded to the high-pitched voice with a clear-cut broad smile while fully awake and with the eyes bright, and even when whimpering and fussing they were able to respond to sounds from without.

At the fourth week a progressive differentiation of vocalisation became apparent, and the moan and whimper which had accompanied the cry face occurred when the child seemed placid and content. To these were added deep throat sounds. By the end of the fourth week gurgling and cooing sounds were in evidence and the mother's voice could arrest crying.

By the fifth week, the stage in which the baby smiles at a face, the mother's voice added to a face elicited arousal most easily. In addition the child tended then to respond to his own vocalisation which was a necessary prelude to imitation. From now on vocalisation became a spontaneous activity 'practised' by the child independently of other stimuli. This autonomy of the activity suggested that the child's own voice was the stimulation to further vocalisation. A nascent selective attention to stimuli had been apparent by the third week when vocalisation was the more frequent response to vocalisation, but by the third month it would appear that sound-articulatory schemata were sufficiently established to ensure circularity of self-stimulus and response. This implies a feed-back of the sensory results of motor discharge which is facilitative to the motor system and gives rise to repetition. Since by the fourth month the child's articulatory repertoire may be comprehensive enough to furnish the phonetic requirements for any language (Moore 1896), he is ready for the circular reaction of communication. He shows by an arrest of movement followed by a spontaneous smile that he has been significantly affected by the imitation of one of his sounds by an adult. In this way the primary body image associated with speech and language is established.

Thus orienting and postural patterns consist of a system of locking-in of neural paths and their pattern of facilitation and inhibition, and competition with other pathways. From this structuring of RAS should emerge such styles as verbal fluency, verbal inhibition and stammering. The general pattern emerges as a result of the autonomic stimulation of movement in sucking and burping (labial elements) and swallowing and regurgitating (guttural elements) and reaches perhaps its final stage in Baldwin's circular reaction (Lewis 1936) which is the dawn of conscious and purposive imitation in speech. Another significant stage during the first two years occurs round about fourteen months when most infants can say a word on request. This represents the beginnings of immediate memory and means that a word is easily available to recall. The importance of this for a capacity to express wishes and to communicate with others in words is obvious. By this time the linguistic orienting response has achieved a complex level but it is comprised of all the elements listed above, any one of which could regain autonomy in future disoriented moments. This is seen in the embarrassed stammer, the shocked indrawn breath, the anxious vomiting before a maiden speech. None of these vocal forms, associated with disruption of established cortical patterns, are new or strange but merely primary forms which have fallen into disuse with the building up of a more mature linguistic orienting reflex. When they occur, 'locking-in' has failed partially on account of over-arousal from autonomic sources and there is regression to an earlier pattern associated with similar situations.

Expectancy is a term closely allied to orienting response. Expectancy is the potential underlying habit, and orienting responses are the summation of the dynamic processes which launch expectancies into overt habitual behaviour. During the first seven months expectancy is not highly structured, but after this age the child suffers if customary stimulus fails to lead to habitual response. Orienting responses die out if this deprivation is too prolonged and symptoms of depressive withdrawal take their place. As Schaffer (1963) remarks, "the infant who at ten months cries for his mother, and who cried for the attention of any person at five months, will have cried for any kind of environmental change at three months". This implies an increasing differentiation or specificity within the general sensori-motor field.

3 *The empathic bond between mother and child*

Schaffer's hospitalisation studies suggest that by the eighth month separation upset occurs because of denied expectancy associated with the customary caretaker.

It has been long realised that the affective bonds established between the customary caretaker and child vary considerably in reciprocal sensitivity. Adequacy on the part of both participants is apparently necessary, and it is the function of mothering to comprehend the optimal amount of stimulation having regard to the child's readiness. A realisation of the importance of this for social development and emotional health is implied in the use of the term 'empathy' to describe the reciprocity of attachment. For Sullivan empathy is a form of psychological contagion which is experienced not only by the mother but also by the child. More exact methods of research have thrown light on the origin of this symbiosis. It is a relationship of attachment which is formed between the child and his customary source of stimulation. Harlow's (1962) baby chimpanzees were reared with heated cushions and wire frame feeders to serve as parent surrogates. If a foreign object was put in their cage they first retreated to the cushion and then investigated the object. In the absence of the cushion, a foreign object brought about an acute access of anxiety. The young chimpanzee showed signs of panic, crouching on the ground with face hidden. In a subsequent report, Harlow (1963) shows that such mechanical contrivances by way of a parent do not educate the baby monkey to become an effective mate because of privation of the necessary social experience. But it was an adequate preparation for a celibate existence among robots. The essential aspect of mothering appears to be some constant form of stimulation calibrated to the child's developing capacity to receive it. For the most part the arousal brought about in a normal family environment is an adequate form of structuring for adult family responsibilities. Yet individuals in the same family can differ enormously in the extent to which they develop normally. Where these differences are gross it in all probability arises from genetic causes. For example, a first child of extreme schizothymic temperament should present a strong contrast to a second of cyclothymic disposition by the time maturity is reached. For the first the parent's inexperience and the child's lack of responsiveness combine to reduce the level of all-round stimulation. Orienting responses leading to complex purposive behaviour in maturity tend to be conspicuously absent. In the case of the second child, the experienced caretaker and the child's capacity for response to stimulation results in structuring on a multiple front suited to varied adaptability later. Most families incidentally provide enough stimulation for normal development, and empathy between mother and child is tempered by the practical exigencies of caretaking. Multiple caretaking of children in institutions usually results in less handling than home-reared infants, but it is possible that young children could make multiple attachments if each caretaker handled them more. This is certainly true in cultures where there is multiple but intensive caretaking of children, as among the Rajputs of Khalapur (Whiting 1963). Here siblings, grandparents and uncles partake in caretaking, and the family is extended much beyond those normal in the west.

Soon after birth the infant appears to indulge in activity for its own sake when comfortable and awake. Hand and arm activity and mouthing take place in all infants whether they are handled or not. It is in the legs and in their co-ordination with the trunk in supporting weight that handling is expediting. Self-initiated activity appears to be enjoyed and is pursued in states of satisfaction. By the latter half of the second year many primary skills such as finger-thumb opposition in manipulation, walking, and the ability to use speech and gesture in simple communication, renders more clear the child's joy in forming schemata. This is an important motivational variable, and novel movements are repeated many times with intense concentration. Activities are discovered by accident, and once the child is ambient he increases his sensorimotor repertoire in proportion to environmental opportunity. The writer once counted the number of repetitions made by a child of twenty months after discovering a new activity. This consisted of stepping up on to a hassock and down again while resting one hand on the arm of a chair. The contrasting effects of the hard firm surface of the floor and the soft less stable surface of the hassock on his equilibrium was a new source of proprioceptive and visual stimulation which prompted thirty-two repetitions. It is clear from such observations as this that the neural schemata which comprise the body image are established with all the accompaniments of delight in learning which is reinforcing in itself. Interest shown by an affectionate adult, if distracting, could be a form of frustration, and it is probable that detachment in the caretaker becomes increasingly important as the power to explore and discover increases.

Although much is known, through studies of privation and deprivation, of the effects of insufficient stimulation, little is known about the effects of overstimulation. The effects of too much stimulation by caretakers would probably relate to frustrating attempts to intervene when the child is embarking on activities of discovery. This could arise from a protective attitude to prevent accidents on the part of an anxious mother or impatience with the child's incompetence leading to premature training techniques. In over-protection, the amount of vigorous activity initiated by the child could mitigate much frustration, and where the child is expedited a precocious maturity will enable him to satisfy caretaking demand without loss. Both, however, are examples of too much parental stimulation in specific areas of experience associated with parental anxiety. In an enquiry into stereotypes in the upbringing of English children seventy mothers of problem children showed a-normal attitudes only in the areas of suppression and overprotection. There were no significant differences in matters of discipline, freedom for the child and freedom for the mother, nor in their position along a dimension of detachment-projection (Hebron and London 1963). The over-protection of young children is more readily understood than an attitude expediting their progress at this tender age, but the writer once knew an intelligent boy whose mother succeeded in teaching him to ride a tricycle before he was two because his walking pace frustrated her. This was a case of successful expediting by an affectionate but impatient mother. His capacity enabled him to meet her demand without experience of frustration. Kagan and Moss (1962) postulate on the basis of their longitudinal study that the critical hostility of mothers before the age of three years is a good basis for achievement motivation if reinforced after the age of six years by expectation that they will do well at school. How far this extended back into the first two years is not clear from their report, but it is probable that such an attitude which they describe as hostility, i.e. impatience at the child's incompetence, would accelerate as the child's competence increased. The manifestation of emergent forms of response in the child is usually noted with interest by the parent which causes her caretaking to move slightly ahead of the co-operation made possible by the current level of competence to which she had become accustomed. In this way she provides, as it were, a moving front of expectation for him, and he comes to align his pleasure at forming new schemata with her approval of his success. Her positive appraisal serves eventually as a conditioned stimulus which evokes satisfaction with his own achievement.

4 *The development of verbal meaning*

A mother's empathic echo of her child's joy is a conditioned sustainer of his efforts beyond the point of first habituation, and on into a more refined level of skill. Her aid in all nurturant activities is usually accompanied by a running commentary of directives and observations. She may recall wandering attention by renewing in some way the arousal jag which is waning, and as his passive vocabulary develops her comments encourage the child to observe his own actions more closely. Such exhortations as 'Mind—you are spilling your milk', accompanied by her correction of his hand position, develop nascent skills beyond the level displayed at a chimpanzee tea-party. By the time a child is two years old and has thus reached the upper level of mental ability of this animal, he has four times as large a passive vocabulary, i.e. 200 or more sound patterns with specific meaning compared with the 50 of a chimpanzee (Kellogg 1933). Add to this the 600 or so words which are added to the child's active vocabulary every successive year during early childhood, and it is clear that the greater refinement and variety of sensori-motor capacity in the human could spring largely from this structuring source in childhood. Arousal by means of verbal communication makes possible an awareness of subtleties far greater than would be possible by purely sensori-motor demonstration and imitation. This is encompassed by directing the child's attention to his actions thereby improving his perception of them. This is particularly true of the sensori-motor components of speech itself, where poor articulation is due to faulty perception rather than motor incompetence (Van Riper 1950). Perception of verbal sound patterns is improved through imitation of correct models and through exercise of function as an active vocabulary increases.

Between the ages of 18 and 24 months, genuine active communication emerges in the form of articulate desire. This verbal expression of wants is in direct line with the gesture language of the first year. At the earlier age, his hand outstretched towards an object finds itself supplied through the anticipation of his desire by the adult. Thus in his perception his mother comes to be regarded as an instrument, a means to an end, and the magic hand gesture acquires a similar instrumental significance. This is a more mature and active form of conditioning than the passive classical pairing of unconditioned and conditioned stimuli. To the perception of the mother as a conditioned stimulus is added his own instrumental activity of command and appeal. This expression passes from gesture into speech in five stages, gesture, gesture and name, facial appeal, interrogative tone in naming the object, and finally a statement of want. The earlier instrumental forms become extinguished through disuse, as more effective procedures are acquired, unless culturally reinforced as in the Byzantine era. There the empress's gestures could be described poetically as the charioteer of her speech (Mathew 1963).

Reference was made earlier in the chapter to the autonomic roots of early behaviour and how feeling mediated by the hypothalamus is fundamentally one associated with approach and withdrawal. The young infant in pain or hunger contracts muscle after muscle as he writhes and contorts his body, but the satiated comfortable child is relaxed and exercises his specific muscles with a predominance of extensor movements. These are the first psychophysiological signs which it is not difficult to align with retreat and approach tendencies. The fact that the noxious and pleasant stimuli are not perceived by the infant is perhaps the only difference. But by about the tenth month the maternal attitudes of acceptance and rejection towards the infant's behaviour become an increasing determinant of facilitation and inhibition. Thus feeling 'evaluation' will have two roots, one hedonistic derived from the soma and the other social. When, in later life, these two areas of value are in conflict, the hedonistic is likely to claim priority in terms of incipient neural facilitation, because these phase sequences will have been established earlier. This suggests that moral socialised conflict, in which subjective good and bad must be reconciled with an objective right and wrong, has its psychogenetic roots in the experience of the child of nine months, for by then 'No' can be effective as a deterrent. Since the parent is the arbiter of right and wrong and also the chief model for language, her significance both as an aid and as a frustrator to the child in his activities permeates the meaning of all the words he first learns. Indeed, it might be said that there is established from this time onwards a strong disposition to endow most words with some significance along a good – bad dimension of value. Thus the early assimilation of a 'core' vocabulary will occur in close association with the valuation of the caretaker in her comments on the child's activities. The most frequently used words will tend to be expressive of a position on the good – bad dimension. More mature variation of meaning within the good – bad dimension demonstrated in the American culture are reputable – disreputable, kind – cruel, wise – foolish, beautiful – ugly, positive – negative, successful – unsuccessful, true – false, grateful – ungrateful (Osgood 1958). This awareness of good and bad has its origins in the period between infancy and articulate childhood, during which the word of the adult elicits predictable behaviour from the child and thus becomes the regulator of his behaviour (Luria and Yudovich 1959).

Since this evaluative aspect of the semantic differential is so consistently pervasive, it should be of interest to note the kinds of attribution which do not partake of it in Osgood's analysis. These are the attributes of tenacity, humour, transparency, speed, size (bulk), sharpness, defensiveness, dryness and ornateness. These lack the affective element of meaning but are alike in that they are well saturated with the next most pervasive thread of meaning in language which is 'potency'. This is a general quality characterised most by hardness, strength, severity, weight and masculinity. This quality of potency will impinge upon the child as he becomes more active in relation to his environment and more able to effect material changes in it. It is interesting that masculinity appears on this dimension, for increased mobility during the second year coincides with increased awareness of the father, who can now make playful approaches to him with more effect, and who appears as more physically potent than mother. During the second year the sensory consequences of movement become more apparent to the child (Wallon 1956), and thus the experiential field is structured to include this new pervasive aspect of meaning. The valuative element is the most fundamental orienting factor in social communication – the element of potency important for the comprehension of the physical world and man's impact upon it.

5 *The motivating effects of unfamiliarity*

A motivational readiness is created in this way at two levels of imagery, the one sensory and the other verbal. Where such motivating complexes are inadequate to meet situations, they are perceived as unclear or ambiguous.

Several stages in response to the ambiguous or problematic may be traced with the aid of two motivational concepts – Berlyne's (1960) arousal jag and Festinger's (1957) cognitive dissonance. These are related concepts, for cognitive dissonance tends to give rise to arousal jags. Both imply that the equilibrium of the organism's resting state is disturbed, and that there is a tendency for it to seek homeostatic balance after this arousal. The arousal jag which is mediated by the ANS is pleasant if not too excessive, perhaps because its reduction is easily encompassed. In psychological terms the slight arousal jag is a relief from boredom. In physiological terms, it relieves the neurones concerned with the maintenance of equilibrium, by giving them a rest pause. It is probably for this reason that fatigue and boredom produce very similar behavioural characteristics, those of lassitude, together with an unwillingness to be motivated by routine stimuli. Over-strong arousal jags are unpleasant because they tend to spill over into random firing, thus disrupting neural organisation as it has been built up in the central nervous system. This prolongs the period of unstructured tension prior to the restoration of equilibrium. Such restoration may occur through dissipation of effects during a pause, as when resting after shock, or by the emergency of superordinate functioning in schemata which have relevance for the external cause of arousal. Return to homeostatic balance has reward value in increased comfort which causes the restitutive behaviour to be reinforced. This strengthening of bonds may be brought about by connections between the amygdala and the cortex which 'remembers' the comfort and reassurance. The related concept of 'cognitive dissonance' is the cerebral source of arousal jags. The dissonance refers to the discrepancy between environmental stimuli and the coverage of neural templates to match them. It is manifest in the alerting of attention which occurs in the presence of the enigmatic and unfamiliar. If the situation is ego-involved or in any way threatening, cognitive dissonance may give rise to an extreme arousal jag from autonomic sources, resulting in panic. This results in the disruption of the whole cognitive apparatus. Where arousal is not too great, the organism searches for familiar clues which will reduce the amount of cognitive dissonance. Naturally jags and dissonances will differ regarding their environmental causes, as growth and development proceed.

These two processes would, between them, account for the fact that learning, or establishing new neural schemata in the CNS is a pleasurable activity (Hebb 1949), particularly when spontaneously inaugurated. This element of spontaneity in learning is at its greatest during the first months and years of life. Then, established schemata are too slight for caretakers to impose their own expectations on the infant's behavioural inclinations. Later, after the establishment of relevant schemata of technical competence, the child may be expected to behave in prescribed ways. Thus most behaviour in early infancy may be regarded as spontaneously induced or passively endured. Conflict between environmental expectation and the infant's behaviour is usually at a minimum. Heaven still lies about him for the most part.

The proportion of passively endured behaviour to spontaneously evoked activity will decrease as sensori-motor schemata are established, but it is possible that to be passively moved is in large measure a necessary prelude to actively moving. This process of the passive induction of behaviour obviously begins in utero, where the structural conditions of gestation prepare the passive organism for future spontaneous functioning. This trend in preliminary exercise of future function has been observed in close detail in the chick embryo (Kuo 1932) and similar trends have been observed in human pre-natal behaviour. Mention was made in the previous chapter of the early development of foetal reflexes subserving the 'following' response. Such passivity, however, is not confined to uterine conditions. In post-natal development also, passive learning, mediated by impingement of the environment on the sense organs, leads to the acquisition of active motor patterns of response. Motivation in the relatively passive stage, dependent on chance stimulation, manifests different characteristics from that of the active stage. Freud's postulation of masochistic and sadistic modes of obtaining reassurance undoubtedly refer to the same rhythm between passively endured experience and that arising from active participation.

As was suggested earlier, passively endured experience is frequently brought about by some form of handling which occasions the sensory stimulation of both the distance and proprioceptive receptor organs. Since it is imposed on the infant from outside his tegumen, there will be an element of surprise in it, with mild startle effects, which is comprised elementally of both cognitive dissonance and an arousal jag largely from autonomic sources. Cognitive dissonance will be provided by the contrast between the resting state and the disturbed state, and the arousal jag by the disturbance of current field tensions.

Handling thus creates an expectancy of what movements should feel like – a kind of proprioceptive expectancy which will be matched eventually in the course of the child's reflex movements. For example, moving one leg at a time when inserting them into a bifurcated garment may be matched in the discovery by the infant of the 'running' movement of the legs while lying on his back. Such matching is certain to occur, because the infant's repertoire of reflex activities cover all possible contingencies of environmentally induced patterning, as was remarked earlier regarding the laryngeal reflexes expressed in babbling, crowing and gurgling. The structuring of this reflex motor system is attendant upon a sensory lead into organised forms and in this sense passive receptivity is psychogenetically prior to spontaneously directed response.

6 *Built-in behaviour patterns and passive learning*

Since some of these structured sensori-motor systems will have developed in utero, they will appear as instinctive or innate modes of behaviour during the first few days after birth. Such reflexes in the neonate fall into two classes – those which appear to be general and unadaptive, and those in which a specific response to a stimulus has biological utility, such as the built-in reflexes of sucking and clinging.

The major structured sensori-motor systems present at birth are sucking, clinging, following, crying and the smiling grimace. The sucking reflex is activated by pressure of the nipple on the back of the tongue; the clinging reflex enables a neonate to support its own weight by its hand grasp when other support is withdrawn; in 'following' a baby touched on the side of the cheek or head will turn to confront the object; viscero-somatic sensations elicit the smiling grimace and crying. Since these responses stem from a hypothalamic source they are unconsciously motivated, but they are accorded perceptual status in the course of time by the response of the caretaker to their appeal. This progressive patterning mediated by cortico-thalamic circuits is so closely geared to the biological needs of the infant, that it may be regarded as an integral aspect of biological inheritance. The absence of the child's true mother merely retards these emergent characteristics.

At all stages of development, sensorily conveyed familiarity is a prelude to effective response, but feed-back from response systems into receptor areas endow the stimuli with meaning, and raises sensation to the level of perception. Thus what the child does changes the meaning of what he perceives. His actions may be spontaneous or imposed from without. For example, the nurturant habit of lifting the infant's lower trunk by a grasp of the two ankles and then separating the two legs while the napkin is fastened causes the weight of the body to be moved from the length of the spine to the thoracic and neck regions and back again. This rocking movement is reproduced spontaneously by older babies in their moments of glee – a kicking out of the legs using the thoracic and neck regions. This may be the result of the feed-back of awareness of limb and trunk movement at a time of enhanced comfort. All the necessary reflex elements were there at and before birth, but they become patterned more explicitly into the glee response which follows some form of arousal by familiar stimuli.

Nurturant rhythm is probably the main source of neural expectancy in infants, and the perception of the parent tends to constitute a conditioned stimulus which signals comfort or pleasure or security. The child's response to her presence ranges from gleeful recognition when she attempts to communicate with him, to a marginal awareness that she is in the vicinity. Her responses to his varying needs are matched by an expectancy within himself, but in prolonged absence of arousal from her presence, many of his orienting responses may become extinguished. In this event the desolation of denied expectancy gives a manifest picture of depression. The validity of hope as a basic psychological drive would seem to have its justification in this regular maternal mediation in the satisfaction of need, operating within a narrow range of variation in time intervals.

The interaction between drive states and stimulation from caretaking is closely geared and it is conceivable that this is a crucial period for differentiation in emotional states as well as in sensori-motor schemata. This may be effected largely by hypothalamic discharge into the amygdala region of the limbic system and into the thalamus. This would result in a differentiation of the circuits between cortex and subcortical systems both sensory and motor. In support of this from the psychological angle, it is commonly held that no mental event occurs without some arousal of the affective system, but it is to be questioned whether this element may not be lacking in some deviant mental events in the psychopathic and in the schizophrenic. Rhythmic regulation such as is exercised through the hippocampal formation harmonises the cortical contribution with the dynamic and less articulated upsurge from subcortical regions. Thus affect and cognition are fused into the same circuit and an affectively toned cognition results. Under stress or prolonged deprivation the circuit is liable to disintegrate into its component parts, in a state of functional dissociation. The earliest bonds between the thalamus, hypothalamus and limbic systems are likely to remain integrated, even when the cortical component cannot operate. This primary awareness is matched by an affect which is as simply structured and which tends to have an all or nothing quality. Thus when the infant is deprived of the cognitive stimulus of the perceived mother, the thalamo-limbic awareness can remain as an unstructured expectation. Her frequent reappearances cause this neural vigilance or tension to fire into cortical regions thus completing the centrencephalic circuit. At a more mature level by the end of the second year the absence of the mother's concern, even when she is bodily present, will be sensed as a disappointed expectancy in the child, and give rise to strong autonomic arousal, expressed in some form of primary appeal such as crying. This is an awareness of 'what-is-not', and such negative responses are often psycho-genetically prior to a knowledge of what is. For example, a two-year-old child who responded positively to the friendly face of a stranger sobered when the same individual spoke to her. The face was a familiar sign – the voice was strange because it was unlike those heard hitherto. A year before this she would have sobered in the same way at people seen as strangers. Her cognitive integration was disrupted by the strange auditory stimulus because it found no matching cortical template, and her cognitive functioning reverted to a form of thalamic processing. Behaviour became temporarily regressive. The eyes ceased to focus intently, and bodily tension suggested an attitude of social withdrawal. She abandoned the play activity to which the stranger made reference. After more experiences of strangers' voices, they will present no arousal jags on account of cognitive dissonance.

This concept of centrencephalic functioning means that every problem situation, which always contains an element of 'what-it-is-not', may be entered into cognitively at either the subcortical or the cortical level of awareness. For example, Hugh Newman an expert in butterflies reported that he may have a great feeling of certainty that he will find the species for which he is searching in a certain spot near by, even when another expert, with greater knowledge of the terrain, denies that it is so. When the hunch proves to be justified, he cannot rationally explain how he came to have it (BBC Broadcast, 17 September 1962). An explanation is afforded by an appraisal of clues at a subcortical level. Similarly one can know that one has a piece of information not immediately available for recall without knowing what it is. Moreover, dream work can elucidate a problem, using symbols which have the same 'feel' about them as the real elements of the problem. It is not improbable that the general feel of the problem is sustained at subcortical levels of the centrencephalic system. Intuitive hunches may be thus examples of centrencephalic short circuiting, knowledge without structured justification. During infancy, this is a normal level of functioning, not because the cortex is temporarily inhibited, but because structuring is not yet sufficiently pervasive to cover most experiential contingencies. Short circuits rather than short circuiting is the explanation. There is an affective appreciation of the absence or presence of clues, which serves to mediate a conclusion of an affective nature, and this reaches expression in crying or sounds of pleasure.

The establishment of cortical vigilance and expectancy increases with experience, and with this enlargement the neo-pallium becomes a source of cortico-fugal activation, competing with the visero-somatic discharge into RAS. The mediation of the limbic system between these two sources of activation may result in the calibration of RAS to accord with the habitual reciprocal activation as it is shared by the cortex and the lower centres. This habitual style of arousal and drive reduction, expressed largely in a tolerance level of activation and resting state, will be compounded out of cerebral and viscero-somatic contributions to the total dynamic flux. In so far as activation is from viscero-somatic sources the style of behaviour which emerges may be regarded as temperamentally determined. In so far as it arises from cortical structuring it will be culturally determined. Individual differences could arise from both sources.

7 *Unselfconscious behaviour*

The Freudian concept of identification is relevant to the theoretical account of motivation during the first two years. The period of strong empathic communication between caretaker and child is considered to lie between the sixth and twenty-sixth months. It is regarded as a biological phenomenon rather than psychological, since it does not occur through the mediation of perceptual activity of a specific sensory kind. This non-specific or extra-sensory perception causes the infant to incorporate the affective coloration of the parent and with it a tendency to assume unconsciously motivated attitudes. It is not uncommon, at about the age of two years, to see an expression on a child's face identical with that of the mother, if she is sad, anxious or aggrieved. Thus a chronically anxious mother inevitably conveys her condition empathically. At this age in all children, experiences will tend to be fragmentary and to occur in a discrete series of momentary states. The result, in a structural sense, will be protaxic or dissociated (Sullivan 1953) and will remain autonomous if not integrated into later systems. Thus all early experience creates potential tension systems, whether well integrated or not, and when the later developed cortical systems become dissociated through sleep or some other cortical depressant, they find expression in the unexpected irrationality of dreams, hunches and unusual behaviour.

At this period of infancy and childhood, the boundary between reality and irreality is at its most fluid. It becomes firmer and less broken as maturity increases, but creative thought can best be subserved by maintaining sufficient synaptic flexibility between earlier and later neural structuring. It is in all probability conducive to the production of the intuitive hunch which creates a new major premise from which deductions may be made. Since empathic communication between mother and child is a kind of prolonged hunch, it is clear that her permissiveness regarding his behaviour and her strictness regarding his conformity will set up the first barriers between reality and irreality, and that a suitable degree of fluidity will be maintained in so far as this is well balanced. Permissiveness-strictness is the most pervasive factor in child-rearing practices (Sears, Maccoby and Levin 1957), and all the evidence suggests that the child retains his idiosyncratic outlook in proportion to the extent to which it is permissive, or to the extent that he is able temperamentally to resist or evade the impositions of parental authority. Unconscious identification with a permissive mother and the incorporation of such an imago would tend to ensure in the adult a benign attitude towards the more playful impulses stemming from his own infantile experience. Identification with a strict mother may contribute to the incorporation of a conditional acceptance of the self which may exclude the playful delight in exploring for hypotheses. For example, if behaviour producing noise and dirt is met by parental rejection, psychological discomfort would accompany behaviour of these kinds in subsequent years. This could result in the careful inhibition of all such behaviour or in a rational control of it. The ghost of the censorious mother stands both within and without, for it creates autonomically mediated anxiety within and challenges from without by the subjective significance it contributes to the perception of situations. Such a mechanism is common to most animals in that punishment can instil inhibition of behaviour. Moreover, as in the case of human beings temperament would appear to contribute an element of style to such responses. For example, Solomon's experimental conditioning of puppies to resist the temptation offered by a dish of boiled horse meat was expressed in as many styles as are found in human beings. Mowrer (1960) reports that some circled the taboo dish again and again, some walked round the room with eyes averted from the dish, others got down on their belly and slowly crawled forward, barking and whining. Those who were timid in approaching human beings and which were most frightened by a loud noise, resisted temptation most easily. It is not difficult to recognise extravert-introvert characteristics in these styles. These conditioned reactions were extinguished (i.e. abandoned) at rates which ranged from six minutes to sixteen days.

An analogy might be drawn between the highly emotive conditioned responses of the puppies to food and the affectively charged parent-child interaction in the business of toilet training. This usually occurs round about the age of eighteen months and by this time the child is vigorous in self assertion and at the same time more consciously dependent for a sense of security. This demand for toilet continence can be traumatic where there is maternal coldness and may intensify feeding problems. It may also increase aggression and retard the acquisition of toilet controls, and the growth of normal shame and guilt (Sears, Maccoby and Levin 1957). Such maternal behaviour militates against the establishment of habitual orienting responses. As Razran (1961) postulates the orienting response in any particular situation is no single reflex but is in all respects "a centrally organized holistic system, of a variety of specifically distinguished visceral, somatic, cognitive, neural and neuro-motor reactions". If these receive a fundamental imprint during the first two years while the motor fibres complete their maturation, it is clear that any highly charged constantly recurring situations associated with all-or-none success in meeting caretaking demands, are of considerable importance. Integration is most likely to be achieved where anxiety levels are kept low. Absence of such disruption is more likely to result in cross-modality associations and patterns of arousal, which orient the organism to act adaptively in the reduction of pressure on the sphincter muscles of bladder and anus. Such orienting habits make for ease in changing the set required where perception passes over into search and exploration. Orienting patterns to be adaptive, however, should be related to a highly differentiated sensori-motor field. This implies that parent-child interaction should be varied and of increasing complexity. The optimal extent of variation in the approach of parent to child is in evidence when she is able to modify it, in accordance with the child's tolerance for the ambiguous. Negativism to maternal demand is discernible as early as eighteen months of age and may be regarded as the beginnings of healthy assertion (Sears 1957). Normally such responses alert the caretaker to a greater awareness of how far her expectations are geared to the child's capacity for adaptability.

At the end of the sensori-motor period of the first two years motivation enters a new phase. Up till now it has been biologically centred, mainly along the length of the alimentary canal. The socially important reflexes have been conditioned at its entrance, the centre has provided the major drive states and at its exit the first stages in voluntary control of a tension system have been experienced. The assimilation of the primary sensori-motor skills of walking, talking, manipulation, and facial expression, have opened up new experiential possibilities. These skills make possible the emergence of a more continuous ego awareness and with it the extension of objective perception.

CHAPTER III

The emergence of selfhood during the pre-conceptual and symbolic phase of the third, fourth & fifth years

I. STRUCTURING THROUGH SPONTANEOUS BEHAVIOUR

1 *Growth in selfconsciousness*

In the previous chapter the basic importance of the body schema was outlined with special reference to the advantage inherent in adequate differentiation. This chapter will be concerned with the further elaboration of this pattern which is effected through the use of the child's private and public language. By the age of two years he can name himself although he cannot yet use the first person pronoun in self reference. He knows the name of many objects in his environment including the parts of his body. He also has a number of evaluative terms in his vocabulary such as good, bad, dirty, naughty, nice. The stage is thus set for the verbalisation of the body schema. Three cortical areas would seem to be progressively structured in this process. Firstly the specific projection areas of the pre-central gyrus subserving somatic sensation and movement, secondly Broca's area anterior to this subserving the sensori-motor aspects of speech and thirdly the parieto-occipital lobe posterior to the pre-central gyrus which subserves the function of speech ideation. At this stage it is possible that the cerebral spheres become selectively structured by spatial and verbal activity, spatial 'ideas' to one side, and verbal associations to the side which subserves the dominant motor functions. The right and left pre-central gyri are heavily structured by the experiences of the first two years and mediate the most elemental aspects of the body schema. Refinements and elaborations could be expected to stem from the more intricate manipulation of spatial objects and from the indication of more subtle differences by verbal reference. The two major types of experience in man are the verbal and spatial, and almost all human functions involve both. The fact that the ideational aspect of each is allocated unilateral space in the cortex may be due to the neural competition between them, particularly as right or left preference is established.

The most significant words used by the child from the age of two years onwards are those which refer to himself, for by naming himself he comes to exist as an object in his own regard. This nascent self concept is made possible by the changing flux of his own experience in association with identical verbal reference to the experiencer. These references are made first by the caretaker, his alter ego, speaking to the child of himself, or to others about him, and later by the use of the personal pronouns by the child. These sound-articulation complexes such as I, we, your, my, our, become nodal centres of redundancy in cortical activation and thus accrete around themselves vast cell-assembly potential, which will establish the awareness of the self as an object, and of the self in action, as a process. In view of this, it was exceedingly percipient of the ancient Egyptians to postulate that Ra created himself by uttering his own sacred name, for this is precisely the way in which the child establishes his capacity for self determination. Piaget has used the terms pre-conceptual and symbolic to describe this phase of development. It is a transitional stage during which the linguistic tools of self construction are perfected.

2 *A private language*

For Piaget and for Freud the symbol was pre-conceptual. This implies that whatever is used as a symbol has a private meaning for the user and in no way derives its meaning from a dictionary definition. In other words it has no significance for social communication and is egocentric and syncretic. The symbolic objects belong together because they happen to have stimulus value for the child and not because there is any reason to attribute time, space or causal relationships to them. The symbol can thus be contrasted with the sign which has value for inter-person communication. But the symbol is in all probability the necessary precursor of the sign because of its value in differentiating the body schema in such a way as to render it amenable to verbal direction. The demands and expectations of caretakers become increasingly complex as the child achieves greater technical competence, and he is hard pressed in some areas of his experience to understand its significance. It would be, in all probability, in those daily experiences which are areas of conflict, that ambiguity would arise. In other words it might be said that his cognitive dissonance regarding these episodes would tend to persist and the arousal jags be of unpleasant intensity. Such tension systems created by a persistent ambiguity will later be resolved by direct verbal enquiry or prolonged observation. During this phase, however, the tension system causes the child to take particular notice of objects analogous to those involved in his problem. The grounds of analogy can be guessed at by the psychological observer, by noting what the child does with the object, as well as from any similarity in appearance. Accordingly Piaget defines symbols as "schemata of action removed from their context which aid in the child's assimilation of reality to his own interests". This means that in children of this age play is an attempt to reproduce a situation which has aroused anxiety. They repeat the play because to do so reduces tension. Such schemata of action thus become reinforced by drive reduction and there is a likelihood of frequent repetition until the ambiguity is resolved. For example, a child of three years was constantly subjected to disappointment and frustration by a pathologically jealous father. In addition, when playing with him, his father was accustomed to throw him up to the ceiling in a horizontal position so that his face came suddenly within close range of it. The tremulous note in his giggle when in mid-air suggested he felt himself to be in danger. In his nursery he was accustomed to play-out this episode, or so it seemed, in a repetitive way by tossing the acorn tassel at the end of a blind cord over a high screen and then running round to the other side to see if it had descended. He would then repeat the process, in reverse, reiterating the action many times. In the same session in which this observation was made the boy placed his teddy bear beside his commode (which was clean and empty), took out the imaginary contents with a scoop of the hand and dumped them on to the bear, making grunting and scolding noises as he attacked. The pattern underlying these actions has its rationale in the parent-child relationship. In simulating parental scolding and punishment with the bear representing himself, he was enabled to experience their role and thus lessen the difficulty he had in understanding it from the receiving end. Since his perceptual structure during the process was likely to be global rather than specific and detailed, self and object would comprise a single dynamic continuum and would include both the element of giving and the element of receiving fused into a single awareness. This kind of perception was described by Wallon (1949) and illustrated by the reactions of a boy in his third year. He was shown the picture of a monkey in a tree thumbing his nose at an explorer, who frowned up from the ground below. The child reacted by both frowning and putting his thumbs to his nose, instead of identifying himself with either the explorer or the monkey. Wallon considered that this confused identification with both characters was analogous to the child who, at this age, when playing coach and horses, whips himself.

He also attributed this immature perceptual level to Janet's psychotic woman, who, in her Nativity delusion, acted the double role of the Child and the Virgin. Support for this hypothesis can be gained in cross-sectional Rorschach studies showing that the developmental sequence of perceptual organisation can be paralleled by that of various levels of psychosis and neurosis (Ovsiankina 1960). Such an hypothesis stems from Freudian theory, and accumulation of evidence suggests that it is a useful way of explaining the play of a child at this stage of development. Stern's (1930) description of the logic of early childhood as being transductive rather than deductive is a reminder that choice of objects for phantasy takes place by transductive association, e.g. a feeling for the bear because it is most like a human and that it is large compared with the other toys. The schemata of action in fantasy, however, tend to repeat the schemata of action experienced in daily family life. It is the fact that 'a transduced' object is used which removes the schema of action from its context and obscures its significance from the naïve observer. These highly dynamic periods of global involvement with objects of interest in the environment afford exercises which lead to a heightened perception of self as distinct from object. It is probable that the dynamic intensity of the fantasy intensifies self realisation at the moment when the child is recalled by some interruption to his familiar sensori-motor world. As maturation proceeds a growing vocabulary and verbal comments on play integrate sensori-motor, affective and verbal systems. By the end of this period he can say 'Let's pretend!' with full consciousness of the distinctions between the fantasy object and the real object, but his global involvement with his symbols is an antecedent of this detachment.

3 *The growth of self-awareness*

The personal pronouns and names of both child and caretaker would tend to give a centre of stability to interpersonal communication and thereby heighten a sense of detachment. They become endowed with meaning provided by all the nuances of feeling and intention, interactive between caretaker and child. At its simplest level each person refers to himself in the third person using proper names, e.g. Mummy do it. Baby do it. The child uses the label for his mother that he has been taught and similarly his own name that he hears her use. The chances are that the accusative case of the first person pronoun will be used next for self reference, because he hears his mother refer to herself as 'me'. Finally, he observes that she refers to herself as 'I' and he accepts this as the model for his own self reference. This transition is effected during the third year and by the age of three years most children are aware of their selfhood as distinct from that of others. In illustration of this Wallon (1949) remarks that "Je puis tout seul!" is a characteristic cry for the three-year-old. In his moments of fantasy this objectivity and independence will tend to merge into the environmental situation because for a young child of this age preoccupying fantasy is regressive. He is busy solving a problem, but his cortex is largely subordinated to an intensity of feeling of a highly idiosyncratic kind for objects in the environment, at such moments. Objective existence and his selfhood mingle and lose their outlines in a schema of reaction which resolves feeling tension but does not in itself bring cognitive advance. A child of two or three who has been filling and emptying a mug with water with complete absorption, oblivious both of self and environment, is in a trance-like condition, and like the sleep walker, is shocked and startled if too suddenly recalled to objective awareness. It might be described as a condition in which the cortical and directive properties of mental life merge in a balanced way with the hypothalamic and dynamic. Neither appears to have a preponderance. Sudden stimulation can cause an immediate return of cortical dominance, the change in sensory threshold being signalled by the primal startle response. Such a capacity for a balanced cortical and hypothalamic interaction is never lost and appears from time to time in states of reverie, when the glazed eye changes to alert brightness at the moment when cortical dominance of a sensori-motor kind is re-established.

4 *Antecedents of mature symbolism*

Since this kind of experience is most characteristic of children during the preconceptual and symbolic period, its functional significance might be guessed at. Theoretically speaking it should result in a facilitation of centrencephalic pathways on the neurological side, and on the psychological in the endowment of sensori-motor verbal schemata with idiosyncratic feeling content. Such transductive experience in all probability underlies the poet's capacity to re-evoke psychological echoes of it in figurative expression. For example

> " . . . An immense slackening ache,
> As when, thawing, the rigid landscape weeps,
> Spreads slowly through them . . ." (Larkin 1964)

In this metaphor, descriptive of release of tension among neurotic women in an American faith-healing session, an experience of empathic mergence of self and environment is implied. It is unlikely that such verbal constructs will spring from deductive activity of a logical kind, but are largely the work of the physiological unconscious. Unconscious motivation would seem to differ from conscious contrivance by the fact that it is not 'thought out'. It may be consciously elaborated subsequent to its appearance, but it tends to spring suddenly into conscious prominence. Bearing in mind that older schemata take priority in areas of conflict, such inspiration may derive from a tension system. In the above example, ambiguity is presented by a strange social phenomenon in the perception of the poet, and he is moved to resolve this in poetic metaphor.

Motives are both energisers and directors and it would seem that both functions are unified in the ANS and the CNS by virtue of the reverberating circuits run between them. Ambiguity is appraised perceptually by the CNS and its significance for the organism felt. In both children and adults, if the latter element involves threat, an arousal jag may be large, particularly if cognitive dissonance is pronounced. Acquired techniques may operate to reduce the ambiguity to some extent, but in pioneer creative work these are not sufficient to resolve all ambiguity, and the individual is thrown back on his own resources. Time and again these have been shown to emerge without rational deduction and to have been born fully fledged from an imageless vacuum, in which the tension of preoccupation has been the only action schema. It can perhaps be assumed that the higher centres subjected to prolonged tension drive renewed circuits between the structuring of infancy and childhood, and, as it were, re-evoke all the successive aspects of differentiation which have led to the individual's present interests. It may be further assumed the tension of this interest would not have arisen but for these residues. Whether this is merely plausible or a valid interpretation, it seems clear that Kukele's dream of a snake having its tail in its mouth was also the pre-conceptual and symbolic counterpart of his formula for the benzene ring. Moreover, the fact that the more elemental experience was an overnight prelude to the sudden emergence of the hypothesis is not without significance. Dream work as first interpreted by Freud shares closely the characteristics of the young child's fantasy during this period. There is a psychological *raison d'être* about both but the symbols are 'chosen' and related into schemata of action according to their suitability for portraying analogously events consciously experienced. The therapist in the consulting room employs the same technique interpreting the dreams of his adult patients as the child therapist does when observing her patients in the playroom. Freud was of the opinion that neurotic structuring of the personality stemmed largely from this period, hence perhaps the importance of observing dream work in adult patients and the significance of fantasy products in children. These inspired hypotheses have never been seriously challenged and are congruent not only with observations in the consulting room but also in the nursery. Sears (1944) when spelling out experimental findings in the field of psychoanalytic phenomena concluded that it was only in support of sublimation that there was no evidence. It is true that Freud's terminology is more comprehensible when defined in terms used by learning theorists, but even such an empirically minded child psychologist as Piaget chose to accept Freud's terminology as a useful label for the thinking of the child between the ages of two and five. In fact, it is in the psychology of middle and later childhood that Piaget makes his unique contribution. He has contributed little to the Freudian thesis concerning earlier ages.

5 *The barriers between reality and fantasy*

Lewin (1952), treading more in the footsteps of Freud than of his gestalt predecessors, postulated two dimensions of experience which he termed reality and irreality. In early childhood these were independent, but irreality tended to become vestigeial with increased experience. He stressed the need for maintaining a flexible capacity to pass from one to the other in the growing child in spite of the contrary necessity for establishing functional barriers between one sub-gestalt and another, in avoidance of delusion. This thesis finds experimental support in the work of Luria (1960) where he observed the development of voluntary obedience in young children when they were asked to perform certain actions at a given signal. He found that at the age of one and a half to two years, commands are successfully obeyed only if the child is not already doing something else, but later, at the outset of the pre-conceptual phase, he can abandon one task for another with greater facility. This is evident also when he is asked to reverse the action he is engaged on, such as taking rings off a bar. The command 'Put them on now!' serves to reinforce the current action before the age of two. In tasks calling for delayed action such as squeezing a ball once when a light was turned on, numerous squeezes were given between the ages of two and two and a half years. If, however, a child of this age was asked to squeeze a ball once in order to turn on a light, he was successful. The sensory feed-back from the light served to terminate the squeezing action.

The relation of Luria's work to Lewin's freudian hypothesis regarding reality-irreality is that reality is imposed on the child largely through caretaking expectations during the first four years. By contrast, irreality is pursued in spontaneous activity. Thus the generic forerunner of voluntary activity is volitional impulse. Both are forms of excluding the irrelevant, but the former is socialised and the latter egocentric. Volitional activity may be pursued to the exclusion of other stimuli as early as the third month, when Wolff (1963) noticed that stimuli tended to be unsuccessful in evoking smiles when the baby was busy with some activity of his own. Earlier than this, whimpering and fussing could be halted by the distraction of the mother's voice. These are examples of the earliest capacity to attend exclusively and of the ability to pursue an activity against distraction. Such observations indicate that a great complexity of functional barriers have been erected throughout the first two years which brings the child to a level of competence in which he can voluntarily abandon his own activities to obey the commands of his mother even if they involve reversed and delayed response. These new competencies in verbally mediated control are not without their own dangers. They increase the chances of the child being asked prematurely to meet difficult caretaking demands, as a price of her affection and his security. Such an attitude tends to erect barriers between reality and irreality of too rigid a nature at too early an age.

The Lewinian view of optimal flexibility implies an easy passage from reality to irreality but with well-defined boundaries between them. Chown (1959) suggests 'permeability' would be a better name for the properties of mental boundaries in the Lewinian sense and this is more congruent with learning theory. Where there is rigidity, it would imply that spontaneously pursued pleasures had been decrementally conditioned by punishment and acquiescence, and highly reinforced by anxiety drive reduction. Too great a preponderance of such decremental conditioning in caretaking would presumably lead to a highly specific response pattern tangential to the child's idiosyncratic motivation. Such specific structuring, combined with a strong dispositional rigidity, could conceivably result in the personality structure noted by Eysenck and Adorno as characteristic of the prejudiced, tough and conservative. Cattell found rigidity to be correlated with submissiveness and lack of character integration. Chown, after reviewing the literature on rigidity, suggests that a 'coefficient of rigidity' from the ratio of stress to strain by analogy with physics should be aimed at. This is reasonable if strain is largely calibrated by disposition, and stress by environmental pressure. Under optimal conditions, the child would emerge from this period with permeable systems, restrained behind firm barriers. Such a personality structure implies that cues conveyed in sensory perception are as numerous and complex as the experience of early childhood was varied and dynamic. This is most likely to arise in a permissive atmosphere which gradually gives way to a balanced disciplinary one. In this sense flexibility implies well-differentiated gestalten within a comprehensive attitudinal system which becomes socially oriented.

A physiological explanation of voluntary behaviour is afforded by recent evidence which suggests that centrifugal inhibitory 'messages' prevent irrelevant impulses from reaching the cortex when the organism is busy attending through some other channel. This capacity for relevant inhibition may be related to what is called intelligence (Tomkins 1960) and may be one of the more important pacemakers for experiential advance. This is congruent with the hypothesis of RAS as a regulator of orienting responses. Each new experience in childhood results in inhibitive behaviour or arrested activity, while search and scansion proceeds. Thus the initial phases of experiences pave the way for the inhibitive barriers which will create new gestalten of reaction. As soon as some response in relation to the ambiguous situation is made, the new structuring permeates other systems which have been involved in the response. It is highly probable then that flexibility is engendered through responses, and that at this level of maturity a permissive atmosphere free from wrath is likely to be the optimal condition for flexibility. Such an emotional climate would allow the child to adjust his already acquired response patterns to new situations.

Flexibility within and between related systems has relevance for the directional properties of motivation, particularly for the understanding of neurotic motivation. A wide repertoire of substitute actions ensures that ambiguity in situations can be the more easily tolerated. Moreover, this very acceptance diminishes anxiety arousal, thus maintaining the set which inhibits all but search for the cues to resolve the ambiguity. The vital significance of the ages between two and five for this process lies in the fact that linguistic development acquires impetus then. An increasing skill in sign manipulation is established and this facilitates the retention of the connection between events in the experiential field, even though these events are considerably separated in time (Mowrer 1960). The effect of such a capacity on cortical differentiation and integration, goes a long way towards explaining developmentally the characteristics of children at the end of this period, when they achieve in all important respects a pattern of behaviour characteristic of the adult members of their culture.

Such developmental trends are related to certain motivated learning contingencies, and in their absence behavioural responses will tend to remain at a level of minimal sufficiency. This circumstantial effect is exemplified in the case of the identical six-year-old twin boys Liosha and Yura (Luria and Yudovich 1959), whose mutual caretaking obviated the necessity for more complex forms of communication than that reached approximately by the end of their second year. This sufficed for all practical purposes, and for them a gesture and the verb 'to drink' served to denote equally a teapot, a cup and water. Remedial measures, which created an objective necessity for more articulate speech, effected a rapid improvement. One of the twins was given speech training and this expedited his progress, but the untrained twin drew level after 10 months. The facilitation afforded by the speech training was most apparent in the imaginative use of language and also in the capacity to correct prepositional errors in sentences. From the viewpoint of motivation, however, the attaching of conditional meanings in fantasy activity is of the greater importance. Play involving substitute stimuli, such as letting a pencil stand for mama and a vase for a tree, was accomplished sooner by the trained twin. It may be, however, that grasp of prepositional phrases is necessary for this. The preposition is a relatively late linguistic form to appear, and since prepositions qualify the main part of the sentence they create a conditional factor. The trained twin was able to correct 'I am writing with an exercise book' at a time when his brother let pass uncritically such statements as 'I was eating with sweets'. In addition, the trained twin arrived more quickly at the critical objective appraisal of pictures, e.g. 'a cat can't *really* play a violin'. This suggests that response generalisation is improved by the linguistic models presented by adults and older children, providing the younger children are emotively involved in communication with them. Moreover, this response generalisation can be made symbolically to any arbitrarily chosen substitute stimulus. When Piaget referred to this period as pre-conceptual and symbolic in character, he was referring to the arbitrary symbol and the instability of conceptual thinking. Yura had emerged from the pre-conceptual phase when he observed that cats do not play violins and also that one writes in exercise books and with pencils. Both examples are evidence of having acquired a conventional constancy of meaning with reference to objects. This made possible a deliberate departure from conventional meaning, accepted as an agreed way of looking at things – a socialised rather than an egocentric fantasy.

II. STRUCTURING THROUGH THE EXPECTATIONS OF OTHERS

1 *Innate and acquired aspects of flexibility*

Barriers between systems and their permeability will obviously depend on learning, but there seems also to be a well-defined constitutional disposition along a continuum of flexibility – rigidity. Cattell's threefold 'cause' of rigidity would seem to indicate that two are genetic, namely, lack of intelligence and innate disposition, while one is acquired in the form of personality difficulties. This would seem to justify Chown's suggestion that rigidity is a multiform rather than a unitary trait. In the present context of psycho-genetics, disposition and caretaking are both significant and interactive factors in determining the flexible adaptability of the organism. In summarising the experimental work on flexibility in thinking Chown remarks that it appears to be easier to reverse a concept than to partially alter it, and that it is easiest of all to stick to the original concept. These three levels of difficulty are apparent in Luria's observations on the acquisition of voluntary motor control in the young child described earlier in the chapter. From this it can be deduced (i) that where a child can with impunity persist in a form of behaviour, he will fail to accept an alternative form; (ii) where inhibition of an erstwhile facilitated form earns freedom from parental wrath, he may suppress the offending behaviour; (iii) that slighter modifications which will permit him to retain the pleasurable aspects of the behaviour and at the same time meet parental requirements will be effected only under special conditions. Such optimal results would presumably depend on a happy confluence of environmental opportunity and congenital disposition, though either alone could facilitate the more difficult adjustment. Luria (1932) observed that the child is 'reactively labile' at the outset of this period. With Cattell, he recognises individual differences among young children in flexibility, along a dimension of lability – stability, according to whether functional barriers appear to be weak or strong. As an example of the relative lability of children at this age compared with later ages he cites their inability to perform slow actions when asked to do so. He regards the postural habits of the child in his third and fourth years as arising from weak functional barriers in sensori-motor systems. As these are strengthened over the space of two years the straddled gait, the sitting stoop and imperfect articulation are replaced by adult patterns in walking, sitting and speaking.

The spontaneous liveliness of this period would seem also to stem from the weakness of inhibitive barriers. The interplay of facilitation – inhibition is not as weighted on the inhibitive side as it will be eventually. Thus from the point of view of arousal, the motivated child of this age appears to be highly energised and tireless. This may be on account of the lower metabolic rate which is present when release rather than restraint of motor impulse is preponderant (Lucas, Pryor, Best and Pope 1933). Further support for this may be deduced from developmental trends in autonomic imbalance under conditions of stress. In younger children, autonomic arousal is seen in changes in blood pressure and heart rate, while at later ages change is greater in palmar skin resistance and heart rate variability (Lacey 1949). This may be due to the inverse relationship between muscle tension movements and skin resistance (Freeman and Simpson 1938). Decrease in skin resistance will be more rapid the more muscle tension is heightened, and in younger children muscular orienting responses or motor set are less readily available at the time of arousal than is the case in later stages of maturity. Hence the maturational change noted by Lacey which could be correlated with diminished lability in behaviour.

Evidence for individual differences in an autonomic pattern of arousal is contributed by several researches. For example, a child's standard score within a sample appears to remain constant under various experimental conditions. Although his measure of autonomic arousal varies from stimulus to stimulus according to its intensity, he tends to retain his ordinal position within the experimental group. This suggests that he has a constant autonomic profile expressible in standard scores (Dykman, Reese, Galbrecht and Thomasson 1959). Several longitudinal studies support this view. Patterns of persistence observed in early childhood were reliably recognised fifteen years later by independent observers (Shirley 1931, Neilson 1948). Similarly, the follow-up study of identical triplets by Sontag (1958) revealed that at eight months the weakest was well on the way to becoming the typical spoilt child. By 30 months each triplet had developed a characteristic life style which persisted throughout nine years of observation. It might be postulated then, that life style is a directional aspect of motivation and that it achieves its mature form in a global sense during this pre-conceptual and symbolic phase. These longitudinal studies indicate that this may be true at least of patterns of persistence and social orientation (Cole 1953) arising from the interaction of disposition and nurture.

The generality of style which emerges in motor responses would appear to be less dependent on nurture, for it is unlikely that, say, expansive movements would be differently conditioned from restricted ones in the small child. As Luria (1932) asserts, the entire output of our thinking machine consists of nothing but patterns of motor co-ordination and the end of all brain excitation is to aid in its regulation. The processes of scanning and exploration depend on bodily support, and bodily integration tends to facilitate the muscular tensions which underlie a course of action. Sustained muscular tone and the control devices which maintain it are essential aspects of cognitive activity (Bentley 1934). The most comprehensive expression of this is posture, and Wallon (1949) regards this as the most elemental aspect of temperamental bias, which according to Sherrington extends to all the tonal activity of the organism.

2 *From symbol to word*

Such a motor theory of thought implies that perception is structured by response through feedback of the perceived consequences of action into receptor areas. Sensation is transmuted into perception by this process. In man this experiential structuring is expedited and refined by the linguistic body image. This too is refined by feed-back and by transcortical association. It is not difficult to regard Luria's (1960) experimental procedure, when he observed the development of voluntary action, as a prototype of what happens in the course of nurture. Verbal direction of the child's behaviour by the mother effects great economy of effort and it is continually used to evaluate and direct his efforts. This may apply particularly to the upper parts of the soma from which social skills derive. The sensori-motor consequences of the child's behaviour are fed into the auditory receptor areas of speech at the same time as they are evaluated and appraised by his mother. If her comments are comprehended, the meaning conveys reassurance even though there may be an element of threat in her utterance for he knows where he stands in the matter. Where, however, a verbal communication is not understood, because it refers to matters not yet experienced, the child is thrown back on symbolic and pre-conceptual techniques in a search for meaning. The symbols of private analogy serve to maintain the system in tension until it is systematically disposed of. An example of this is seen in an intelligent girl of four whose parents were moving house for the first time since her birth. Arrived at the new house, she used all the pieces of paper she could find to make a large tight parcel, layer after layer carefully wrapped each in the next. When it was quite large she heaved a deep sigh and set it on one side turning to other activities. Interpreted symbolically it can be deduced that this activity, heavily charged with affect, both reflected the strange activities of her parents and at the same time activated a schema of gathering together the pieces of the fragmented home to which she had been accustomed. The terms associated with moving house were devoid of motor consequences for her which she rapidly made good in her simulated packing-up.

The parents' activity of commenting on the child's behaviour is converted into retort and spontaneous comment by most children during the fifth year. By this age children will sit round a table and talk to one another with some fluency. A year earlier this is less evident and symbolic play more frequent. Gesell has remarked on the spurt in the acquisition of a vocabulary during the fifth year and once this stage is reached the pre-conceptual symbol is rarely used, though conventional 'signs' may be used to construct a fantasy which expresses some problem of emotional import. The hymn of hate of Karl Menninger's four-year-old boy is a reflection in part of adult comment directed against himself and in part an expression of his hostility at being thwarted and compelled. His chant was used to beguile himself during his daily bath, and it is highly probable that the amusement of his caretakers conditioned him to elaborate the theme. It runs thus:

"He will just do nothing at all,
He will just sit there in the noonday sun;
And when they speak to him, he will not answer them,
Because he does not care to.
He will stick them with spears and put them in the garbage.
When they tell him to eat his dinner, he will just laugh at them,
And he will not take his nap because he does not care to.
He will not talk to them he will not do nothing.
He will just sit there in the noonday sun.
He will go away and play with Panda.
He will not speak to nobody because he doesn't have to.
And when they come to look for him they will not find him,
Because he will not be there.
He will put spikes in their eyes and put them in the garbage
And put the cover on.
He will not go out in the fresh air or eat his vegetables
Or make wee-wee for them, and he will get thin as a marble.
He will not do nothing at all.
He will just sit there in the noonday sun."

Much of this phrasing was in all probability a repetition of frequently heard verbal patterns and may represent adult justification for the use of compulsion, e.g. He must eat or he will become thin as a marble. He mustn't climb the railings or he will run the spikes into his eyes. He mustn't play with the garbage if he doesn't wish to be put in himself with the cover on too! The impulse to repeat this chant in his daily bath could be regarded as an endeavour to resolve the conflict area of caretaker-child interaction through verbal rehearsal.

The child was imitating the adults around him and it was an adaptive modification in so far as he both satisfied himself in symbolically reversing frustration, refusing to meet adult demands, and at the same time amused his tormentors thus ensuring tolerance and admiration. His enjoyment of the social acceptance of his chant is presumably a form of behaviour regarded by Freud as at a sublimated level. This aspect of his theory of sublimation is more tenable than his ascribing it to the deflection of sexual energy, unless infantile sexuality be interpreted philosophically rather than psychologically, as a kind of elixir for living.

Such verbal skills in the four-year-old develop to an optimal extent if language activity is associated with relevant sensori-motor experience during the two preceding years. Passive learning devoid of motor involvement is relatively ineffectual in bringing about verbal assimilation. Children in their third year learn the names of things from two to three times more quickly, if they are allowed to handle them while hearing the names (Razran 1961). This could be explained in terms of summation, for presumably sensory feed-back from motor areas would strengthen neural firing into the speech centres, and thus bring a greater cortical area into a state of increased activation. Since permissiveness of the caretaker at this age is largely that of allowing freedom to the child's impulses, the importance of this dimension of child rearing cannot be overestimated in relation to speech development.

3 *The antecedents of abnormality*

Recently, several cognitive styles have been identified with various patterns of child-rearing. Those which have received particular attention are: (i) tendencies to display more divergent than convergent thinking; (ii) the rise and fall of I.Q.s, and (iii) differences in achievement motivation. Permissiveness and unconditional acceptance of the young child characterised the parents of divergent or unconventional thinkers, while a more rigid expectation, which imposed success as a condition of acceptance, was found among those of convergent (formal and logical) children. Similarly parental expectation of success was found among those children who had high N-ach and rising rather than falling I.Q.s. This is precisely what is to be expected in terms of learning theory. Such cognitive styles will be discussed more fully in later chapters, but it is appropriate to mention them here, for this is probably the period during which parental expectation sets its formal seal on the broad outline of the child's motivational style in cognitive endeavour.

Such cognitive controls have their counterparts in both normal and maladjusted social behaviour. Approach and withdrawal tendencies will be emphasised or diminished by the style of parental acceptance and rejection. Approach is implied in behaviour disorders which cause disruption. These are boisterous, disobedient, attention seeking, un-co-operative, ruthless, combative and negative in attitude. Avoidance is a common feature of behaviour suggestive of inferiority feelings, a tendency to be flustered, lack of self confidence, anxiety, aloofness and shyness (Peterson et al. 1961). The two groups of traits are commonly referred to as extraverted and introverted respectively and are attributed to neuroticism along this E–I scale. The physiological counterpart of the trait is the Pavlovian dimension of cortical excitation-inhibition. Another theory regards E–I traits as arising from early conditioning. It is probable, however, that both theories are correct, for it is notorious that caretakers themselves are quickly conditioned into preferential modes of upbringing by the effectiveness of their techniques in the case of any particular child.

The most withdrawn attitude is seen in the rare cases of pre-psychotic autism. In these, passivity, day-dreaming, sluggishness, inattentiveness, clumsiness and poor concentration are so pronounced as to suggest that the activation system is weak. Such traits are found in children suffering from dementia praecox. The fact that advanced cases suffering from schizophrenia can be caused to function normally by oxidation of nerve tissues and revert to the pathological, torpid condition as soon as administration ceases suggests it is a deficiency disease bringing about dendritic impairment (Chang 1952). A curious feature of schizophrenic information processing is the extraordinary wide span of attention or immediate memory span contrasting with the poor appraisal of cue significance. This causes immediate and delayed recall to function almost entirely in a rote fashion. The schizophrenic may read accurately but not comprehend what he is reading, he may play long tune sequences while being unable to read music. In his case, problem solution and reasoning may be retarded by as much as three or four years while attention span may be eight years in advance of the average level. The anxiety neurotic among children presents precisely the opposite picture. Attention span may be retarded several years while cue significance is readily appreciated (Highfield 1945). Thus a predisposition to attend in a certain manner characterises children in each abnormal category, and it appears to be a safe conclusion that this will affect their information processing and thus their approach to their social and material environment.

The most general behavioural characteristics associated with excitatory potential are threshold, duration and stimulus generalisation (Wittenborn 1957), and from this it would appear that most differences between groups manifesting extremes of excitatory potential, could be interpreted in terms of these three areas of cognition. It is suggested, for example, that a child suffering from dementia praecox is lacking in the third characteristic (stimulus generalisation) but is particularly strong in the first two, while the chronically anxious child is weak in the first two aspects (threshold and duration) but less impaired in the third.

A-normality of cognitive controls will be a contributory factor to the ecology of child rearing. Variations in the 'appeal value' of a child from the point of view of his caretaker will inevitably arise from his responsiveness. Where there is a lack, the warmth of the mother-child relationship will tend to be reduced. This is Sear's (et al. 1957) third factor of child rearing and it is clear that it may be important in the etiology of schizophrenia. It has been identified in family conditions which give a sense of rejection from birth, constant rebuff and disapproval in early childhood, all leading to a feeling of immense loneliness (Thomas 1955). Causally prior to these environmental conditions, however, there is the fact of the child's passivity and failure to respond to stimuli in a way which will evoke affectively toned responses in the caretaker. In the absence of normal empathic communication between parent and child the only kinds of interpersonal conditioning which become instrumental to the child's sense of security are often the bizarre ones, because by such gestures the child 'frightens' the parent into a state of concern. For example, at the age of three years symptoms of acute bronchitis which evoke increased nurturance in the parent may be prolonged functionally into asthma and be used recurrently afterwards to avoid unpleasant impositions of a disciplinary nature. Similarly, infantile grimace and gesture may be perpetuated to preserve the patient from environmental demands which are unpleasant to him (Highfield 1945, Louttit 1942). From these observations it may be deduced that styles in the processing of information during the first two years are an essential etiological feature of both abnormal and normal patterns of motivation.

Where response potential is normal, learning contingencies at appropriate times appear to be the main causes of variation. During the pre-conceptual and symbolic phase children become aware of their models in a more comprehensive sense and acquire sufficient technical competence to imitate them. The function of caretaking draws the child into active participation, and thereby structures patterns of social cooperation in sensori-motor and verbal areas. From now on, the structure of the environment makes a more specific impress on the personality. The attenuated interpersonal environment of the institution child is as specific in its effects as that of the normally situated child. For example, Freud and Dann (1951) observed children who, at the age of three to four years, became institutionalised and whose caretakers changed frequently. They report that the children formed strong attachments with one another and with no one else, presumably because of their mutual caretaking.

Such affectional attachments between mother and child have, as it were, three strata by the end of the pre-conceptual period. During the first half of the first year the child comes to attend to the mother with expectancy of customary arousal. By seven months deprivation of the mother's constant caretaking results in separation anxiety. From attentional habits the baby's next big advance is towards response control, weighted as much on the motor side as sensory discrimination was important for the first structuring. Finally, a third 'layer' is added of more social significance by the acceptance of the mother as a model, to be imitated by children of both sexes. These levels of assimilation are inaugurated by the parent's observation of the growing competency in the child. Sears (1957) observed that negativism in young children of eighteen months on account of inability to comply reaches its peak at about three years as an overt need manifestation. By the age of five years, individual differences in achievement behaviours are pronounced. This may be easily observed in strongly extraverted children as they try to construct something such as an aeroplane with chairs, dustbin lids, planks, etc. Sometimes the furore of activity suggests that a need to achieve motivates it. This arises from a growing capacity to reach constructively towards a more distant end. Such constructive activity of the fourth year may be as designed to resolve ambiguity in the child's perception of his environment as the simpler fantasies of the third year, but whereas the earlier was concerned with ambiguity arising from caretaking demand, the later may be concerned with efforts to gain understanding of less intimate relationships, e.g. the big brother or father who is concerned with aeroplanes and discusses them in the home circle. The earlier conflict between libidinal needs and the ego needs of self-esteem and achievement reach a crescendo at the end of the third year. It lessens thereafter, as dependency is replaced by the greater competency which makes longer periods of self amusement and social play possible. In view of this, parents manifest a change of attitude from one of emphasis on warmth and protection to one of detached and permissive appreciation. This results in a greater consistency of approach geared to the child's desires. Frustration of them tends to arise from rational caretaking expediencies which can be explained verbally and reiteratively until they are understood and accepted by the child as reasonable. Where the parent is incapable of detached consistency, the child's own efforts cannot so easily resolve the ambiguous aspects of his environment and there is considerable habit interference (Wolfe 1951). Most normally situated children have resolved the ambiguity presented by a rewarding and punishing parent by the end of their fifth year, but where this ambiguity is increased by parental inconsistency the period of assimilation is protracted. In the latter case, gestalten are structured to include inconsistency or unpredictability as a social expectation and this increases their complexity. Since most social relationships are stable and predictable in their implications the nervous indecision of the neurotic person is socially mal-adapted, but the assimilation process which set up the expectation of caprice was a normal one. Wolfe's habit interference refers to a normal habit structure. The neurotic habit structure consists of expecting inconsistencies and reacting accordingly without self committal. Nuttin's (1953) definition of the self as a 'pattern of ego-world relations in a state of tension' could be enlarged to include the stratification brought about by each aspect of the world to which the child is exposed. The family environment of the pre-neurotic child could conceivably inculcate an expectancy of instability in intimate social relationships, while the stimulus of school and neighbourhood resulted in stable habits. The earlier stratum would predispose the individual to later marital and familial instability and the latter to adequate relationships at work and play. The Freudian hypothesis that the age of three was a mid-point of the so-called oedipus complex is a relevant consideration here. It involved the incorporation of the joint-parent imago at first with a subsequent identification with the parent of the same sex. This is reflected in Hunt's (1961) dictum that after the age of two years one of the important learning contingencies for optimal development is exposure to adequate models. The child's observational maturity is sufficiently advanced by this age to facilitate an understanding, in broad dimensions, of the general effect of father's presence and absence on his mother's concern or relative 'indifference' to himself. When their mutual concern and preoccupation exclude him, in his perception, he is anxious at feeling peripheral to his mother's regard. Hence the so-called oedipus rivalry. This much is supported theoretically by learning theory. The genitalia are likely to be involved only where they are allowed to obtrude strongly into the experiential field at this age, as in punishment for masturbation. This would be more probable in nineteenth-century middle-class Vienna than today and may have entered frequently into the fantasies and dreams of Freud's patients. This renders Freud's use of the term 'the genital period' to be less meaningful than those of his oral and anal phases. Moreover, his postulation of a sadistic component in these is also likely to be less evident because of the changes in weaning and toilet training habits. It is reasonable to suppose, however, that the child will make instrumental use of actions which affect the parents, however bizarre they may be, if these are useful in reducing his loneliness. For him parental concern of any kind is preferred to indifference. So-called sadistic behaviour could be equated with instrumental conditioning in such instances. Its bizarre and varied forms could arise from the idiosyncrasies of parental vulnerability to sadistic attack, as perceived by the child.

4 *Cultural impact through the family*

Each family, however, is situated in a cultural context which influences the child's intimate environment by stressing the value or danger of certain forms of caretaking. Today psychological theory percolates rapidly into the home and perhaps does much to mitigate the danger of over-specific structuring. But this is because psychologists are aiming at norms of adaptation to a society which demands flexible adaptability. The criterion of normality is a social one. The psychology underlying say nineteenth-century upbringing was conveyed by rigid axiom, based not on tendency or potentiality but on hard and fast rule of thumb, e.g. 'Spare the rod and spoil the child' and all the generalisations implicit in the Struwelpeter. This caretaking attitude gained acceptance because it appeared to be successful in producing personalities who would be capable of applying well-defined principles in a stable well-structured socio-economic environment. The main dimensions of caretaking are in all probability the same then as today and as in all ages. They would appear to be normally distributed rather than U-shaped, and the only difference between epochs would be measured by a shift in the position of the mean scores on such continua. This is apparent today in sub-cultural comparisons. Most of the families in one sub-cultural group can be paralleled by instances in another. But a few more in a particular group are particularly affected for better or for worse by some genetic or circumstantial factor which may also be responsible for socio-economic classification. Hence the slight shift in mean scores.

Between racial cultural groups there may be more fundamental differences. In some, the family unit is more extensive and caretaking is multiple. In some dependency is prolonged by late weaning, constant porterage on someone's back and instant gratification. This would seem to indicate that transfer of motivation from libidinal to ego needs would occur at a varying maturity level. Such early antecedents could conceivably give rise to variation in personality structure which was not reversible. Two extreme contrasts of this kind may be seen in Fischer's American New Englanders and the Okinawans as described by Maretzki (Whiting 1963). Caution must be observed in deductions based on anthropological evidence, and the authors in these cross-sectional studies confine their remarks to description of fact with a scrupulous avoidance of interpretation of cause-effect implication. Such descriptions, however, could facilitate comparative longitudinal studies of character structure.

During the pre-conceptual and symbolic phase, boys change their parental identification. Social suggestion and his own observations cause him to accept his father as a model. For the girl, a continued identification with her mother is encouraged except under a-typical circumstances. It is commonplace that girls may be brought by incremental conditioning on the part of parents to regard the male role as desirable, and similarly boys may be decrementally conditioned to avoid the male role, where the mother abhors it. In the usual course of events the change of identification is expected only of the boy. During the fourth year, boys tend to become unpredictable in their behaviour with a stronger tendency to exhibit shyness and aggression. Bayley and Schaefer (1960) attribute this to the change from a maternal to a paternal identification. Presumably, in imitating his father's aloof independence he retreats from mother's erstwhile welcome expressions of affection and at the same time comes to expect the privileged consideration which the wage-earner enjoys and so powerfully elicits. At this age, it is possible that a feeling for law and order stemming from an observation of the father's example may lay the foundations of future avoidance of delinquency. This may account for the fact that Wilkins (1960), in his cross-sectional study of the antecedents of delinquency, found that the peak of post-war delinquency occurred among boys who were deprived of their fathers through war service during their fifth year. Kagan and Moss (1962) in their report on the Fels longitudinal study suggests that the period between three and six years was less significant for mature behaviour patterns than the caretaking of the first three years and influences after the age of six. They postulated a sleeper effect which caused the relationship between antecedent behaviour and consequence to remain covert. In explanation of this, it is to be asked whether the clearer emergence of two parents operating as a unit, especially in the case of boys, causes a fundamental restructuring from libidinal to ego-type motivation. This would cause the parents-as-perceived-by-the-child to be more important than child-as-perceived-by-parents. Later the more predictable child as perceived by parents exhibits additional behaviour correlated with earlier caretaking, because caretakers are able to resume their preferred style. For example, it was found that the fostering of dependency during the first three years in boys, followed by expediting expectations after six, was the best achievement antecedent. In girls hostility (i.e. criticism of her efforts) during the first three years followed by expediting after six was best. It is clear that if the intervening period witnesses a transfer from libidinal to ego orientation it will be one of transition and parent-child relationships will change. Thus the 'sleeper effect' may arise from a fundamental re-orientation during the interval between infancy and childhood.

By the end of the fifth year in the average child the context of selfhood is sufficiently well integrated to make possible voluntary recall after considerable intervals, and it then becomes possible to expose him to formal teaching outside the family circle. It might be said that he now possesses what McGeooch (1939) described aptly as an autobiographical index. He knows where he belongs and where he is valued and can carry about with him a subliminal set of expectations based on this. The autobiographic index is the psychological context of selfhood. McGeooch postulates that this consists of (i) an environmental element; (ii) an interoceptive body image; (iii) an ideational context. This is regarded as forming a general attitude complex which is normally very stable and is the groundwork of all recall. The selectivity of attention and the interpretative function of perception depend on it. It implies an integrated state under conditions of arousal. Where this integration is lost in later pathological conditions such as the Korsakoff syndrome, there is an inability to recall the immediate past. In this psychotic condition due to brain damage through alcoholic excess, the less mature memory function of recognition may operate without the ability to recall voluntarily. For example, if the patient is pricked and immediately after a second attempt to prick him is made, he will take evasive action, without remembering the first prick (Clarapede 1911). Similarly if the patient is given the name and address of the doctor, he will be unable to recall it immediately after, but will be able to recognise it in a list of other names and addresses (MacCurdy 1928). This inability to carry about with him a body image and an ideational context tuned to environmental cues reduces him to a functional level which is characteristic of the third year. He is disoriented in time and space and subject to illusion because of impairment of the integrating function of the cortex. The continuity of the self is lost, psychologically speaking. This process of disintegration is seen in reverse in normal learning. Material which is newly learned will be recognised before it can be recalled voluntarily. Moreover, new material will tend to be assimilated more readily, where there is a well-integrated background of similar knowledge (Hebron 1957). This is congruent with the view that brain damage and a resultant loss of integrated functioning underlies the behavioural inadequacies in alcoholic psychosis.

By the age of five, the symbolic process has become sufficiently superordinate in its function to facilitate verbal communication, not only between persons but also within himself in the form of internalised speech. Thus, towards the end of the fifth year, the average child has acquired all the kinds of skills necessary for achieving full maturity on a front as broad as cultural opportunity will allow.

CHAPTER IV

Motivational patterns during the intuitive phase of the sixth & seventh years

I. THE STABILISATION OF THE CAPACITY TO ATTEND

1 *Egocentric and socialised speech*

Freud's view of the sixth and seventh years of childhood as a continuation of the oedipus phase, during which autistic fantasy is progressively replaced by an acceptance of reality, is congruent with Piaget's experimental findings. These conclude that thought processes are intuitive rather than rational, yet grounded in a well-maintained awareness of self as distinct from environment. This intuitive phase, to use Piaget's term, opens with a well-defined body image which has been elaborated into an ego-environment system. In addition a relatively simple verbal superstructure reflects his sensori-motor affect systems at all points. He is thus capable of keeping up a running commentary on his own behaviour in much the same way as his parent had earlier provided such a commentary. Such verbal accompaniments during the intuitive phase are regarded by Piaget as egocentric, since the child is not concerned about whether the listener understands what he says. He may derive pleasure and reassurance as he chatters in the presence of an adult or another child, but emotive noises of concurrence and sympathy usually satisfy him. The development of socialised language stems as usual from the expression of urgent need and gives the child experience of the instrumental value of language. Moreover, he experiences a new pleasure when his thoughts and feelings are reflected back to him in social intercourse. By the time he is six years old most of his utterance is socialised. He can then live on a reality plane socially as well as through his instrumental manipulation of the environment to suit his needs. To be realistic in social relations it is necessary for him to be able to put himself at the viewpoint of another. This leads to the abandonment of earlier methods, in which caretakers were part of an instrumentally conditioned set of satisfiers, for techniques which imply knowledge of the probable reactions of caretakers. This level of behaviour differs from the previous conditioned patterns by virtue of its verbal direction and the behavioural complexity it engenders.

It would seem then that social maturity and language development are two descriptions of a single process and it explains why a social maturity age of six years is an experimentally derived norm of 'reading readiness'. It follows upon the establishment of socialised speech as demonstrated by Piaget's observations. This implies that for a child to understand what is required in the reading process he must first place himself at the viewpoint of the writer of the book and regard it as a means of communication to him from another. Children who have not reached this stage may be helped to understand the printed word as a means of communication if they provide the text from their own fantasies or experience, e.g. each saying what one of his own drawings is about and having the words he utters printed underneath. The teacher thus acts as an intermediary in the child's egocentric communication with himself, and facilitates a passage to the correct orienting response to reading materials.

The emergence of socialised speech is made possible by a change of 'set' or orientation whereby attention is concentrated on the recipient of the communication. This is perhaps the outcome of attention directed outwards under arousal conditions of frustration. Such energising arousal may produce scanning behaviour, followed by neural overspill into a schema subserving the right word to unlock his hearer's understanding. This neural process, when it becomes habitual, may be regarded as the appropriate orienting response of linguistic communication. It is a necessary prelude to voluntary obedience. This skill, as Luria has shown, begins to be evident at the outset of the pre-conceptual phase. During this phase it reaches a level which is immune to contra-suggestion, enabling the child to attend selectively against the pressure of dominant sensory impressions. This phenomenon has been observed experimentally in Piaget type research, with its pedagogical pattern of demonstration, question, answer, and also in similar studies by Russian psychologists. The latter are of the Pavlovian stimulus-response type, and are couched in the terminology of conditioning. Both are for the most part cross-sectional studies and their different research-techniques are mutually illuminating.

2 *Verbally mediated orienting responses*

The experiments reported by Zaporozhets (1961) on the orienting responses of young children demonstrate this. For example, Martsinovskaya taught groups of children between the ages of three and seven to react by key pressing to first the strong component of a visual stimulus, such as a red circle on a pale yellow background or a bright green circle on a grey background. The colours of the figure ground composition were then reversed so that the child was required to react to the lower-toned figure on its higher-toned background. The results suggest that whereas all the children in the age range were able to orient themselves selectively to the tonally dominant elements in the stimuli, correct reactions to the designated cues which were tonally weak did not stabilise until the seventh year. By this age all but 10 per cent of the children were consistent in their responses to the visually non-dominant stimuli. It might be said then that the verbal direction of the investigatory-orienting activity in these experiments brought about an intensification of the weaker stimuli which was not indifferent for behaviour. There was a distinct improvement in the responses of the children during the sixth year for all were able to react selectively to some extent to the weaker element though 30 per cent were not consistent in this. The age five to six appeared to be a transitional stage in orienting selectively against the suggestive power of strong stimuli. By the seventh year it would appear that most children's motor systems have become amenable to regulation by a verbal system of elective connections, and the impulsive unspecific role of speech as a clarifying accompaniment of activity disappears (Luria 1960). It is replaced by verbal rules which mediate responses to signals, and voluntary movement becomes regulated by internal speech. This makes possible a refinement of motor behaviour which may achieve the level needed for the most exquisite end results in both ethical and artistic spheres, and brings about more adaptable responses in human behaviour. In this connection, it is interesting to reflect on the reason why electrical stimulation of the motor areas of the cortex in conscious patients does not arouse a sense of voluntary movement although a movement is made. It is, perhaps, because the element of verbal intention is lacking and these integrating mechanisms prerequisite to voluntary planned action, subserved by to and fro cortico-subcortical neurone circuits, are not evoked when specific motor areas are surgically stimulated (Penfield 1954).

3 *From orienting reflex to learning set*

Since verbally mediated orienting determines the direction of subsequent voluntary behaviour, it will be of general significance for motivation, and it is to be expected that a new trend in motivational pattern should ensue upon the appearance of this newly matured capacity. For example, it is to be expected from this time onwards that competences and established techniques would become more binding reasons for following one course of action rather than another. It is common experience that this increases with age, but it might be regarded as achieving a prime place among motivational factors by the end of the intuitive phase. For this reason, an analysis of learning parameters must include and give prior place to the formation of an orienting basis for the learning which is to follow. The intuitive phase is important as a bridge between the orienting responses of autism and the more socialised and perceptually objective appraisal of externality through voluntarily embraced and verbally expressed terms of reference. Learning of this kind which conforms to prescribed criteria, rather than to those of transductive association, must be initiated by an orienting process which is complex, consisting of a preliminary representation of the product, and of the process itself, together with a system of reference points which allow a task to be performed (Gal'perin and Talyzina 1961). This implies some past acquaintance with the situation which evokes the orienting reflex. The acquisition of such capacity to learn should be encouraged step by step in the remedial teaching of children who have failed to assimilate arithmetical concepts in their first year at school, i.e. during their seventh year. Gal'perin has attempted to do this by formulating the principles of remedial teaching along these lines. He considers there are five successive types of situation to which the backward child should be exposed. These recapitulate the normal ontogenetic stages in assimilatory development and thus facilitate the passage from the orienting reflex to the learning set. The first and lowest level of acquaintance is casual and undirected. The child is incidentally exposed to the stimuli which are later to represent meaningful integrated units of experience. In the quantitative field of arithmetic the stimuli would be the concrete materials such as shells, beads, counters which will later be quantified, and the digits which will later be used symbolically. The recent pronouncements of Gal'perin on this stage has long been recognised in English schools and is exemplified in the sorting of a medley of such materials into separate categories or in the making of patterns with such materials embedded in plasticine and so on. This is an expressive stage and is frequently associated with nursery rhymes and jingles which introduce number. Acquaintance with the shape of the figures is effected by tracing, or feeling and guessing when blindfolded, or by matching. Under normal developmental conditions this stage is incidentally enacted in the family environment through hearsay and the normal transactions of everyday life. Where, however, the child hears little conversation of this kind or ignores it because of a chronic condition of anxiety, this privation will be reflected in a delayed start on formal arithmetic.

Gal'perin's second stage is designed to effect response generalisation in distinction to the stimulus generalisation effected in the previous stage. In this, the child learns to make relevant physical responses with concrete objects such as counting with sticks, arranging cut-out numbers in order, sorting objects into classified groups and labelling them with digit tablets. This stage is normally incorporated into the curriculum in British schools. It is one in which the symbol is associated with the generalised experience of quantity. That is to say the number is recognised as being independent of the kind of thing counted.

The third stage is occupied with the mastering of actions on the plane of audible speech. Here the aim is to replace concrete operations with verbal ones. An aid during this stage is the adoption of a conventional concrete method of depicting each quantity. For example, the arrangement of ten in two groups of five, each of which clearly demonstrates the composition of five, since five is the largest number which can be grasped perceptually in one mental act. Larger ones require two mental hops such as that six is one more than five, or two threes, or that seven is three and four.

During the fourth stage of Gal'perin visual perception is replaced by imagery, and in addition, the sensori-motor speech responses are muted, first into whispers and then into speech imagery. Thus the child transfers action to the mental plane by rendering the overt responses covert. During this stage, eye movements may be seen operating frequently as though numbers and objects were projected in space and incipient articulation may be present in lip movements.

The fifth and most mature stage marks the elimination of these covert orienting responses and their substitution by the immediately available end result. The stimuli now anticipate immediately the response, presumably in neurological terms, by direct firing into association areas which may by-pass the specific projection systems. This may involve the structuring of two association areas, the parieto temporal lobe which probably transforms the input systematically into the recognisable, and the frontal which may be responsible for the appraisal of the correctness of the response (Pribram 1960). Where the child is in doubt about the correctness of the response, a return to the fuller, more primitive stimuli processing occurs spontaneously or, more usually, may be instigated by his teacher.

Gal'perin's analysis of the process of assimilation might be paralleled by Piaget's, though differently expressed. His first stage would result in a sensori-motor schema of number devoid of sign language. The second stage sees the integration of a sign language and the sensori-motor schemata of objects in the environment. In the third stage this integration is intensified. During the fourth stage feed-back of an auditory nature is avoided. This lessens the sensory elements of the schema and facilitates the fifth stage in which the intervention of this system either in overt speech or covert imagery is eliminated. Thus the minimum of cues comes to evoke the correct response. It is the final stage which Piaget describes as a formal operation while the fourth stage is a concrete operation and the first three stages contribute to the half group. The half group is the intuitive schema which is rigid and ungeneralised and therefore cannot be reversed in process nor applied in the solution of problems.

These concepts of Piaget will be discussed more fully in the next chapter. Here the Russian approach is more profitable because of its emphasis on mode of entry to problems in response to verbal cues which is largely acquired during this phase. Moreover, Piaget's adoption of terminology peculiar to logic and the philosophy of mathematics (Young 1911) has made for difficulty in understanding what they mean in a psychological context. He may have been led to do this because his experimental approach to thinking was first carried out in children's understanding of reasoning and quantity.

4 *Persistence and concentration*

The developmental importance of the intuitive phase for the study of motivation is twofold. Firstly, it ushers in a more effective facility in the selective raising and lowering of thresholds to stimuli in accordance with verbally expressed criteria, and secondly, by virtue of this, persistence and concentration are established as habits of mind. Both environmental expectation and private inclination combine to exercise these two functions, the former being the pacemaker for persistence and the latter for concentration. Persistence is largely regarded as a character-trait and is epitomised in the concept of Webb's 'W' factor, while concentration is the hall-mark of the strong ego and the anxiety-free mind. The character trait of self-control implies persistence in planned voluntary action beyond the point of inclination for the sake of achieving a desirable end.

This is to be distinguished from concentration which implies intensity of immediate and on going attention. Persistence may be present when concentration is fitful, but normally the two traits are highly correlated. The pursuit of intrinsically motivated tasks evokes strong concentration. This kind of preoccupation was noted by Meier (1933) as being a characteristic of his sample of creative artists, and it may be that the intuitive phase is the period in the life-cycle when interest and some degree of technical facility make for intensive investigation of a single phenomenon. It has its antecedents in preoccupations of earlier periods, but the intuitive phase ushers in technical competences which simulate adult skills and is therefore more closely geared to creation and discovery. At this age both intrinsic and extrinsic motivation will tend to stretch the child's persistence beyond the extent of his inclinations. He experiences coercion more frequently, and this insistence of caretakers develops the child's capacity for persistence in tasks not immediately of intrinsic interest to him. This is a significant aspect of will-power as introspectively studied by the Louvain school (Aveling 1931). The acceleratory influence of parents and teachers during and after the intuitive phase inculcate what might be called habitual levels of application, and these through becoming aspects of self regard become also calibrators of motive. In an achievement oriented culture, persistence until ends are reached is highly applauded, and this is particularly so in those areas of achievement which command the best rewards such as the intellectual, the athletic, the mechanical and the artistic (Kagan and Moss 1962).

Culturally valued areas of achievement tend to provide cues which lead to lowered thresholds. The less reinforced areas of cultural expectation yield stimuli which are not so readily perceived. It is difficult, however, to know whether it is reinforcement or frequency of experience which results in lowered thresholds. It is probably both. It is important therefore to canalise the flux of attention in as varied a manner as possible in order to increase the range of lowered threshold potential. For a broad-based education, which provides potentially lowered thresholds to widely different classes of stimuli, it is of obvious importance to avoid intensive specialised attention to specific classes of stimuli. In this way, the individual's energy is free for deflection into a wider range of interests. Thus during the intuitive phase among insightful educators, little is taught with accuracy at the formal level. Instead formal symbols are more fully associated with meaning through the perceptual and motor activity of the learner in relation to the objects, which the words denote. This is relevant to the first three stages of assimilation as outlined by Gal'perin above, and brings the child to the stage of Piaget's half-group. This is the purpose of the so-called project method commonly found in the modern schools for pupils in this age range. In projects, activities lead to the building of one complex whole which can be given one name such as 'Our village', 'The harvest' and so on. In maturity the verbalised concepts 'Village life' or 'Harvest' will form the starting point for analytic detailing of their respective aspects, but at this stage the construction is concretely and practically built up so that it may become an integrated awareness subsequently, capable of analysis into many parts. This applies also in the acquisition of motor skills. During the intuitive phase a skill such as driving a nail in with a hammer is much more speedily acquired if attention is oriented towards the manner of performance of the action rather than on the result of the action. Later, perception of the target evokes the correct action more readily (Zaporozhets 1961). This is another example of the endowment of objects with meaning and significance in terms of the child's activity in relation to them. Percepts and concepts alike are grounded in the hindsight which follows on sensorimotor experience. But this hindsight becomes tomorrow's foresight. Through experience of the means whereby the end is attained, the image of the end result comes to mean the steps whereby it may be attained.

II. THE STABILISATION OF THE CAPACITY TO CONFORM

1 *Regression and progression under stress*

A child hiver hovers in and out of reality with ease during the intuitive phase though his irreality is usually a closer reflection of the real world than when he was younger. This is particularly so when he is disoriented by a stress situation to which he must become habituated. Regression to a kind of thinking typical of pre-conceptual fantasy is not uncommon, and this was illustrated in a fantasy sequel in two stages by a boy of seven years who was badly disturbed by a change from a normal home environment to a regimented institution. He and his younger sister had been admitted a year previously when the family had been deserted by the mother. The persistent aggressive and refractory behaviour of the boy called for therapeutic measures and he received play therapy for a month. Constructive and imaginative play flowed easily from him and one Friday he began a drawing saying he would finish it at the next session which was on Monday. The Friday's drawing was quite elaborate

FIGURE 2a. *Fantasy drawing of a boy of seven years*

FIGURE 2b. *Continuation of the fantasy drawing of a boy of seven years*

and is shown in Figure 2a. The sequel drawing on the Monday is shown in Figure 2b. It was drawn in three sections each occupying a page, the third of which was on the back of the second. The drawings of Figure 2b were regarded as a continuation of the stream which was terminated by the right-hand margin of the page of Figure 2a. The stream is widened to form a sea or lake from the left-hand margin and narrowed again at the right-hand margin three times in Figure 2b. The format and contents of the drawings of the second session can be traced to recent experiences, but that of Figure 2a is more pre-conceptual in fantasy level, though executed with the technical competence and facility of a child of normal maturation. The sequel is a good example of progression from a regressed projective condition to a more normal level of control and adjustment to reality.

He verbally reported on the picture of Figure 2a that it was the castle of the King and Queen whose soldiers, sailors and servants were guarding them in the grounds and on the water. The plan of roads was in all probability derived from those of the cottage homes in which he lived. Most energy was expended on the water which was extended a section at a time and shaded in energetically with a pen and then with a pencil. The bridges and steamer provide transport facilities over the water barrier. In the front garden of the castle are two outsized flowers on each of which sits a butterfly.

A freudian interpretation of this day's fantasy would consider the King and Queen as prototypes for parental figures and the butterflies as the two children shut out from their parents' regard. This may have been an experience encountered prior to leaving the family circle, now confirmed by admission to the Institution. On the whole the picture reflects dynamic assertion of a libidinal type. The smoke from chimney and funnel, the marching soldiers and the vigour of the water suggest resurgent anal and urethral aggression. The disposition of the patches of water is reminiscent of patterns formed by these natural functions. If this interpretation is relevant, it can be seen as a theme carried over in sublimated form into the drawings of Figure 2b. These were inspired by a drawing made on the blackboard in school by his teacher of the Mediterranean Sea in illustration of the Hellenic myth of the war between the young and old gods, and the giants created by the latter. In the first map of Figure 2b there is an island where the castle stood in Figure 2a, while a ship off-shore without its aggressive funnel is roughly in the same position as the first steamer. In the second section of Figure 2b the island is diminished in size but contains a diminished nonsmoking image of the castle. The live volcanic island may be representative of repressed aggression, and was reported by the child to be one of those beneath which a giant is buried as in the Hellenic myth. An experience of the weekend is reflected in the coastline where the letters 'pli' are distinctly incorporated. The patient was unconscious of this, and it appears to be a case of automatic writing. Further support for this is seen in two repetitions, also unconsciously executed, in the third section where 'plc' and 'plo' are distinctly incorporated. When these were pointed out to the patient he said he had seen a policeman in the garden of the police station where he had peeped through the hedge during the weekend and he was wearing no helmet. This had been a shock of surprise to the boy for he had never before seen a policeman so bereft of this insignia of authority. In this last section of Figure 2b the island now 'fits' into the shape of the coastline and is harmoniously integrated with it. This perhaps reflects a condition of acceptance of the external pressures which control his id propensities. Certainly after this month of therapy he became a model pupil, amenable to persuasion and alertly co-operative, over a follow-up period of two years. This complete 'cure' suggests that the patient was suffering from the effects of temporary deprivation but that he had never been seriously privated at home during the sensori-motor and pre-symbolic phases of development. The intensive therapy assisted him to resolve the ambiguity of his self perception in relation to this environment which failed to satisfy his expectations. He was very extraverted temperamentally, and in his anxiety condition betrayed a tendency to dissociation as seen in the incorporation of the letters from the word 'policeman' in the coastline and in the clear parallel between his phantasy construction and his deprivation. This was seen also in his play on another occasion when he constructed a woman without conscious intention – moving associatively from the placing of one piece to another. The first stimulus was a sentry box about 4½ feet high. Around this he draped a hessian wigwam decorated with a wool embroidery. Some large wooden beads commonly used in the teaching of arithmetic, an inch in diameter, were strung where the hessian contacted the roof of the sentry box. Finally he fixed the drawing of a face on paper to block in the aperture showing above the wigwam. The roof of the sentry box looked now like a peaked hat. When the therapist suggested the patient had made a lady like his mother, he accepted the remark with a laughing assent. This remark had healing value, for it was a communication between patient and therapist which integrated the patient's sense of desolation and his ego-involved creativity into harmonious co-existence. Neurologically speaking the cortical structuring of the present activity became part of the cell assembly subserving his sense of loss. This was brought about by the phase sequence driven between the two from the association area of the cortex subserving speech ideation. The therapist's 'interpretation' drew a dissociated cell assembly into the general matrix of cell assemblies, thus rendering it susceptible in some part to the superordinate direction of the verbal centres. It is clear from the content of these fantasy drawings that the boy made advances and retreats between new and old vantage points in his behaviour, analogous to the frequent returns to earlier stages when assimilating cognitive skills, as in the learning of arithmetic. Reversion to the concrete props to computations are equivalent to a regression to a transductive type of imagery in self expression as was used by the boy in Figure 2a above. Although seemingly more complex than the schematic later stages of Figure 2b, it has a lower ontogenetic status, for the structure and relational juxtaposition of the objects drawn is characteristic of the thinking of a child in his fifth year or earlier. This fact is disguised by the technical competence of the representation. It is a pre-verbal way of thinking in a child mature enough to think in words at a fully social level of communication. He was quite capable of discussing his plight in his separation from his parents, but had failed to accept the alternative society had offered. His caretakers came thus to be regarded with hostility and aggression, as frustrating what he desired. They acted in ways contrary to his expectation, and new expectations had not been formed, for the institution caretakers had failed to condition him positively to theirs. Thus the schemata of his old relationships had not been brought forward, as it were, in a transformed condition through integration with more recent ones, but this process was inaugurated and expedited through play therapy using the permissive and interpretative techniques described above. It is perhaps of interest in assessing motivation in this boy, that at the age six to eight years children are more prone to return to tasks when they are frustrated in completing them and that boys are more prone to do this than girls (Allport 1962). It would seem then that at this age tension systems tend to persist more than at other ages.

It is during the intuitive phase that the child is exposed to wider cultural stimuli in school and neighbourhood. He is now capable of orienting his behaviour in accordance with the verbal instructions of another and can persist for longer in repetitive tasks. He is, however, relatively incapable of deflecting energy into alternative, and equally satisfactory, means of solution because of his relative ignorance. There is thus a functional rigidity about the need to return to the same incomplete task, and if an alternative solution is sought it is likely to be regressive. The experience of the next few years, however, will introduce him to technical competences which should increase his repertoire of possible behaviours.

This flexible adaptability is brought about by feed-back of the effects of response into the perceptual awareness which evoked it. Thus perceptions become increasingly cue laden as a result of active behaviour in relation to them. This causes both stimuli and responses to become generalised to one another because the daily situations of children are more similar than different. But these systems become more complex as they learn to react to the nuances in their environment. In time, equivalences are seen between more diverse stimuli and between various behavioural consequences. Finally, the customary responses to one class of stimuli can be transferred to the solution of new problems. This is a graduation which is observed in all good caretaking and teaching. The first exercises of the skill are based on closely similar stimuli and call for identical responses. Gradually, differences are widened between examples, but the diversity is not so great as to prevent the child from recognising equivalence. Finally, a new process is introduced which though different is facilitated by a transfer of the behaviour structured at earlier stages. As maturation proceeds the amount of transfer to each new process increases, but at the same time the new process must be practised in a relatively constant form. Thus, it progresses from the generalisation of stimulus and response through equivalent forms, to a readiness for transfer to a still more complex process. This kind of learning prior to the intuitive phase is largely incidental and undirected by adults, but such verbal direction as there has been has taught the child to orient his attention in accordance with the criteria of adult instruction. In the common school this directive element in learning is a more frequent occurrence, and it is not surprising that I.Q.s are most upwardly mobile during the intuitive phase (Sontag et al. 1958).

The acquisition of more complex and flexible stimulus-response systems is encompassed by forward and backward swings between maturational levels, as well as through recently acquired lateral association. For this reason as Murphy (1947) insists all developmental levels of thinking are always present and co-existential. Thus regression is a useful device for calling on an earlier mode of response when a more recent one proves inadequate. It may be a crude adaption from the viewpoint of the detached observer, but it serves the child in extracting him from a present impasse, whatever the long-term consequences may be. It is of educational value for nothing alerts a positive caretaker more quickly than regressive behaviour in the child for whom she is responsible. It is a releasing stimulus which causes the caretaker to examine more closely the nature of the child's frustration and so enables her to obviate the necessity for suffering the pain and inconvenience of his misdemeanours, and anxiety concerning his happiness.

During these years, children are prone to enter enthusiastically into projects but fail because of their lack of techniques to achieve what was envisaged. Thus the fluency and verve of this period which is an important element in creative thinking tends to disappear as formal education places increasing emphasis on accuracy and control, re-emerging again in adolescence when these are acquired (Burt 1962). Corrective discussion then during the intuitive phase limits creative spontaneity yet at the same time provides the necessary technical know-how for future creative activity. This has caused many educators to call for a delay in the demand for accuracy and neatness until the intuitive period is over, i.e. until the age of seven years. Free activity methods are advocated in which corrective discussion follows upon the child's spontaneous endeavour to create, when he needs help. Thus fluency is facilitated and training in accuracy and control made intrinsic to the child's own projects. In so-called progressive schools for part of the day the carefully planned programmes of the teacher lead the children by the gradual stages advocated by Gal'perin into knowledge of the technical skills of reading and arithmetic, while for the remainder of the day the only restraints experienced derive from the media of the optional creative activity. By this means the spontaneous groundwork of conceptual thinking is freely laid, thus facilitating the assimilation of related 'taught' concepts.

2 *The antecedents of mature concepts*

Concepts are always operational in function, i.e. they are a generalised stimulus-response complex and are so because they are amenable to linguistic formulation. They appear, however, to pass through a number of well-defined developmental stages on their way to maturity. These have been outlined by Vygotsky (1962) as three-fold. The earliest syncretic stage is one in which there is an incoherent coherence in that the most diverse elements are incorporated into one inarticulate image. The binding force depends on the child's lowered threshold for aspects of the percept which are in some way analogous to his own affectively toned object relations. In this stage there is a free stimulus generalisation which is as yet unfettered by response mediated significance. The valuation by caretakers of the child's responses provide the most pervasive 'bonding' influence during the syncretic stage. It is a stage in which conditioning through the social reinforcement of praise and blame is conveyed by the emotional climate of acceptance and rejection in the home. This was Gal'perin's first step in assimilation.

The second stage witnesses greater differentiation of the autistic bonding into sub-wholes, each of which illustrate his own needs. There is an attempt to assimilate actively a quality which is inherent in the object to the satisfaction of his own needs. This kind of thinking is prevalent during the pre-conceptual phase described in the previous chapter. For example, a doll will serve as an object of aggression because it is like a person and small and therefore can stand in relation to the child as he does to the adult. Moreover, its inanimate lack of response renders it safe as an object of aggression. All these qualities are inherent in the object but are such as to consort well with the child's needs 'to practise' those aspects of experience he is assimilating. The more his experiential front matures and becomes structured, the greater the degree of coherence and plausibility entering into his choice of the objects with which to fantasy. This brings the conceptual level to its third stage designated by Vigotsky – a pseudo-concept. This stage of assimilation is comparable to the half-group of Piaget and the third stage in Gal'perin's description.

The pseudo concept is the kind of thinking most prevalent during the intuitive phase. In this, a certain kind of perceptual relationship is adhered to as the characterising factor. This differs from the true concept, however, in that the perception of the relevant relationship is lost to sight when the perceptual matrix is altered in appearance but not in substance. This is largely because there is insufficient maturity to inhibit the irrelevant from appearing in the focus of attention than because of failure to attend to the relevant. It is thus a rejecting and dismissing capacity for what is redundant in a percept which must be acquired – the raising of the perceptual threshold for 'what it is not' – a capacity for ignoring the irrelevant. In infancy the strange and unfamiliar bring about greatest arousal. The reverse is true of more mature orientation where orientation and arousal is towards the relevant. The negative arousal and aversion of the earlier arousal jags in the presence of the unfamiliar is now converted into cognitive occlusion of the irrelevant through raised thresholds. These are raised through the agency of the learning or orienting set adopted at the outset of the behavioural cycle, and as has been shown above this capacity achieves an effective maturity in voluntary behaviour during the intuitive phase. This new skill in learning to learn facilitates the acquisition of the true concept.

Orienting responses to relations of difference are acquired earlier than orienting responses to relations of likeness. Normally a child is articulate about differences in his sixth year, but the verbal formulation of likenesses is a more mature skill and appears a year later. This illustrates the greater maturity called for in the suppression of the irrelevant. If he is asked in what way an apple and an orange are alike he persists in giving differences such as 'One is soft and the other hard' during the sixth year. It is clear that these are the obvious points which strike his attention, and that he cannot eliminate them from his mind in order to seek the less obvious likeness. He may have experienced the fact that they both have pips and that each will roll like a ball, but his use of the word 'like' as a superordinate director of attention is not developed and thus the earlier type of experience claims priority in the comparison. The perception of differences is implied in orientation towards the dominant figure in Martinovskaya's study of orienting responses. The stimulus was one of strong contrasts. The perceptual selection of the tonally weaker part of the stimulus according to instructions indicated greater maturity. The perceptual figure-ground pattern was more congruent with thalamic processing. The selection of the lower-toned element as a stimulus for response involved a verbal reversing of the primary process. In a sense, the perception of differences is a matter of contrasts – one sensation throwing another into relief. When seeking similarities the child is reacting to the non-dominant sensory aspects of the pair of objects in juxtaposition. Seen thus, in terms of sensory processing, the selection of the non-dominant aspects as criteria would seem to involve a raising of sensory thresholds (or imaginal ones) for the more obvious figure-ground characteristics. The child who persists in giving differences when similarities are asked for is unable to orient with the help of his verbal system in this selective way. Such attributes as hard-soft, sweet-sour are sensorily in a figure-ground relationship, even as a yellow patch on a grey background.

This tendency for the perception of differences to constitute an antecedent condition for the perception of similarities appears in broad outline during the first two phases of development and again during the third and fourth. Between the sensori-motor and the pre-conceptual periods a transition is made from the sensori-motor startle and a cognitive-dissonance withdrawal reaction to the use of 'feeling analogies' and approach reactions. In the third stage which is now under review, an ability to use the term 'different' in orienting responses precedes the correct use of the term 'like' in voluntary direction of attention. Facility in orienting towards the like features of his environment enables the child to profit from exposure to situations involving generalisation and application of rules. The acquisition of this level of skill terminates the intuitive stage in thinking. This does not mean that at the age of six years intuitive thinking is abandoned altogether. It is merely a matter of over-all proportion. In any future learning situation there will be an intuitive phase which will be prolonged in proportion to the situation's novelty. Moreover, there is more likelihood of a bewildering syncretic stage if the situation is entirely unfamiliar. Naturally, with increase in experience, unfamiliar situations decrease in incidence, and it is for this reason that the intuitive phase is located at the ages of five and six years. After this age, most situations have become sufficiently familiar to lessen the chances of syncretic and intuitive reactions.

3 *Experience and maturation*

From these considerations it can be deduced that the two most determining characteristics of the intuitive phase are firstly the internalisation of speech which covertly sustains a course of action in progress, and secondly the ability to distinguish the essential from the inessential in a schema, by stabilising it in verbal terms of reference. Words, however, come to have different meanings according to the context in which they occur, and developmental studies reveal that this is geared to the kind and frequency of experience the individual encounters. This is seen clearly and simply in the variety of meaning associated with the word 'some'. With children in the intuitive phase 'some friends' means about five and 'some trees' about twenty. This implies two differing contexts of experience. Distinctions between expressions are also sharpened with increase in experience. For example, the expression 'nearly always' is not clearly distinguished from 'scarcely ever' at the age of seven, but by eleven years the former connotes a frequency four times as large as its opposite in meaning, and among adults twenty times larger (Cohen et al. 1958). Variation of meaning with change of context can be described as an increase in response generalisation, for the same verbal response is seen as appropriate to a large variety of stimuli. Thus linguistic sophistication is dependent chiefly on response generalisation, and by virtue of this the naïvety of childhood is left behind.

One important experiential area which becomes sophisticated during the intuitive phase is realisation and acceptance of sex role. This is facilitated in all probability by the new-found competence to operate independently on a social front wider than the home and family. It would be particularly so where there is less than two years spacing between siblings, for then each plays with the other's friends. Similarly, if the siblings are of the same sex there is more likelihood of a wider social experience. Where they are of the opposite sex the boy has a greater advantage than the girl, for girls who are friends, tend to play nearer to one another's homes and are thus available to brothers when at home (Koch 1957). Sibling relationships due to accidents of sex and birth order of this kind introduce relative richness or privation of experience which will cause the social response generalisation of members of a family to vary proportionately. Such acquired facility can be an important element in social motivation in more mature years.

4 *The relationship between social and verbal development*

This new phase of experience is reflected in the verbal system in Osgood's semantic differential (1958). His second and third dimensions of meaning are potency and activity, and they resemble in large measure the stereotyped conceptions of male and female traits. The terms highly loaded with the potency dimension are large, strong, loud, heavy, bass, rough and rugged. Those with highest loadings for activity are agitated, sharp, ferocious, tense, hot, angular, active and fast. These two types of meaning suggest they arise from a layer of experience which intensifies at the time when sex role is recognised by children as such (Kagan and Moss 1962). It is significant perhaps that the age of five and a half is the peak age for desiring a change of sex (Subes et al. 1954). Thereafter the opposite sex may be envied for the advantages it enjoys, but desire for change of sex is less frequently found. Awareness of sex role is expedited or retarded by the attitude of adults in the family towards it. This is reflected in the mean ages at which different socia-economic groups reveal its presence. Working-class children are sophisticated in this respect a year or two years earlier than middle-class children (Rabban 1950). This may be because the roles of the two parents in domestic life tend to be more sharply differentiated among the working classes. Such slants to experience are important for future social motivation in choices of companion and mate, and in style of managing social relationships generally.

The more differentiated perception of others brought about by the broadening of social relations with peer and adult groups exposes the child to much more varied stimulation. Mention was made earlier that one of the most important predicters of success in assimilating reading skills at this age is social maturity (Gesell et al. 1940). From this it would appear that fluent oral intercourse with others inculcates the notion that words are a means of communication and that speech sequences are made up of separate words. This undoubtedly occurs by virtue of the variety of settings and tones of voice and idiosyncrasies of pronunciation which are to be met with in conversation with a wider assortment of persons. In view of this, however, it is difficult to explain why boys represent between 60 and 100 per cent of reading disability cases (Bennett 1938). Boys have a wider social fare than girls according to the findings of Koch (1957), and some other reason of a more deep-seated kind must be found to explain this. There are probably several reasons, but a sex difference in two factors of reading readiness may be detected. In the first place the motive for compliance to adult demands may be differently oriented in boys as Kagan and Moss (1962) have suggested. Since more mothers foster dependency in their boys by waiting on them and acceding to their requests for nurturance, their sons are willing to learn in order to oblige a loving caretaker. Girls on the other hand tend to be more critically reared through infancy and early childhood, and are therefore accustomed to comply with the wishes of caretakers as a means of achieving security. These emotive factors will underlie the acquisition of learning sets or orienting habits in the process of reading, for the social situation of teacher and pupil is more akin to that experienced by little girls at home than by boys. It is thus more possible for teachers to accelerate girls and so bring them safely through the initial stages of learning to read, which are the crucial ones at which most remediably backward children are halted. Boys who have been fostered in dependency are not accustomed to the impatience of adults such as that of a teacher with a failing child. Thus the blame attached to error sets up a cognitive closure against a threatening environment, for they have not been conditioned into error avoidance as their sisters were. Where this is the case and the boy is of normal intelligence, it is often sufficient to create for him a permissive social atmosphere which lowers his resistance and so enables him to learn. This was exemplified in a boy who had been reared by his grandmother and aunt on the death of his mother, but returned to his father, who had remarried, when he was three. The stepmother was a sturdy forthright woman with little natural tenderness of demeanour, and when two years later the boy began to attend school he acquired no reading skill at all in the course of three years. This led to a psychological investigation whereupon he was found to be of above average intelligence but showing signs of long-standing anxiety. During subsequent sessions with a woman therapist, he freely fantasied, expressing hostility and aggression towards her such as burning her at the stake while he galloped round on a white charger. These fantasies were acted, and he explained what he was doing as he acted. In a very short time he was unloosened cognitively and was able to respond to the reading lessons provided by the school. Thus, without any teaching but after play sessions at a child guidance clinic, a stubborn non-reader may begin to make progress for the first time. The covert nature of obstinacy and the raised perceptual thresholds which accompany it, cannot be directly observed by teachers, but the probability of their presence may be deduced when intelligence and the case history are known.

A second reason for the relatively large proportion of boys among backward readers may reside in the greater chattering propensities in girls. In boys, fluency in conversation tends to decrease with age more sharply than it does in girls. A survey of the incidence of chattering as a cause of disruption of lessons was made by the writer (Highfield and Pinsent 1952). In this the incidence of notorious chatterers in school at the age of seven was 41 per cent in girls and 36 per cent in boys. By the age of thirteen there was 32 per cent among girls and only 16 per cent among boys. This reflects, perhaps, a cultural expectation that boys should be restrained in speech, and that the effect of this is apparent towards the end of the intuitive period. This would deprive boys of the exercise of verbal fluency which is a supporting characteristic in the reading process. It is indeed a striking fact that it is the rare girl who ends her primary schooling in Britain with a reading age inferior to her mental age, but among boys there are usually a minimum of 15 per cent who do so (Highfield 1951).

During this transitional period between early and later childhood, self perception receives its cultural imprint, in that awareness of role becomes a significant aspect of self-other relationships. In normal children at this age there is a delight in the fantasy assumption of roles both familial and extra-familial, as is delightfully portrayed in Robert Louis Stevenson's 'The Lamp lighter'. Here a feeling evaluation for role is very evident. This assimilation is valuable not only for choice of role but also for responsible understanding of others who occupy such roles. Being at the receiving end of another's role needs as much understanding as actively occupying one. Nietzsche's (1886) view of the ego as a grammatical illusion fails to take into account role mediation in development, and Murphy's (1947) conclusion, "Self perception in light of role makes up personality", is more apposite. The hypothesis that without linguistic terms of self reference conscious selfhood would not emerge would seem to support Nietzsche's dictum, but there is danger here in the logical fallacy of defining a phenomenon in terms of its genesis. The psychological structure of language and the power of flexible reference which it facilitates is built upon a set of existent relationships in a cultural matrix. These transcend the individual and comprise the meaningful context in which he moves. The condensed significance of words derives from many sensori-motor experiences within this matrix. For this reason, as Pavlov emphasised, an individual's decisions verbally formulated have the potency of 100 of the conditioned pairings by which animals are trained (Leontev 1961).

This is perhaps an appropriate point at which to consider conditioning as a form of learning for it appears from the evidence that the conditioning of human beings becomes progressively more difficult as the verbal systems mature. In conditioning, the nature of the conditioned stimulus is not subjected to change on account of the response. It is linked to the unconditioned stimulus rather than to further stimuli evoked by the response such as an awareness of environmental change wrought through the agency of the response. When verbal systems are operative, however, the perceived effect of responses automatically spill back into stimuli through their complex networks of association. This precludes the simple automatism of conditioning. Conditioned responses may be acquired during the pre-verbal period of development, but these would tend to appear only in regressed behaviour when verbal direction of thought failed to solve a problem. If such regressive behaviour continues to be reinforced because it is effective it is likely to persist, as it does sometimes where caretaking is naïve. Where, however, the front of caretaking expectations move with the child's competence to respond to cultural norms, regressive behaviour is decrementally conditioned by disapproval or becomes extinguished because it is ineffectual.

5 *The effect of caretaking on achievement*

Every child enters the intuitive phase with an oedipal legacy which will affect profoundly his attitude to authority figures in extra-familial relationships. Oedipal rivalry can be fostered and strengthened as a pattern of adjustment if the parents stimulate it through their rivalry for the child's regard. Aggressive habits of dealing with frustration between the ages of three and eight years can be engendered strongly in such a family structure. Thus a two-fold technique of obtaining satisfaction can develop, first by appeal to the opposite sexed parent in defiance of the rival parent, and then by turning to the rival parent whose jealousy may have been aroused by the preference shown for the opposite sexed parent. In such strategies the child acts at two levels which are mutually reinforcing, the oedipal or id level, and the ego level (Bender 1943). By the age of six he may encounter the frustrations of school in the same way. He fails to compete and achieve through a generalisation of the same pattern. In this the school is played off against the home, with the parent at one moment taking an attitude of acceleration and at the next interceding with school that the boy shall not be made anxious. Such a child is continually conflicted about the degree of autonomy he can maintain and fails to acquire an internalised model for more mature behaviour which does not seek special privilege. In houses of low moral and cultural standards, deviant behaviour in such children is more likely to offend against the law, for they tend to meet all frustration with massive defiance by the time they reach adolescence. Children who have resolved their conflicts with authority figures in this way might be regarded as privated of the kind of experience which is necessary for achieving adult status in western democracy. Such a future citizen might be at an advantage, however, in a culture or situation in which an astute and ambiguous path had to be traversed between rival factions. The ultimate criterion of good adaptation is a cultural one.

Some other highly specific effects of caretaking are seen in studies of changing I.Q. levels in children. Hunt's dictum (1961) that the great need of the child between the ages of four and seven is "ample opportunity for corrective discussion" is supported by the experimental finding that there is an average increase in eight points of I.Q. in children who enjoy a democratically oriented home environment. The criterion by which the home was graded for its democratic qualities were whether pains were taken to justify policy, whether children participated in policy making, whether appropriate answers were given to children's questions, and whether there was also an appreciation of excellence in performance. Further evidence in support of this finding was afforded by non-democratic families. Where there was an emotional climate of active hostility and passive neglect, there were small decreases in I.Q. over a three-year period (Baldwin, Kalhorn and Breese 1945). Two influences would appear to be operative, the nature of reinforcement and exposure to verbal discussion. Presumably in homes where children's I.Q.s tend to rise, incremental conditioning is more preponderant than decremental and there is more exercises of verbal function. Where the tendency is towards a falling I.Q. a reverse trend is to be expected because of hostility and passive neglect. Of these two influences – reinforcement and practice – it is probable that the practice of cognitive skills is the more important, for these are what are measured in an intelligence test. This accords with a further finding, that warm democracy when compared with a more detached variety, yielded no difference in mean I.Q. It would seem then that discussion of pros and cons in a family situation may provide exercises in problem solution, in perceptual organisation and integration of evidence, and in acts of communication, and these are the kinds of cognitive activity which are measured in an I.Q. test. Hence the increase in I.Q. among those who enjoy a democratic atmosphere. This necessity for appreciating fully the viewpoint of another expedites the normal departure from egocentric self expression at this age. In most children between the ages of six and eight there is a marked increase in the spontaneous offering of explanations. At six to seven, 50 per cent of children completely forgot to name what it is they are speaking about. A year later only 16 per cent omit this. Again, at the earlier age, the absence of temporal and logical order in explanations is the rule, while between seven and eight it is the exception (Piaget 1952). It would seem then that the important learning contingency during the intuitive phase is discussion between adults and children if maximum development is to be procured. The higher I.Q. of upwardly mobile working-class groups compared with those who are downwardly mobile may be also as great as 8 points of I.Q. (Hebron and de Samardick 1962), and it is to be wondered how far this stems from differing types and degrees of intercourse between parents and children.

Attitudes to achievement and independence begin of course with the self-initiated activities of the first two years such as reaching for things at a distance, attempting to hold the body upright and creeping. But these are weak predictors of achievement behaviour, perhaps because they are genetically determined. More reliable prediction resides in style of caretaking before three and after six according to the longitudinal evidence of Kagan and Moss (1962). Escalona and Heider (1959) and McClelland et al. (1953) also give evidence of the correlation between parental expectations and achievement.

The intuitive phase is one of acceleration because of the increased exposure of children to the nuances of a competitive society. As Eisenstadt (1956) remarks society is 'achievement oriented' while the family is 'kinship oriented'. But of course the family will be influenced by cultural norms and will view the child through the projective lens of identification and accelerate him in order that the identification may be comfortably intensified. Thus kinship and achievement orientations usually merge during the latency period, and it is expressed in the parent's appraisal of the child's performance at school and in the subtle inculcation of prestige values. For this reason men acquire prestige increasingly in the perception of the child. Father is the boss, because he owns the home, and because he has to work for a living (Kagan 1956). Prejudice too is assimilated between the ages of four and seven when it is part of the climate of opinion to which children are exposed. The large majority of children, by the end of the intuitive phase, are aware of prejudice as such, but accept it as correct (Radke, Trager and Davis 1949). Children unquestioningly accept a teacher's attitude as right even though it may occasion them discomfort. The fact that they will inevitably perpetuate the techniques used is demonstrated by the fact that in the sixth year a child's doll-play is correlated with his teacher's style in classroom management (Levin 1955). These attitudes acquired pre-operationally may never be rationally questioned in subsequent life.

On these counts it is not surprising that at the end of the intuitive phase, the main dimensions of personality are for the most part identical with those of adults (Cattell and Coan 1957). Verbal direction of behaviour has raised volition to the status of will, and an extended vocabulary makes possible knowledge in respect of objects, and phenomena which have never been encountered. The child now has a basic vocabulary which is grounded in direct experience. This is an aid to the construction of new situations which can be explained in terms of his past experience. By the eighth year it may be assumed that the child enters upon a second phase of social initiation – that concerned with the technical aspects of his cultural inheritance. Motivation from now on will be largely subordinated to competence rather than inclination, and ego involvement in areas of achievement will become less and less fancy free. The intuitive phase witnesses the last fling of imaginative childhood during which anything could possibly be true, and after which 'Let's pretend' is thrust into the straight jacket of technique and reality criteria. Thus as Smith and Stone (1961) remark, "The stress of striving to master the world leads to a cognitive theory of behaviour and development – indeed to a cognitive theory of conation."

CHAPTER V

The development of practical rationality between the eighth & twelfth years

I. THE COGNITIVE PROCESSES

Motivational variables in adults have been classified into two categories by Cattell and others (1962) according to whether (i) they derive from wishful-thinking (autism) or (ii) from resources of competence and knowledge. In the second and third chapters the roots of wishful thinking were described, while in the fourth a transitional phase was depicted, one in which competence and knowledge alternated with autistic-thinking in the motivation of behaviour. The present chapter is concerned with the ascendancy of competence and knowledge as the major motivational category to which wishful thinking becomes geared. During this phase regressive behaviour tends to be less frequent because more techniques are available for the resolution of problems presented by the environment. Thus autistic-thinking becomes increasingly forward looking in contrast to that of earlier phases. In these there was greater necessity, in the absence of alternative techniques, to rely on the effects of protest and social appeal. Moreover, autistic thinking is rendered purposive in a conscious sense during this phase, through the maturation of cognitive skills such as verbally mediated orienting responses and an increase in attention span. These make possible operational thinking as described by Piaget. In this, reversible operations, and the awareness of the continued identity of an object, even when its appearance changes, give rise to reliable and consistent conclusions, immune to the suggestion of chance impression. Since it seems appropriate to concentrate on cognitive skill as a motivational variable, this phase will be termed that of concrete operations, after Piaget.

1 *The nature of operational thinking*

For Piaget, operational thinking is an on-going mental process in which past stages are held constantly in dynamic relationship with the psychological present. This is effected by feeding back into them some of the arousal from current stimuli. Thus a continuous awareness of the identity or consistency of the object is maintained in relation to the self. From this it can be seen that a perception of identity is dependent upon reversibility. It is as though a story is being unfolded and the listener checks up on the identity of the characters by a glance back at antecedent information. Where habituation is established this glance back is effected by neural servo-mechanisms which operate at a subconscious level. In cognitive processing of a deliberate and purposive kind such reversibility and maintenance of identity is a function of orienting or set. Where thinking is voluntary, the verbal instructions trigger off the appropriate systems of orientation. Where it is involuntary, the same mechanism operates, but in a series of associations having no relation to any purpose. For example, should a person undertake to think of a grey circle on a yellow background, only these cues will evoke response in operational thinking. If, however, the subject is dreaming of a grey circle and sleep is suddenly interrupted by the first tinny clang of an alarm clock, the dream image could conceivably change to a familiar grey object which made such a sound, for instance – a dustbin lid. The stimulus changed the dream but certain qualities of the gestalt remained. Even in dream images then, there is some maintenance of identity and some reversibility, but it is mechanistic and dependent on associative paths already existent in a neural matrix associated with experience of grey circles. From this it can be seen that identity and reversibility is a characteristic of neural transmission, and that what Piaget calls operational thinking is the voluntary direction and control of this associative phenomenon by verbal stimuli. A break in such sustained direction betrays itself in overt behaviour by a non-sequitur or an irrelevancy which can be as inconsequential as dream sequences.

The experimental work of Piaget has demonstrated stages of maturation in the capacity to think operationally. These appear to depend on the amount of experience afforded by the verbalised situations of everyday life. For example, a young child constantly hears references to his behaviour in quantitative terms, implying more, less and equal. At first, these tend to refer to continuous and discrete quantities such as his drink and sweets. He is less exposed to quantitative remarks on time and weight continuities and less still to volume and prediction. It is not surprising, therefore, that operational thinking about quantities emerges in this order. It is highly probable that Piaget's norms are experientially determined and that if a cultural or geophysical mutation threw early emphasis on experience of weight, thinking in this field would become operational at an earlier age than the tenth year. The evidence suggests, however, that wide individual differences exist in the ages at which operational thinking is in evidence. In Piaget's work, an exceptional child of four may give as operational a reply as the majority of six-year-olds. This may reflect a genetically accelerated development or merely that this particular situation had caught the child's interest. Isaac's (1930) Malting House studies were among the first to demonstrate the effect of interest in the immediate environment on children's thinking in producing mature patterns. Her work was corrective of the then current impression that Piaget's norms were immutable criteria of readiness to learn. Her young subjects at Cambridge were for the most part the children of dons and they thus tended to move in a family context of alert observation with its correlated language. This may have been an expediting experience in her subjects. Family discussion appears to facilitate verbally directed orienting responses and an increase in a tool vocabulary for this purpose. As Leontev (1961) remarks, providing a child is acquainted with the concrete meaning of ice, snow, wind, crack, howl, drift etc., an arctic landscape may be spread before his view.

Piaget's operational thinking is a form of Hull's reactive potential in which habit strength ensures its reliability but in which drive level may account for precocity in its appearance. Habit strength causes a well-established operational schema to be activated by the merest relevant stimulus. On the other hand nascent schemata can be thrown into operational integrity in quite young children where there is emotive preoccupation with a particular circumstance, i.e. by drive level. Undoubtedly, both types of reactive potential contribute to the formation of operational schemata, but for Piaget, thinking was not regarded as operational until it was invariably in evidence, in situations which were not highly motivated autistically. All his experimental procedures were the ordinary pedagogical ones of question and answer. Under these circumstances he recognised two stages of assimilation before the child becomes concretely operational. The first is characteristic of the pre-conceptual and symbolic phase, and the second is more frequently in evidence during the intuitive phase.

At the earlier stage, the child gives evidence of recognition of a fact but he is unable to manipulate it in a changing context. This process Piaget describes as a half-group, because it lacks the operations of identity and reversibility of the full-group. This precludes any use of the fact in problem solution or as a major premise in deductive reasoning. If, for example, the number concept 7 is at the half-group stage of assimilation, seven objects may be correctly counted but the number will not be seen as consistently applicable to the same objects should their spatial context be changed by a different grouping. Piaget tested this, not by asking a question concerning equivalence, but by suggestively asking whether, with the changed arrangement, there were now more or less. This stimulus question acted as a decoy, as it were, if the child was unable to maintain in mind that the objects were identical with those designated before their rearrangement.

From this example, it can be seen what Piaget meant when he postulates that identity and reversibility are criteria of operational thinking. The past state of the object, designated by the number, must be seen as equivalent in quantity in its present form. In terms of the physiological psychology of Hebb (1946) the assimilation which leads to the half-group stage would stem from stimulus-response phase sequences being frequently fired along neural pathways. This would result in automatic habits rather than concepts. They are less useful than concepts because they are related only to specific and relatively simple situations. For example, a child of low intelligence can learn to recite his numbers without being able to use them to reason with in any simple way. For this, knowledge of the numbers must have reached the full-group stage. In neurological terms this means that a number of phase-sequences have been integrated into a cell-assembly. This occurs when experience of the label 'seven' has been undergone in many different situations. These varied significances result in a neural integration centred around the neural counterpart of the word seven. The cell-assembly, then, is the neural correlate of both operational thinking and the concept. It has a relatively differentiated structure because it has arisen from the discharge of phase-sequences each highly similar yet also different in some respect. The common core of the phase-sequences integrate to form an area of common meaning and import, which is also associated with variety on its fringes. The only part of each phase-sequence which is identical with all the others is the sound-articulation complex 'seven'. Thus each variation in experience associated with this symbol gives rise to a phase sequence which overlaps with its predecessors. These common association paths create an integrated and complex cell assembly which is responsive eventually to the stimulus 'seven' in any of its concrete manifestations. The cell-assembly then is one of potential phase sequences and the number of these, cohering 'within' it, determine the extent to which it is operational.

Any word which is rendered easily applicable to a large variety of like situations is ready for use in more abstract verbal constructions. Piaget claims that the point at which a child is ready to abandon the half-group stage for fully operational thinking may be observed when the experimenter questions the truth of an incorrect answer. At this stage, the child gives the incorrect answer hesitatingly and a repetition of the question often causes him to change to an assertion of equality in spite of the suggestive lead of the question. This marginal stage Piaget called pre-operational. The hymn of hate of the four-year-old boy (Chapter III) could be regarded as a stringing together of half-group phrases recognised and learnt by heart from his caretakers. This is seen perhaps in his use of the third person pronoun rather than the first in declaring his 'intentions'. At a later stage of maturity phantasy itself may be spontaneously questioned by the child and an operational level concerning make-believe arrived at. For example, a child in the intuitive phase, running beside his father and imitating a pony, may remark 'Little colts do hold their father's hands, don't they?' This is evidence of a pre-operational stage about make-believe ready to pass from half-group to full-group status.

It is customary nowadays to refer to the reinforcement of behaviour in children, and as this is a term deriving from the theory of conditioned reflexes a comparison of Piaget's operational thinking and Pavlov's unit of behaviour is relevant to a discussion of this phase of concrete operations. The main difference would seem to stem from the fact that the conditioned stimulus has no effect on the response beyond evoking its occurrence. The conditioned stimulus arouses expectancy for the advent of the unconditioned stimulus and for this reason it does so best when presented slightly ahead of the natural stimulus. The same is true of instrumental or operant conditioning. In this a conditioned stimulus evokes a conditioned response and together they are instrumental in producing the unconditioned stimulus and the unconditioned response. For example, a circus horse perceiving his trainer's covert or overt signal (conditioned stimulus) taps a specific number of times with his hoof (conditioned response) and then perceives sugar (unconditioned stimulus) and responds by eating it (unconditioned response). His tapping was instrumental to producing the reinforcing reward. The reinforcing element is the pleasure in eating the sugar. But the conditioned sensori-motor arc, of sign and tapping, remains in its pristine condition apart from the fact that it is more likely to occur again after the reinforcement. Such conditioned behaviour would be called by Piaget a half-group, because it stems from a recognition which is irreversible and rigid. It is analogous to the counting of seven by a child who is unable to recognise the sign as applying to this and all groups of seven things. In him too the response is highly specific and ungeneralised, reinforced usually by praise.

Operational thinking, on the other hand, is made possible by the fact that perceived consequences of response are fed associatively into the stimuli systems which evoked the response, bringing about their re-evaluation and the complexity of their cue significance. This happens with greatest facility when someone discovers a fact about a symbol or object on his own account. For this reason heuristic methods of teaching are of value, because attentional and response systems are equally aroused. Reinforcement occurs when the spontaneous response is effective in reducing the arousal attendant upon ego-involved stimulation. The difference, then, between teaching by drill methods and teaching heuristically arises from this source. When spontaneous interest is present, responses derive their reinforcement from the perception of desired effect and also draw more widely on the individual's established cell assemblies. In contrast, rote learning is as specific as the conditioned reflex, because the response does not of itself change the future perception of the stimulus. Where a response is problematically related to a stimulus, it has an effect on the stimulus in the perception of the problem solver. This perception of effect, termed feed-back, implies that a neural link is established between the perception of the stimulus and the perception of the change in its condition wrought by the response. A simple example of this is the spontaneous discovery by a child that nought if added to seven does not alter it. When the results of such insightful learning are compared with the rote learning of the same facts, it is shown invariably that they are retained longer. Adequate reinforcement then in human learning refers to the probability that an idea will be recalled, or a response repeated, by virtue of the fact that it has associative connections with many other items, each of which may instigate the reproduction. This definition is by implication synonymous with operational thinking.

2 *The interaction between verbal and sensori-motor functions*

During the phase of concrete operations, the generalising function of language ensures a double feed-back from perception of response into stimulus, the one concrete and sensorily disclosed, the other verbal. Since words are more amenable to exact definition than sensations and actions, sensori-motor responses are subject to greater differentiation by virtue of this associative interaction. This virtually excludes the possibility of the classical form of conditioning.

If this is so, the existence of phobias among adults must be explained, especially in view of the fact that they can be cured by reconditioning, from an aversive to a positive attitude. It would seem that such fears should have been dispelled by feed-back of innocuous effects in the course of experience. An irrational fear of feathers for example is difficult to sustain, having regard to all their pleasant contributions to human experience. A plausible explanation could stem from the way the early traumatic experience associated with feathers was handled by caretakers. If the panicking child's perception was disrupted by high arousal, and if the caretaker responded only to the panic in her comforting, the chances are that the stimulus itself would not be perceived as innocuous. In comforting a child when frightened of something which is harmless, it is necessary to demonstrate that it is so. A feather stroked with pleasure by an adult and placed on her garment will later be stroked by the child and used for adornment. Panic responses, however, can have more subtle effects where the adult is usually withdrawn in her attitude to the child. Should the signs of distress rouse her to greater warmth, she is unwittingly reinforcing a fear of feathers. Panic at the proximity of feathers becomes unconsciously instrumental to evoking caretaking warmth.

Such phobias doubtless stem from the early years in which perception is easily disrupted by high anxiety arousal and when there is a close dependence on the caretaker for a sense of security. By the seventh year the development of verbally directed orienting responses facilitates both public and private discussion of fears. By this age, pre-operational thinking is sufficiently developed for a comparison of past and present states to be made. This reduces the child's vulnerability, and irreversible malfunctioning becomes a remote contingency. This was noted by Freud who postulated the antecedents of neurosis to be located in the earlier years.

If it were desired to choose a single manifestation as a best indication of this degree of maturity, it would undoubtedly be in the opinion of the writer the orienting response. The child's capacity to orient himself voluntarily towards a task set by the verbal direction of another person opens the way to the acquisition of the tools of learning during the phase of concrete operations. This capacity has been long maturing and it is not difficult to cite antecedent intimations of its emergence. For example, it is already nascent when, at about fourteen months, a baby can be relied on to repeat a word with which he is familiar at the request of an adult. But the chief importance of the orienting response at the outset of the concrete operational phase is the capacity to reverse established forms of response by verbal direction. The experiments of Martsinovskaya mentioned in the previous chapter demonstrated this. Luria's work referred to in the third chapter demonstrated the same capacity on the motor side at an earlier age. Social orientation is established in a similar way, and it is clear that instructions by others cannot become instructions to the self until speech is more socialised than egocentric. To be able to voluntarily reverse natural inclination implies a socialised capacity for understanding another's point of view and for accepting it as one's own. This enables the child to identify himself with the expectations of others.

3 *Formal learning and cultural trends*

At the outset of the phase of concrete operations, most experience which has accreted will have been gathered under the child's own momentum and in relation to caretaking demands. After the age of six years, however, it is usual for adults to attempt to mould the child more closely into a structure they consider to be correct. Without doubt, this customary change is grounded partly in the child's more mature capacity for response and partly in the need to produce literate and competent workers by the time adolescence is reached. It is impossible in practice to dissociate maturational levels from cultural expectation, but it is unlikely that social pressures could shift norms more than six months either way. For example, in this country in 1926, Burt was able to discover ten words which could be read by at least half the school population in their fifth year. This is no longer possible because of the later ages at which children are taught to read, but by the ninth year the standard of reading implied by the test is the same today as it was in 1926. Thus, although the formal teaching of the skill was delayed in order to preserve a permissive atmosphere among young children, norms were lowered for only the first few years.

Cultural and familial expectations press upon the child at the outset of the phase of concrete operations and expedite the acquisition of more effective learning sets and orienting responses. As perception becomes more selective and attention more relevantly directed the variability of response in relation to stimuli decreases. After the consequences of innumerable responses have been fed back into their sensory and verbal origins, the sensori-perceptual and motor primary systems become capable of acting independently of the verbal sensori-perceptual and motor systems. Finally the mechanics of speech in their turn are subordinated to the schemata of the ideational systems. At this stage sensori motor components are short-circuited, with only a marginal and perhaps redundant awareness of imagery. Imagery may be evoked, however, at points of frustration where phase sequences follow less facilitated paths. These successive stages mark the progress from Piaget's concrete operations to formal operations. The concrete attitude may be defined as a tendency to react to the immediately given object or situation with its relationships implicitly realised. The formal attitude implies reaction not so much to sensory impressions of the object or situation as to its classification or conceptualisation. Naturally the age at which formal operations emerge will depend on the age at which their concrete expression was established. For example, concrete groupings of a quantitative nature are among the earliest to appear, but by the time the sight of 7 and 5 means an automatic immediated awareness of twelve in a child's mind it has reached the formal level. Given the usual amount of experience, this abstract or formal level of assimilation will be reached during the so-called phase of concrete operations while other quantitative skills are still pre-operational or concretely operational. Thus during this period of middle childhood, Piaget and others have demonstrated the gradual emergence at successive ages of concrete and formal levels of operation culminating in the twelfth year in a general formal level for all the basic skills of the culture. This is not to be regarded as a terminal point in growth but as the beginning of a predominantly abstract attitude in approaching new features in the environment.

Piaget's researches and those of his followers have elucidated, by description and by the establishment of norms, such stages in learning to learn. These may be regarded as levels of readiness for the average child in the countries where the researches were promulgated, i.e. the western world where education after the age of six is compulsory and more or less standardised. Readiness for formal education in some of the major assimilatory areas could be codified thus:

1 Learning a number system – the seventh year, Piaget and Inhelder (1941)
2 Learning a reading system – the seventh year, Piaget (1952)
3 Calculation of time, speed and movement – the eighth year, Piaget et al. (1946a), Piaget et al. (1946b), Fraisse and Vautrey (1952)

4 Causal thinking – the eighth year, Piaget (1930)
5 Drawing involving symmetry – the tenth year, Raban (1952)
6 Calculations of weight – the tenth year, Piaget and Inhelder (1941), Lovell and Ogilvie (1961)
7 Scientific thinking – the twelfth year, Deutsche (1937)
8 Prediction in terms of probability – the twelfth year, Piaget and Inhelder (1951), Keats (1955)
9 Calculation of volume – the twelfth year, Piaget and Inhelder (1941)
10 Understanding of religious forms – the twelfth year, Hollingworth (1930)
11 Understanding the content of religion – the sixteenth year, Hollingworth (1930), Goldman (1962)

The concepts of developmental psychology in so far as they have reference to norms, must include an appraisal of the structuring brought about by the common school, but the findings concerning child development during the last fifty years has done much to correct misapprehension concerning readiness for formal education. At first the effect of this was to delay a formal approach, but more recently there is a tendency to recognise certain areas of study as suitable for the curricula of younger children. Notable among these are the earlier teaching of foreign languages and introductory courses in general science (Bull 1957).

The attainment of an operational level of thinking in a perceptually disclosed area of experience depends perhaps on the integration of language and the results of activity. For example, the term 'weigh' is perfectly understood by children in its practical implications as soon as they can play with scales, but the verbally expressed realisation that substance weighs the same irrespective of its shape does not emerge until the tenth year, and until it does the child cannot be expected to compute and reason on paper about weight problems. But it is the spontaneous process of weighing which teaches this. It is thus appropriate to stimulate this process some years prior to the tenth year. From observing a limited number of cases the writer would suggest that a child with an I.Q. of 140 may weigh with ardour and persistence if given scales at the age of six. For the average child the comparable learning contingency may be eight years, but more research is needed to discover the correct ages at which pre-operational learning contingencies should be made available. A hint is perhaps afforded by the finding of Riess (1946) that conditioned responses generalise to homonyms at younger ages but in the eleven-year-old only to synonyms. According to this, 'wait' tends to be regarded as equivalent to 'weight' at seven years, but by the end of the phase of concrete operations only a synonym for 'weight' such as 'heaviness' would be effective. This implies an extension of vocabulary associated with weighing and it is a problem which calls for research to discover whether such an extension is best effected pre-operationally or after this stage is reached, if learning is to be expedited. The evidence suggests that operational thinking may be tested with the simplest of vocabulary and from this it can be deduced that an extension of vocabulary is best effected after the operational level has been reached. In this event the verbalised technical system would become integrated with a previously integrated sensorimotor schema and its correlated rudimentary symbols. This is analogous to the hierarchy of sets apparent in learning any complex task (Gagné 1962) in older children. At the outset the patterns of subordinate learning sets may differ widely from child to child, but the formally prescribed uses to which a term is put standardises the processing. This reorganises the subordinate learning sets and so reduces individual differences at all levels of the hierarchy. Thus experience which had been gained under the impetus of pre-operational individualistic interest is rearranged into a processing system which codifies response to accord with cultural norms.

4 *The growth of concepts*

In the building up of verbal concepts negative instances also have their part to play. These arouse cognitive dissonance, and under the influence of heightened attention they are frequently points of departure for a new concept. At the same time they strengthen cognisance of the concept they negate. In fact concepts may be learned experimentally from all negative instances, though the presentation of only positive instances results in more speedy learning. The mixed presentation of both positive and negative instances results in an intermediate speed of assimilation (Hovland and Weiss 1953). Mixed presentation is more closely representative of everyday experience, for erroneous judgment on the part of the learner ensures the inclusion of negative instances. A negative instance may be regarded as a mistake by the learner without it being clearly seen as an exception to the rule. At a more mature level, however, it will be realised why it is an exception. Realising that it is not correct is a necessary prelude to recognising the nature of its not belonging. Hence the necessity to expose children to the possibility of frustration as a growth measure. It has been demonstrated in the case of gifted children that failure to accelerate them and thus expose them to the risk of error leads to lazy and careless work habits (Margary and Eichorn 1961). This might be explained as a privation of the learning contingency associated with the motivational value of cognitive dissonance. This would appear to be contrary to the connectionist conclusion of Thorndike that an erroneous association is likely to recur by virtue of the fact that it has been made. This is undoubtedly true when the temporal juxtaposition of stimulus and response are in question, but it applies to rote learning rather than conceptual learning. For example, mistakenly supposing that $3 + 3$ is 7, when seen as a negative instance, can sharpen awareness of the composition of 6 and also of its relationship to 7. The same principle applies generally to any negative instance of a concept which is seen as such. Errors thus generalise to their own related truths, to result in much incidental learning.

The ability to recognise a negative instance as such emerges after an operational level has been reached. In fact it implies the reversibility of operational thinking. For example, as Goldman (1962) has suggested, two stages are discernible between the ages of seven and eleven in the assimilation of religio-ethical concepts. Up to the age of nine the vocabulary necessary for the expression of rules of conduct is acquired, and thereafter generalisations on moral conduct are in evidence. The concept of fairness was examined by Goldman using the story of the drowning of the Egyptians in the Red Sea as a stimulus. Before the tenth year of age, his subjects justified the happening in terms of retributive justice with no attempt at relating the punishment to the crime. After this age, there was a realisation that it was rather hard on the Egyptians but that God was regretfully compelled to act unfairly by the exigencies of the situation. This more mature level is tantamount to postulating a negative instance of distributive justice because the punishment does not fit the crime. This suggests that during the secondary stage of concrete operations an awareness of bi-polar constructs, in the form of opposites and contradictions, emerges. Their lack of congruence as cohering attributes present an ambiguity or dissonance which the individual endeavours to resolve under the impact of the experimenter's questions. Doubtless left to his own devices, the incongruity of ethical principle and the treatment meted out to the Egyptians would not bother him, but the enquiry showed the capacity for resolving such contradictions to be developed rudimentarily by the tenth year. By this stage an explicit kind of negative instance has emerged – the simple opposite. Unfair is seen as an absence of fairness. Spearman postulated the recognition of similarities and opposites as a capacity commensurate with a person's intelligence. In developmental terms it might be said that where this capacity matures at the fastest rate the highest I.Q. should be found. The fact that the capacity for the perception of differences or similarities appears to alternate as antecedents to one another suggests that the perception of negative instances of concepts improves the perception of what constitutes the positive elements and vice versa. But the recognition of negative instances tends to reach the operational level prior to awareness of classificatory likenesses in any learning area. For this reason 'It is not fair' is a more common judgment during the phase of concrete operations than an imputation of fairness. The ability to generalise in both positive and negative terms ushers in the causal-logical state of interpreting phenomena. Most of the evidence such as that contributed by Piaget (1950), Anthony (1940), and Alexander and Adlerstein (1960) suggests that this type of thinking becomes facilitated in most children at about the age of ten years. A necessary prelude to this matures during the eighth year when sensory and imaginal sequences can be seen as occurring without a break over an interval of time. For example, retaining the sequential thread of a story or of the emptying of one vessel as it fills another are examples of an operational comprehension of continuity in time. Piaget has demonstrated that this concrete operation is mature in all but 10 per cent of children by the eighth year. He tested this by getting children to tell back a story and by asking them to arrange a number of drawings of water at various levels in a flask so that the emptying sequence was in a downward direction and the filling sequence in an upward. It is clear that identity and reversibility would be involved in this feat. The minority of children who did not seem to possess this facility by eight years of age was of a proportion commensurate with the dull and back section of the population of 85 I.Q. and below. This is a reminder, as Deutsche and others have shown, that mental age is a better guide to the operational level to be expected than chronological age.

5 *Special abilities and disabilities*

An hypothesis worth investigating perhaps is that until the age of ten, I.Q. is a better prediction than chronological age, whereas after this chronological age or length of experience becomes increasingly important (Brennan 1962). This consorts well with Burt's (1943) finding concerning the diminishing contribution of intelligence to mental abilities and the increasing importance of opportunity as measured by length of schooling as age increases. Thus, during the phase of concrete operations special abilities and disabilities emerge. These impose limits on the extent to which intelligence paces assimilation in any cognitive area. For example, after the age of six years, a spatial ability emerges which combines differentially with intelligence as a determiner of success or failure.

Since competence is of prime significance as a motivating force during the middle and later phases of development, individual differences in the various modalities of experience are relevant to the discussion, because of the abilities and disabilities associated with them. The modality most explored is perhaps that of vision, the most important for distance reception. M. D. Vernon (1954), commenting on Flugel's work on oscillation, remarks that the extent of voluntary control of reversible perspective varies in different individuals and is never complete. She concludes that some process of alternating excitation and inhibition may take place in the CNS which is only partly under voluntary control and is beneath the limen of conscious awareness. A similar elemental phenomenon has been explored more recently by Ditchburn (1956) in the field of physics where drift of retinal images has been shown to occur during fixation. At a certain point in the drift from foveal fixation correction is brought about by a flick movement during which sensory reception is occluded. This neural servo-mechanism has been observed to differ markedly among individual adults. Individual differences of this elemental kind would seem to be more constitutional than acquired and in close association with the general activation system of the organism, in so far as it affects sensori-motor processing during the first two years. It is not inconceivable that some such mechanism underlies individual differences in spatial ability. It is clear then that individual styles in sensory processing begin to take perceptible form at approximately the same age as orienting reflexes become amenable to verbal direction. Thus the period of common schooling begins with the dice loaded against or for success in some subjects (Schonell 1946, Hebron 1957, Mackay and Vernon 1963, Hudson 1963). These strata of perceptual tendencies affect the mode of entry into situations and can profoundly affect the orienting process itself. They form part of the more covert aspect of motivation, which gives rise to approach and retreat tendencies in psychological attitudes. The cumulative effect of temperamental preferences for some activities more than others is evident in more than 30 per cent of children by the time the age of twelve is reached (Hebron 1957). In these, one or other of the primary mental abilities (Thurstone 1958) is weaker or stronger than their general level of attainment would predict. The large majority, however, maintain even profiles of ability in all the major mental and scholastic areas for which standard learning contingencies are provided.

Since most individuals, if sufficiently motivated by prospect of reward, can overcome specific disabilities (Fleishman and Hempel 1954, 1955), it must be concluded that the initial failure arising from some built-in perceptual weakness conditions the child decrementally to avoid such tasks, either through passivity or through substitution of some more readily rewarding activity. In learning situations the former is sometimes termed apathy and the latter distractibility, and the problem of inadequate concentration fall into these two categories. In fact it might be said that one of these two attitudes to failure characterise learners according to their position on the E–I dimension, extraverts being more distractible and introverts more apathetic (Highfield and Pinsent 1952). The effect on personality of repeated failure in specific learning situations was clearly demonstrated when the writer asked eight specialist teachers in a girls' grammar school each to assess the personality of ninety pupils in their twelfth year. Marked disagreement among the assessors occurred only in those cases where a pupil had obtained a failing mark from the deviant assessor in the annual examination. This particular assessor perceived the pupil as less well adjusted than the others. Such attitudes to specific learning areas and in rarer cases to learning in general are in the making during the phase of concrete operations, and anxiety may be set up in children at all ability levels. It can be specially marked among children of high I.Q. because although the disruptive effect of anxiety is similar at all levels the impoverishment thereby seems the greater where there was former excellence (Sarason 1960). It would seem then that extrinsic sources of motivation, such as reward and punishment, are important for pupils who find difficulty in establishing orienting responses in the various learning areas. By the age of seven years the majority of children are fully responsive to the verbal reinforcement of behaviour through favourable comment. For example, in a three-choice experiment with marbles Stevenson and Weir (1961) found that a single reinforcement of the correct choice was adequate for 70 per cent of their sample at the age of seven. This was present in only 15 per cent of their three-year-old sample. After seven, there was very little improvement for the incidence of correct response had risen only 5 per cent by the age of nine years. This quickness to learn from a single example signalled as correct, also reaches its peak then at much the same time as orienting facility and habituation to certain kinds of sensory processing.

6 *The development of will-control*

The orienting response studied by the Russian school might be contrasted with the concept of learning set. It would seem that genetic factors are most likely to introduce individual differences in orienting response systems while environmental influences would tend to bear more heavily upon the formation of learning sets. Orienting responses have relevance for entry to situations and are therefore influenced by genetically determined states of perceptual processing. Set refers to the prolongation of a course of activity thus initiated. For simple and immediate behaviour, orienting response and set are synonymous terms. For more prolonged sequences orienting responses may be taking place all along the line thus re-energising set. Set, then, may be a comprehensive function which includes initial and subsequent orienting reflexes, particularly at points of ambiguity and choice. Without the capacity for sustaining prolonged sequences of behaviour facility in initial orientation is of little value to the individual's social security.

Until the age of five years orienting responses and exercise of set are largely under autistic direction, but from the age of six there is social expectation that compliance with the demands of longer projects shall be sustained. For these reasons, as Peterson and others (1961) observe, normal development before six is facilitated by warmth, affection and freedom from wrath, while after that age a considerable amount of parental firmness is necessary. After the age of six years children in general tend to receive a considerable amount of firm direction from parent surrogates, in schools and other institutions to which they may become affiliated. This external support affords increased exercise in the formation of learning sets and thus expedites the growth of will-control. Cattell et al. (1955), in studies of the nature-nurture type, suggest that among children will-control is for the most part environmentally determined, but that general neuroticism, somatic anxiety and surgency-desurgency were more constitutional. Constitutional characteristics appear to be important for clarity of attention, while will-control refers to the dynamic aspect of its endurance in any behavioural act. Thus, constitutional factors tend to affect the mode of entry into situations, while will-power maintains involvement beyond the point of satiation. The permissive aspect of child-rearing in the caretaking of the very young encourages the spontaneous direction of attention, while the external support of insistence by caretakers maintains a train of behaviour in its course, thus inculcating a facility in orientation and set in relation to more remote ends. It would appear that from now on until adolescence, cultural expectation concerning education transforms the capacity of the future adult to endure in tasks until they are effectively completed.

Willingness to persist in imposed tasks is to be contrasted with initiative in seeking change of activity. Lewin (1935) reports investigations into satiation points for imposed tasks, such as drawing moon faces, and studied the willingness of children to turn to alternative self-directed tasks. These findings suggest that the child's willingness to abandon imposed tasks when allowed to, in favour of self-imposed tasks, increases steadily between the ages of eight and eleven years. The tenth year ushers in a marked increase in capacity to initiate sequences of behaviour dictated by independent decisions about what to do next. During the year prior to this age the average child soon tires of following his own inclination, but is as willing to persist in activities suggested by an adult as he is in his tenth year. By the eleventh year, however, there is less willingness to persist in imposed tasks in a spirit of passive compliance and a greater capacity for self-directed occupation is apparent. The trend then with increasing maturity is first to need direction of activities, and to be compliant in situations of imposed occupation. During this phase, persistence at self-imposed tasks is not great. In the second phase, round about the age of nine, children are usually more adept at amusing themselves but are at the same time amenable to the direction of adults in their activities. By the age of ten, however, there are greater proclivities for self initiation and direction of behaviour and less inclination to persist beyond the point of satiation in tasks suggested by adults. It would seem then that the period between the ages of five and ten is a transitional one for the conative dimension designated by Cattell as will-control. At the outset the child is amenable to direction, and out of this experience emerges a capacity to initiate and persist in his own projects. This implies that during the phase of concrete operations the child becomes habituated to persist in tasks which are not of intrinsic interest to him, such as those associated with learning to read, compute and write, thus preparing the ground for a more complex approach to the organisation of his own affairs. This competence, once acquired, ushers in anew the fluency so necessary for a creative approach to the environment. The spontaneity of adolescence, however, must be contrasted with that of the intuitive and earlier phases, because whereas the latter was possible because of the relative absence of functional barriers between systems, the more mature spontaneity is grounded in the adequacy of a technical competence made possible by their presence. The fluency of immaturity has fewer reality checks, that of maturity is facilitated by technical competence.

II. MOTIVATIONAL PROCESSES

1 *Behavioural styles and patterns of child-rearing*

Social learning during the phase of concrete operations is expedited by the matured ability of the child to put himself at the viewpoint of another in communication. By the eighth year, as Piaget has shown, 73 per cent of his conversation is social rather than egocentric and he is therefore able to judge situations from three viewpoints namely: (i) as he thinks they ought to be; (ii) as others think they ought to be; (iii) as others believe them to be (Staines 1958). The interaction between the first two sets of schemata, an awareness of his own and of other's imperatives, may be regarded as contributive to his strategies expedient to living comfortably. The third is a catalyst which tempers his working hypotheses to accord with some ideal standard, where he is strongly identified with persons who hold such beliefs. On the other hand, he may use his knowledge of the beliefs of others in the interests of expediency to encompass his own ends. Between the ages of seven and eleven, however, the stage is one of concrete practical realism. He learns to be shamed when found out rather than to suffer from the guilt of infringing internalised moral rules. The avoidance of detection may be cunningly pursued because of a clear appraisal of the opinions and belief of others. Such strategies are exercises leading to techniques for dealing with situations which are threatening. Where, however, the child has satellised successfully to parental and other authority figures, he will tend to incorporate their values and beliefs. The difference between the incorporation of earlier years and that of the period of concrete operations stems from the fact that standards and rules are assimilated within a wide matrix of social expectation rather than the more sporadic familial conditions of early childhood. These techniques or rules of conduct at first imply that adults are capricious Olympians who meet out punishment and reward to suit their own ends. Later this develops into a view of a responsible authority who distributes reward and punishment according to merit.

These trends in development proceed at different rates for boys and girls respectively. The reasons for this sex difference are becoming more clear as a result of recent longitudinal studies of caretaking styles such as those of Kagan and Moss (1963).

Mothers who fostered dependency in their boys during infancy and early childhood, but expected good results when school-days began, were most successful in inculcating a desire to achieve. In girls, however, criticism and conditional acceptance in infancy and early childhood was the most significant antecedent, providing they were accelerated after the age of six years. This may underlie the tendency for boys and girls to enter the phase of concrete operations with different patterns of motivation in work-related situations. In a nation-wide survey of behaviour in schools (Highfield and Pinsent 1952), which included the 20 per cent at each of the two extremes of adjustment to classroom requirements, it was clear that girls are more frequently capable of satisfactory application and resource than boys between the ages of seven and nine years. By the age of ten years this sex difference in application is no longer apparent and the resourcefulness of boys surpassed that of girls. These trends are indicated in Table I. The sex

TABLE I

Proportions of children showing satisfactory powers of application and resource in English and Welsh schools

Area of Behaviour	Age groups and Sexes					
	Boys			Girls		
	7 & 8 N = 583	9 & 10 N = 583	11 & 12 N = 900	7 & 8 N = 504	9 & 10 N = 504	11 & 12 N = 900
Application	47·8	55	63·2	55·5	54·2	64
Resource	56·3	60	68·3	60	56·7	62
Together	52·0	57·5	65·7	57·7	55·4	63

differences for application in the youngest age group and for resource in the eldest are significant. Among the resourceful attributes were self criticism, objectivity and purposeful persistence when failing. These contributed most to the eldest boys' superiority. Planfulness was significantly more prevalent among the youngest girls.

The results of this survey might be taken as indicative of the effectiveness, for school behaviour, of caretaking styles in the nurture of boys and girls respectively. As is usual of course when the social indices of age and sex are applied, the groups are more alike than different. It is probable, however, that the major source of differences arises from bias in caretaking habits on the dimension of permissiveness – strictness. This would appear to influence the way the child comes to process information (Tomkins 1960). The more permissive atmosphere increases his chances of acquiring more differentiated schemata, and in this way his chances of becoming objective and self critical are increased. In addition he is likely to have more opportunity for discovering independent and unique solutions to problems (Getzels and Jackson 1962). If the thesis of Kagan and Moss is correct, that mothers tend to be more strict with their girls than with their boys in early childhood, it is to be expected that their resource will be less, and their powers of application precocious. The results of the survey in schools suggest that something in the order of one girl in twenty may receive this sex-biased treatment.

It is reasonable to suppose that learning styles in matters of application and resource are more acquired than of genetic origin. In areas of behaviour concerned with control of anger and aggression, genetic differences between the sexes would appear to be more decisive. It is well known that the hormonal and skeletal structure of the male predisposes him to greater physical assertion when compared with females taken by and large, but as the Fels longitudinal study suggests styles in aggression are reinforced to suit prevailing cultural expectation. The girl is permitted verbal gratification of hostility while boys may more freely resort to fisticuffs. In schools, at the outset of the phase of concrete operations, between the ages of seven and nine years, 32 per cent of boys and 22 per cent of girls among those who presented behaviour difficulties to their teachers were quarrelsome. By the age of eleven this sex difference had disappeared, and in both sexes 20 per cent were so designated. These findings are based on cross-sectional surveys, but the samples were large and representative and the differences between age groups are probably indicative of a developmental tendency. As each sex was quarrelsome in its own style here, the greater proportion of the aggressive tendency among the younger boys is probably indicative of a genetic tendency towards aggression retarding the emergence of controls in boys more than girls. These quarrelsome children of both sexes were more frequently in evidence than those who presented problems because they were too dependent and retreating in the face of hostility. Of the latter there were 6 per cent and this remained constant throughout the period of schooling. This approach-retreat dichotomy of reactions to frustrations in school life presents a strong suggestion of extravert-introvert characteristics. The fact that there were more than three times as many children showing the extravert response is in all probability due to their selection as problems. A slightly non-conforming extravert is a more manifest and dynamic problem than a slightly non-conforming introvert. The latter is more easily reinforced in a decremental direction and so ceases to be a problem sooner, as well as being a less obvious problem pupil because of his introverted style (Highfield and Pinsent 1952).

There would seem to be three major interacting sources of variation producing behaviour styles namely, cultural expectations, genetic factors in the child and genetic factors in the caretaker. Inter-cultural comparisons should present least ambiguity because of the randomisation of the other two factors and their interaction. The genetic element in caretaking, however, is confused by the fact that the child may or may not inherit the caretaker's temperament. Theoretically speaking, it is presumed that this will occur in the larger proportion of children. In this event a parent of introvert disposition should produce restrained and non-ebullient children compared with those of extravert disposition. These tendencies should emerge in a cross-sectional comparison of caretaking style, and the response of a child to teacher caretakers at the outset of school life.

A study of this kind was made of the characteristics of 191 difficult children between the ages of six years three months and eight years eleven months in rural schools, and in this work parental style in upbringing was also assessed (Highfield and Pinsent 1952). It was found that rigid punitive parents tended to have restless distractible children needing control in school, while lax indifferent parents produced apathetic listless children needing stimulation. These trends are statistically presented in Table II. It is possible that these behavioural patterns have their roots in some constitutional similarities between parent and child, and are reinforced through learning during infancy. As Dollard and Miller (1950) suggest, an infant who is fed when he cries is more likely to learn an active manipulative orientation towards drive reduction compared with one who is frequently left to 'cry himself out'. Under the

TABLE II

Showing percentage differences with respect to treatments required in the classroom between children subjected to various types of home management as compared with children in normal home conditions

Types of home management		Classroom treatment required					Attention	
		Reassurance	Stimulation	Insistence	Criticism	Control	Confused	Distractible
Repressive	Obedience rigidly enforced	—	24·0	28·7	—	—	—	—
	Full retribution exacted for wrongdoing	—	—	39·5	—	29·5	—	32·5
	All child's interests directed by parents	—	—	—	—	—	—	23·8
Slack, irresponsible	Commands not followed up	—	35·6	27·8	15·9	—	33·9	—
	Querulous reproaches only	18·2	29·7	19·8	—	—	39·3	—
	Whims gratified as the way of least resistance	—	32·2	18·0	—	—	28·5	—
Aloof, unsympathetic	No regard paid to child's interests. Child has to fit in with parents' convenience	—	28·7	31·7	—	—	27·2	—
	Parents aloof	21·7	36·7	29·6	—	—	24·1	—
	No. of significant differences	2	6	7	1	1	5	2

latter condition he may acquire more readily a predisposition for a passive and apathetic reaction to strong drive stimuli. Thus a tendency to lax indifference in the caretaker is likely to produce apathetic children on experiential grounds. The survey suggests both types of children constitute a large proportion of school misfits in the early stages of schooling. Parents who are much preoccupied with their children either punitively or overprotectively produce overactive children on the whole. These are so preoccupied with their own activities that they make a retarded adjustment to classroom requirements. Parents who are more withdrawn in their caretaking (and so would tend to leave the child to 'cry himself out') produce children who need stimulation because their attention is not well concentrated and alert. This suggests that parental temperament has led to a style of caretaking which has reinforced the same dynamic styles in their offspring, particularly when they were of similar temperament. The independent observations of a psychologist during the administration of the Terman Merrill Scale suggested that 39 per cent of these children would achieve normal attentional habits after a longer period of schooling, for they responded well when they were the sole concern of one person. In 28·8 per cent of cases, however, the observations of both psychologist and teacher concerning the child's a-normality were mutually confirming. Of the 191 difficult children from rural schools, i.e. the entire difficult population of the schools from which the sample was drawn, 113 were boys and 78 girls. This proportion of 3 : 2 is in the expected direction and indicates a statistical sex difference in behaviour which becomes more marked as maturity is approached. The origins of this phenomenon have been discussed earlier in the chapter and would appear to arise from the greater willingness of girls to respond with effort even when criticised for failure. Boys show stronger achievement motivation when they are expedited by people whom they like. The findings of Maxwell (1961), in a cross-sectional study with retrospective assessments of caretaking, have relevance for the pattern of expediting achievement between the ages of five and ten and a half. His neurotic children of ten and a half years differed in their ability to arrange pictures in sequential story form (Wechsler's Picture Arrangement Test). These differences were correlated with the extent of overprotection or indifference which had been accorded to them by their parents. Maxwell's measures of caretaking style, however, referred only to experience from the sixth year and after. Parental indifference was negatively related to success in the test and overprotection positively. This is further evidence that intercourse between parent and child fosters the realisation of antecedents and consequences in the appraisal of events.

Intercultural comparisons between American and Western European samples serve to throw into relief the effects of social expectations and styles in caretaking. Boehm (1957), using Piaget's interview techniques, compared Swiss and American children between the ages of six and sixteen years and found national bias was discernible in several respects. American children tended to be emancipated earlier presumably because of the greater permissiveness of their parents. Related to this was their greater dependence on peers than on adults. This would follow too from the importance ascribed to popularity as a status symbol in the U.S.A. Another trait related to the comparatively greater American bias towards permissiveness in child-rearing was the more pronounced independence of judgment and freedom of thought in that sample. The American children would more frequently experience this activity in their family and social environment. A fourth conclusion of Boehm was that the conscience of the American child tends to be developed earlier in life, to be more autonomous but less complex. This could be explained by the greater dependence on peers for status and a sense of security. In a culture such as the Swiss where adults set standards and criteria of conduct for a longer period in the approach to maturity, and where in addition children and adolescents remain more closely dependent on adults for security, it is clear that more complex models will ensure the growth of a more complex conscience during adolescence. There is probably a general tendency today for children to change to peer identification earlier because of the greater economic emancipation in an affluent society. America is in the van in showing a move towards a more extraverted pattern of life on this account. Eysenck's (1959) comparative norms show an American sample to have its mean at +0·33 sigma of the English sample. This may indicate a significant cultural shift towards an extraverted pattern of life in the American nation compared with the British. Further suggestive evidence of the extent to which American children are less specifically structured by school influence is afforded by a study of classroom behaviours by Hebron and de Samardick (1962). In this, a time-sampled count of English children's and teachers' responses were compared with a similar one made by Anderson and Brewer (1946) in Chicago. The results suggested that the child in America tends to be less regimented in school. A more recent comparative study of adolescents in their thirteenth year (Butcher et al. 1963) showed the same trend towards greater social extraversion in the American schools.

2 *The disruptive effect of anxiety*

Towards the end of the phase of concrete operations cultural pressures and social expectations regarding achievement intensify, particularly where crucial decisions are made concerning future educational courses. In America this occurs two years later than in Great Britain. This highlights the importance of test-taking attitudes and the need to achieve. These areas of experience tend to become threat-laden after the age of eleven. Such new strains will be met with the resources built up during infancy and early childhood. One of the earliest schemata involved will be the body image. The fact that the body image is covertly operative is seen in a positive correlation between test anxiety and a lowered threshold for perception of bodily injury (Sarason 1960). Since anxiety is largely an autonomic response, bodily sensations are its inevitable accompaniment. For this reason the test anxious child is more likely to be aware of his covert responses such as restricted breathing, cranial distension, heart tension and muscle tremor than of the nature of the external situation, which includes the task stimulus and accompanying instructions. These stimuli, extraneous to the test task, mean an extension of the number of channels along which the child is attending, and thus a narrowing of perception of the test ensues. Orienting responses tend to be tentative and of short duration under such stress. Where a test occupies a short space of time, disruption at the orienting phase will result inevitably in fewer items being attempted, and it is not surprising that Sarason reports a negative correlation between such a test as Thurstone's Primary Mental Abilities (seven to eleven years) and one of test anxiety. A test situation appears minatory to the test-anxious child, and Sarason's findings support the dictum of Dollard and Miller (1950) that "the social context provides the conditions of learning as distinct from the technique or principles of learning". Perceptual or attentional attenuation is brought about by the extraneous somatic stimuli of autonomic arousal, and it is probably for this reason that sporadic and inconsistent error in calculation has long been recognised as an anxiety symptom in children.

It may well be that individual differences in temperament are correlated with differing degrees of test anxiety. This would account for the fact that mesomorphic children tend to do less well in crucial selective examinations at the age of eleven years. The mesomorph might be described as a muscular extravert, who tends to experience high autonomic arousal which expends itself through the emergency functions of the soma. This may explain why correlations found between Mesomorphy and success in the selection examinations for children at the age of eleven years were as high as −0·44 (Parnell, Peierls, Stanley, Westropp 1955). This disadvantage is not apparent at university where presumably after much reassurance through examination success his high drive level may increase his chances of a good degree (Child 1950). By this age the intelligent mesomorph is more sophisticated to test situations.

3 *The need for achievement*

Success in tests which are intensely ego-involved is to be distinguished from the general need for achievement experienced by children in everyday life. Their readiness to perceive and appraise situations in terms of achievement is regarded by experimentalists as a projective measure of the importance they attach to it. They will be moved by stories in which the hero achieves something difficult more than children without a strong need for achievement. Moreover, when presented with suitable ambiguous pictures, they will tend to read achievement motivation into the unstructured aspect of the picture. Usually N-ach is measured projectively through ambiguous pictures or uncompleted stories (McClelland et al. 1953). Low N-ach as measured by such techniques was found in two types of children, those who were genuinely indifferent to achievement and those who wished to avoid failure. These two types are to be distinguished by their levels of aspiration or assessments of their own potential competence according to Atkinson (1958). He showed that in simple psycho-motor tasks such as ring tossing, maze tracing and dot connection children of nine years of age who had high N-ach scores were willing to take only moderate risks in estimating the level of their performance. In other words they were more realistic in their assessments of their own powers than those with low N-ach who chose tasks which were either too easy for them or too difficult. Atkinson interpreted these trends as indicating two ways of avoiding failure on the part of the low N-ach subjects. Those who set themselves easy objectives were not put to the trial, those who aimed too high could be excused failure on account of the difficulty. An alternative explanation could be that the low N-ach subjects lacked general experience in making careful judgments, because they were either too conditionally or too protectively reared in matters involving practical tasks. This privation in the exercise of judgment could account for unrealistic levels of aspiration. This lack of judgment may be analogous to the poor self perception shown in the lie items in personality inventories. A high lie score in the Children's Manifest Anxiety Scale seems to be associated with the same experiential lack in judging. The child is preoperational in his self perception, and his opinions are swayed by the authoritative atmosphere of the statements. Presumably sound judgment by the child concerning his own powers will stem from having performed many similar activities in the past. These tend to give rise to schemata relating to his sensorimotor or social potentialities. It is not so much that he takes only moderate risks in his aspirations as that he has acquired knowledge of himself, and is capable of applying it in the experimental situation. The experiential privation of low N-ach subjects from their first excursions into problem solution during early childhood would tend to militate against the development of orienting responses associated with aspiration. Indirect support for this thesis may be inferred from the positive correlation between increase in I.Q. between the ages of six and ten years and competition with peers. Manifest independent attitudes towards peers and adults also correlates positively with increases in I.Q. (Sontag, Baker and Nelson 1958). Such attitudes are fostered largely in the home by the balance between maternal hostility, protection and acceleration. The antecedents of achievement motive as observed in the Fels longitudinal study (Kagan 1956; Kagan and Moss 1962) appeared to depend mainly on acceleration, by an ego-involved parent, of attitudes to achievement between the ages of six and ten years. But they suggest that underlying the achievement motive of boys is the wish to please a loved object while girls may be more frequently motivated by the wish to feel secure and wanted because of competence. Thus high general achievers as early as their tenth year tend to be sensitive and responsive to socialisation pressures, and have largely accepted adult values (Sarason 1960), but the antecedents of these attitudes appear to differ somewhat in their frequency and proportion among boys and girls respectively.

In the lower ranges of ability, sex differences in learning are also found which could possibly be related to differential styles in child-rearing. Table I above suggests that boys more frequently than girls fail to acquire normal habits of application during the first four years of the common school between the ages of five and nine. Girls may more frequently succeed in acquiring such habits, perhaps because of the greater frequency of the conditional acceptance which they experience, an acceptance dependent on degrees of competence in the early acquisition of basic self-help skills. For this reason, taken by and large, girls, even among the slow maturers, tend to achieve nearer to their optimum in schools subjects. In spite of their frequent failure they are motivated to persist in complying with teacher demand. Boys, who may be less frequently conditionally loved in infancy, have less motivation to please a caretaker at school who is a threat to his equanimity.

A further consideration of sex differences in the mean lie scores on the Children's Manifest Anxiety Scale (Castenda et al. 1956) are of interest having regard to this theory of differentials in caretaking of the very young. If a small lie score is taken to mean objectivity in self perception, it would seem that boys tend to be more precocious than girls in this until the age of eleven years. This may be because they are not so anxious to regard themselves in a favourable light. In addition to this delayed capacity for self appraisal, girls produce significantly higher anxiety scores than boys between the ages of nine and eleven years. In this, however, cultural factors may outweigh the familial ones as a structuring influence. By the age of nine, the average boy has experienced some four years of identification with his father, and thus will have acquired the masculine view that expressions and admission of anxiety are a weakness. Where circumstances and family expectations are such as to cause a girl to change from a predominantly maternal identification to a paternal one, the same culturally imposed standard would tend to be adopted.

The relationship between anxiety and social popularity may be indicated by the negative correlations found by Castenda and his co-workers (1956) between scores on the Children's Manifest Anxiety Scale and sociometric measures of popularity. The pooled correlation for all age groups and both sexes was −0·32. The peak of the negative relationships was reached at the age of ten with a correlation of −0·75 for girls and −0·52 for boys. A year later, however, the correlations were insignificant, +0·01 and −0·16 respectively. This suggests that by the end of the phase of concrete operations children by and large have canalised their anxiety drive into socially acceptable behaviour, and that their self-perception in relation to the expectation of others has matured sufficiently for them to maintain an adequate balance in face-to-face situations. This increase in self and social perceptiveness is indicated by changes in choice of friends among the gifted. Between the ages of seven and nine, gifted children tend to have as many friends outside their ability group as in it. By the age of eleven, however, the social distance between himself and the less gifted begins to widen. His earlier incorporation of adult standards earns him adult approval, and to the child of average ability he begins to appear as an out-grouper (Kaluger and Martin 1960). From now on the social acceptance of the gifted child within groups of lower intellectual status comes increasingly to depend on specific roles of service and contribution rather than on a liking for him as a person. He tends thus to be respected while being socially rejected, an attitude which he will be tempted to reciprocate. In view of this, it would seem to deprive adolescents of a very necessary learning contingency by separating children into schools according to ability. By exposing children of each ability level to the structuring influence of all the others, the necessary skills which have been acquired in practical guise before eleven years of age may be developed into greater complexity both concretely and verbally at subsequent ages.

It is perhaps true to say that from now on no act is performed without in some degree involving role behaviour (Cattell 1963). Similarly it might be said that no problem is solved without a chain of orienting responses being evoked. These have been acquired during the first ten years of life and by their means the symbol has matured into an autonomous directing force which can dispense with its sensory and imaginal origins. This 'sentience', as Spearman called it, assumes primacy in function only when the symbolic system proves inadequate in new learning, and even then but fleetingly. It has been the function of concrete operations to produce this formal or symbolic level of operation.

CHAPTER VI

Adolescent motivation and learning

I. COGNITIVE DEVELOPMENTS

1 *A definition of adolescence*

The term adolescence refers to a vaguely defined period which might be regarded as beginning during the twelfth year and ending early in the third decade. The defining criteria can be grouped into four main categories – intellectual, emotive, physiological and social. Those of an intellectual nature have been demonstrated by researches of the Piaget type. These have shown changes from concreteness to abstraction, and formal operations, which facilitate abstract thinking, emerge during the twelfth year. Emotional criteria might be best described in Freudian terms as a libidinal resurgence, according to which behaviour becomes imbued with stronger affective dynamism. The third category, afforded by physiological criteria, are seen in the changes in bodily structure and function characteristic of sexual maturity. Finally, there is the effect of a shift in social pressure and expectation, which produces a fourth category of behaviour characteristic of the adolescent as a marginal person, moving between the spheres of the child and the adult. The interaction between these four sources of variation is indefinable, but it is perhaps true to say that the extent of variation is dependent more upon individual differences in intellectual growth and social milieu than upon affective and physiological characteristics.

Assuming adolescent growth to occur between the eleventh and the twentieth birthdays, the mid point of this period coincides with the so-called terminal age of intellectual maturation. After this age, the bright adolescent tends to grow away from those who have matured at an average or less than average rate, particularly in the cognitive skills. These show a greater capacity for abstraction, a larger vocabulary, greater depth of verbal meaning, complexity of imagination and facility in generalising (Conrad 1944). Such marked qualitative differences are already apparent by the age of twelve years, not only when the above-average children are compared with those who are average, but also when the average is compared with the below-average (Hebron 1957). By the sixteenth year, however, all but the slowest maturing 10 per cent have acquired at least a twelve-year level of capacity for abstraction. At the other end of the distribution curve, the acceleration of mental growth has lifted the top decile into a capacity for abstraction and generalisation which differentiates them permanently from 90 per cent of their fellows. Moreover, the prolongation of educational opportunity for this gifted minority intensifies their a-normal development until, in the perception of the majority, they are inevitably regarded as out-groupers, as members of minority groups in society at large. To some extent this has been their experience from the age of nine years onwards, but a greater capacity for self perception brings a clearer realisation of exceptional role and social purpose during the second half of adolescence. These qualitative differences in both organism and environmental circumstance call for a separate consideration of the gifted adolescent as such, and this topic will receive more detailed attention in the following chapter.

In the previous chapter it was postulated that the main motivational variable prior to adolescence and after the intuitive phase is technical competence. By the onset of adolescence, however, in addition to liking to do what he can do, the individual is more open to the stimulation of opportunity and differential reward. He is now capable of understanding more distant goals in which self enhancement and self preservation are united in pre-vocational stirrings. During this period he discovers more clearly to what extent he is like all other teenagers, like some teenagers and also like no other individual. His unique awareness of himself emerges as he finds himself assuming roles in the various social groups into which he is directed, or to which he becomes voluntarily affiliated. These bring about more differentiated self perception mediated by the emergent expectations of others concerning him. His status in society is clarified as a result of group membership, particularly through experience in the common school. For example, if the grouping adopted in his school is heterogeneous for ability, the average and less skilled adolescent is able to accept his status more realistically in that his self estimation tends to be lower and his humility enhanced (Margary and Eichorn 1961). This is encompassed by observing the manifest achievement of others, and even the most gifted realise the challenge of near competitors which threaten a disturbance of the self image. Such experiences as may be inconsistent with the perceived structure of the self are examined in imaginal rehearsal with greater facility during adolescence, and the self concept is revised to assimilate and include them. One of the most facilitating factors in this process is exposure to adequate adult models who may demonstrate unwittingly a style of solving similar everyday problems, in a manner which displays the cardinal virtues of their particular culture. In this way motivational patterns and techniques in terms of age, sex, occupation and so on will be acquired which tends to establish adult significance and status. As Murphy (1947) has expressed it, "Through such serially enacted roles, as through a tube, he makes his way to old age." Presumably, the simile of the tube is intended to convey both the security and the limiting aspect of role. It is limiting because to understand what must be done and to conform to social expectation reduces autonomy by removing the chance to enter equally attractive but incompatible roles.

2 *Learning in role situations*

During the first half of adolescence until the age of fourteen years roles are seen as highly specific to situations (Hartshorn and May 1930). Practical experience of role brings the adolescent into touch with peer values, and performance is seen as good, bad, mean, generous, wise, foolish and so on through the prism of teenage jargon. In this way role experience becomes integrated into a stereotyped sentiment formation which imposes its taboos and appraisals on both the consequences of actions and the means whereby ends are reached. From the ethical point of view knowledge acquired in this way should proceed from the half-group stage of recognitory judgment to a set of acceptable practices associated with each role and labelled with some generalising terminology such as decent, respectable or disgusting. Such practical insight might be regarded as concretely operational, but it differs from the concrete operations of middle childhood, in that the thinker can discuss the behaviour and justify his opinion of it. Such justifications are not usually highly logical and tend to be dogmatic, and few get beyond this in their grasp of ideals. It suggests a point of view suited to a limited power of questioning (Hollingworth 1932). How far this is due to the cessation of opportunity for general discussion of ethical niceties after the sixteenth year and how far it may be a genetically imposed limitation cannot be determined. There is no doubt, however, that more prolonged training in the logical appraisal of religious and ethical concepts would raise the general level, without affecting individual differences within groups.

In most adolescents concepts can be used operationally, although the ability to define them may be lacking. This increases the importance once more of ideal models who present in their personality and behaviour practical exemplifications of what is admirable. Ego-involved situations, which give experience of mature techniques and attitudes, are most likely to arise through the natural entry of such persons into adolescent groupings. Where adolescents are privated of good models, this gap can be filled only by the dedicated and socially apt adult. Between the ages of twelve and eighteen there is an increasing tendency to wonder specifically about ultimate destiny (Kuhlen and Arnold 1944) and other imponderables, and this renders them vulnerable to the opinions of those on whom they depend for guidance. Since the national mores rest upon a concept of the destiny of man in terms of moral responsibility and self realisation, adult examples and precepts provide the adolescent with topics for critical appraisal and objectives for acceptance or rejection in social and personal ethics. But, as has been implied already, this means for most of them an acquaintance with what Tolman has termed the 'utilitanda' properties of concepts, and it is left to the more gifted minority among them to pass beyond these functional and concrete forms, to those which are abstract and attributive.

3 *Concept formation*

An example of a fine gradation from the functional and practical to the relatively abstract can be seen in two levels of difficulty in the abstract words which are required to be defined in the 1938 revision of the Stanford Binet Scale at the twelfth and thirteenth years respectively. To be able to define 'constant' is regarded as a year more mature than success in defining 'connection'. The latter is more easily defined in concrete and functional terms because the action of connecting is implied in the abstract form of the word. There is no such readily available practical image for 'constant'. In the Wechsler Vocabulary Scale, a superior level of definition in terms of abstract generalisation is accorded two marks. Where the word is correctly defined in concrete and practical terms one mark is allowed. This shift from concreteness to abstraction and generalisation may be reflected in significant shifts in reading skills at the age of fourteen years. Buswell's (1922) researches revealed that there is a long plateau for such skills as measured by the constant number of regressive eye movements per line between the ages of eight and fourteen years, but there are signs of a distinct improvement after this age. The number of fixation points per line also remain stable between ten and thirteen years but improves significantly at fourteen years, in the population at large. It is more than probable that this shift into greater fluency is subserved more by an increase in the meaningful content of words than by an improvement in specific occulomotor skills, or by an extended vocabulary. More abstract and generalised meaning would render reading for content a more facile activity, because phrases, sentences and paragraphs would tend to be processed through pre-integrated channels. Bartlett's (1958) comment on Head's theory has relevance here: "He considered that he had irrefutable experimental evidence that past responses continued to have a direct functional significance in the shaping of present behaviour, not as stored traces of reaction, but as organised response groups to which he gave the name of schemata." Such organisation would lengthen the span of attention and so render reading more fluent.

Marked increase in verbal facility both in speech and reading opens the adolescent mind to broader perspectives of cultural implication, because of the abstract conceptual nature of the vocabulary at this level of maturity. Abstract generalisations are apprehended as having not only verbal content but also response patterns which have been organised into schemata through experience of roles. In this way abstractions, acquired verbally through the integration of verbal elements, are brought into associative relationship with their motor response counterparts. It may be this dual approach to integrated knowledge which explains the sentimentality often manifested by the adolescent. This is especially so in the verbally fluent female, for she is able to use phrases and express affect in relation to her utterance which may have little counterpart among the individual's utilitanda. Verbal substitute systems may be used also in phantasy flights from present reality, with as much verve as the imaginal and prelogical symbols of the intuitive phase. In fact adolescence might be regarded as a second intuitive phase poised between the concrete realities of middle childhood and the practical implications of adult values. It differs from the earlier intuitive phase in that its cognitive unreliability does not stem from breaks in the continuity of thought. It is more in the nature of an inconsistency which arises from the facile use of two systems, the verbal and the practical, prior to their experiential integration. The phrases which express moral, social, economic or political stereotypes of the culture may not be understood in all their practical implications, but they serve to classify concrete instances and to express positive or negative affect in relation to them. This stage represents an upper level of development for the average citizen. The formal operation of Piaget indicating a maturity level of twelve years is a mode of thought within reach of 90 per cent of the population (i.e. all with I.Q.s of 85 or over).

For these, a viewpoint concerning cultural matters is possible varying in complexity and subtlety according to the speed and level of mental growth during the first sixteen years of life, and, of course, according to the learning contingencies which had been made appropriately available. Cultural norms rather than endocrine changes are both the instigators and architects of this development.

In western culture the three conflictful motives tend to be aggression, dependency and sexuality (Kagan and Moss 1962) and it is therefore to be expected that 'concept formation' as distinct from 'concept attainment' (Bruner et al. 1956) will occur most readily in these areas of experience. For concept formation to occur the individual must be motivated spontaneously to attend to certain classes of events, and this is more likely to take place in these three areas. Other concepts relating to these areas will be 'attained' through the various educational media of the culture. These may or may not be integrated into those formed spontaneously. For the most part, however, 'attained' concepts are those relating to the technical competences required in vocational and personal living, and these are largely motivated by a competitive need to achieve (N-ach) reinforced by the status and prestige rewards of success. This causes N-ach to be geared to conventional needs, and one of the current major problems of education is to foster spontaneous formation while inducing the passive assimilation of taught concepts. Concept 'formation' is to a large extent idiosyncratic in its end results and is to that extent an original creation on the part of the learner. Attained concepts are not discoveries in this sense, though they may include an element of idiosyncratic hindsight. Most original thinking of any complexity includes both elements, since the original thinker of today stands on the shoulders of those of former times. Thus, attained concepts provide the culturally established background against which pioneers in thought may contemplate their 'empty categories' (Bruner et al. 1956). In other words, hypotheses are largely formed and validated by virtue of reorganised attained concepts.

4 *Intellectual growth*

The term 'empty category' may be regarded as the adolescent equivalent of 'cognitive dissonance' at earlier ages. Cognitive dissonance brings about affective arousal and of course continues to do so at the adolescent level of maturity. At this age, however, the dissonance is created by an awareness of the discrepancy between verbal stereotypes and the know-how of putting them into practice. In scientific spheres this is represented by the problem for which a hypothetical solution is sought. In everyday experience such problems are concerned with social deportment and appearance, and all the other aspects of a mature persona in the Jungian sense of the word. In other words, the adolescent is concerned with the image he presents to others which will result inevitably in a revised self evaluation. For Bruner, the empty category is a means whereby we go beyond the conventional grouping imposed on the segments of nature that we have encountered. It is a vehicle for exploring the ambiguous interstices of experience and is distinguished from the arousal of cognitive dissonance by a positive effort after meaning (Bartlett 1958). It is more than the heightened attention accompanying a diffuse awareness of 'what-it-is-not', which characterises cognitive dissonance in its more elementary forms. The motive to categorize has been termed by Tolman 'placing need' or the urge to identify and place things, presumably within the field of an established mental gestalt or schema. Hilgard emphasises the relief categorizing brings through increase in stability and clarity. Woodworth's 'will to perceive' is of the same order. Klein's 'epistemophilic urge' is the forerunner in infancy of the empty category or the effort after meaning. It appears to be primarily an inductive process (i.e. generalising from instances) which establishes its own major premise for deductive purposes. For this reason, perhaps, Thurstone's efforts to identify the primary mental abilities were successful in producing an independent dimension of inductive reasoning, though none for deductive reasoning was apparent. This suggests that it is the ability to induce major or superordinate premises, which make possible the recognition of the class members from which the major generalisation was experientially derived. Thus generalisations are arrived at after a number of observations of events and because of this fresh instances are relegated to their correct category. In this way, experience produces well-ordered thought processes.

The psychological validation of hypothetical categories discovered by the thinker is encompassed by four means according to Bruner. These could be regarded as indicative of four levels of maturity. The first is termed validation by 'affective congruence'. This subjective type of validation is commonly known as faith, when its lack of complete objective justification is appreciated. It is valuable in that it holds thought constant in its course, while other avenues to validation are sought. It is this element perhaps which preserves the integrity of the self in the presence of criticism threatening to self esteem. Affective congruence is also seen in the unjustifiable intuitive leap which is buttressed by a sense of conviction. In its most extreme pathological form it is seen in paranoia but at the level of normal functioning, i.e. culturally acceptable, it permits the acceptance of such unknowable absolutes as God, the dignity of man and Hell. The validation of values as such stems from this source of affective congruence, and results in the most pervasive area of semantic meaning (Osgood 1957). The great exponent of its psychological importance was Jung (1940). The insecurity of the adolescent, poised between childhood and adult status, renders him prone to use this form of validation. His very ignorance throws him back on this more primitive method of validating hypotheses, but the reorganisation thus effected is likely to be wholesale rather than piecemeal, thus safeguarding the unity of the self structure.

A second source of psychological validation of categories is that of consensus of opinion within the group to which the individual is affiliated. This type of acceptance is established as a tendency in middle childhood but it tends to be abandoned as a major motivating force during adolescence, when the individual becomes achievement oriented. N-ach implies competition, which militates against unquestioning gang coherence. Validation by consensus of opinion is a socialising trend which is strong throughout the middle years of childhood and early adolescence. It persists into adolescence, however, among boys who cannot find role and status within the usual organisations provided by school and club. The pre-adolescent gang is a-scriptive and it coheres loosely. The members gain mutual recognition by the manifestation of qualities such as daring and courage rather than by role significance (Crane 1956). In contrast the adolescent gang establishes its hierarchy of status and role and so provides a socialising milieu parallel to that sought by the non-deviant boy. Underlying the individual's acceptance of the validity of group opinion is the suggestive influence of affective congruence. This causes him to feel that the group is the right one for him and this maintains him within it.

Consensus of opinion is a valuable categorising activity in that the self becomes more complexly perceived through knowing how it appears to others. Its behaviour is valued along a finely graded continuum of reaction to all the commoner forms of social intercourse. Where the individual derives much of this experience from a-normal social groups, the characteristics valued by him will be especially subject to distortion in the maintenance of self esteem. For example, when Amos (1963) compared a number of self estimates of boys with independently obtained estimates of the same traits, he found his adolescent delinquent group tended to be unrealistic only about their physical strength and prowess. The self-estimates of non-delinquent groups lay nearer to those of the judges. It is possible, that this particular quality has special significance for delinquent groups because of a preponderance of mesomorph types, i.e. muscular extraverts, among them (Sheldon et al. 1949). Validation by consensus of opinion then might be said to clarify self-perception on both cultural and sub-cultural planes.

The third type of validation of categories postulated by Bruner is by the 'method of consistency' which gives rise to an awareness of general as opposed to specific classificatory criteria. For example, it is consistent to group together flesh, fowl and fish for all are general terms. If, however, 'good red herring' is substituted for 'fish' there is a sudden change from detached abstraction to homely specificity. This surprise element gives the quirk of humour to the saying. The proverbial silliness of adolescence may stem from an increase in seeing society in an unsophisticated way, and much of their humour turns on their unconventional appraisal of it. Frequently, humour depends on departure from an expected consistency, and the comic frequently depends on a deviation from a norm, as for example when something mechanical and inanimate looks human or when something human looks mechanical. The laughter rises on an affective way of realised incongruence. The shared joke is possible because of consensus of opinion concerning what should be the norm. But the norm itself has been established experientially through the observation of criteria consistently related to a word or phrase. It is characteristic of adolescents, where they congregate and communicate freely, to change both norms and phrases with considerable frequency. Adult observers have difficulty in understanding how the new concepts came to be validated among them with such facility.

This validation by the method of consistency usually means accepting a stimulus as a sign of classificatory significance in an environmental context. Piaget's formal operations depend on the maturation of this ability to a level in which the sign can be used instead of the environmental stimuli, and the words become as it were substitute significates. Concept formation of this kind is clearly seen in the activities of the adolescent collector and taxonomist. These are verbally directed, the objects and specimens depending for their significance on the implications of their labels.

From consistent classificatory activity of this kind, 'ultimate criteria' are developed in the form of more or less succinct generalisations. This constitutes for Bruner a fourth type of validation. The ultimate criteria of adolescence change with developing self perception, but at any stage, the term refers to the subjective opinion of the thinker that the particular characteristic is a sine qua non for his purpose. Ultimate principles of conduct are inherent in the culture, but consistent adherence to such values are manifestations of post-adolescent maturity. Whether they emerge at all in practice depends on how far familial models reflect what is best in the culture. Ultimate criteria can be used cognitively, however, even if they are not implemented in the person's own behaviour. Much social cement derives from knowledge of ultimate criteria on the part of those who are not concerned to direct their behaviour in accordance with them. But when such criteria are part of the intellectual aspect of sentiment, the adolescent cannot offend against them without loss of self regard.

Ultimate criteria would seem to derive from the other three validating activities. For the average person most ultimate criteria stem from affective congruence and consensus of opinion, and consistency is restrained within these limits. For example, when hard pressed to justify categorising in the sphere of morals, the adolescent tends to make such statements as 'it seems right' or 'it is only decent and proper'. At a higher level of complexity the same sentiments are justified by a more elaborate conceptual super-structure relating to human nature, divine nature, expediency or free will which integrates ultimate criteria into a nascent philosophy of life. Most adolescents, however, proceed little beyond the logic of middle childhood which is that of class inclusion and serial ordering, in which part and whole and the specific and the general are distinguished (Inhelder and Piaget 1958). They tend not to form concepts which constitute for them ultimate criteria but they can assimilate them as working guides to behaviour.

5 *Belief and its implementation*

Moral beliefs constitute ultimate criteria but the range of situations to which they apply in any one individual depends on how they have been acquired. Most experimental observation leads to the conclusion that they are rudimentary and platitudinous in most cases, and are attained rather than formed spontaneously. The capacity to apply moral beliefs is quite undeveloped at the age of sixteen in the average boy or girl. High agreement and certainty concerning them usually occur on statements which express middle-class codes of conduct in stereotyped language. About 20 per cent of adolescents do exercise autonomy of moral judgment, however, while the remainder are either adaptive and conforming to the expectations of those around them or unadjusted and defiant about moral issues. The unadjusted group comprise about 16 per cent of the population, and the defiant 4 per cent, according to the findings of Havighurst and Taba (1949).

Failure in moral adjustment among adolescents could stem from a number of privations such as arises from separation anxiety before two years of age, poverty of adequate adult models before six years, and rejection by or failure to be exposed to the peer group in middle childhood. All or some of these could result in a weak sense of ego-identity in adolescence. Whether the child adjusts retreatingly or aggressively may depend on temperamentally induced style. By the age of sixteen years the adolescent boy or girl who has acquired appropriate ways of behaving in a necessary modicum of situations in the areas of sex, extrafamilial independence, vocation and morality has to that extent a mature ego-identity. This constitutes a dependable cognitive map which affords freedom from undue anxiety.

The details of this cognitive pattern of ego-identity may be seen to some extent in the work of Moss (1955) who asked 233 young adolescents to judge descriptions of sixty behaviours with respect to appropriateness and importance. Girls placed greater importance on inhibition of anger and aggression in public, consideration for the feelings of other people, kindness, inhibition of romantic activity in public, courtesy and neatness. Boys placed greater emphasis on provoking interesting topics for discussion, finishing tasks quickly and efficiently, ability to solve problems, knowledge of the world and perseverance. These sex differences are, of course, a matter of bias and are not absolute, but a girl wishing to compete in a masculine sphere would need to have acquired this masculine bias and vice versa.

Models for feminine behaviour are more immediately available than those for the masculine, because the role of wife and mother are an essential aspect of family life, and for 90 per cent of women these are regarded as the avenue to status. In the enquiry of Douvan and Kaye (1957) only one girl in ten had any serious commitments to a job that might be regarded as a career. But in choice of vocation the presence or absence of models among the young person's intimates is of vital significance. Hollingshead (1949) found that 77 per cent of her highest economic class opted for the level of vocation of their parents, in business and the professions, while only 7 per cent of those in the lowest economic class aspired to such vocations. Moreover, most in the lowest economic class drift indecisively into wage earning, while only 3 per cent of the highest fail to make a decision. This attitude of indecision in such a large proportion of the lowest socio-economic group is significant when it is realised that vocational interest has become fairly stable by middle adolescence (Carter 1944). It implies retardation in one important area of ego-identity from which the under-privileged tend to suffer. Vocational guidance can to a large extent ameliorate this drawback as pioneer work in this area of applied psychology has shown. In Birmingham (England) school leavers directed into jobs according to cognitive and emotional suitability for them changed their employers far less frequently than those who were not so directed (Allen and Smith 1932). In the middle classes such guidance occurs within the child's immediate entourage.

The three main styles with which adolescents identify successfully are those of self direction, submission and conformity. Those who produce a sense of ego-identity along all or one of these lines may be accorded high moral status. Failure to develop a consistent style is regarded as evidence of low morale, but in the opinion of Havighurst and Taba (1949) most unadjusted adolescents have been prevented by adverse circumstances from achieving a reasonably good reputation in spite of the capacity to do so. The patterns of circumstance which give rise to styles in the implementing of belief have been studied mostly in terms of socio-economic class and sub-cultural groups. The historical accident of American immigration has stimulated enquiry into ethnic prejudice and concepts such as 'the marginal individual' with his characteristics of over sensitivity, extremes of emotion, and sensitivity to the shortcomings of the group from which he stems. Similarly the 'authoritarian personality' with its rigidity, rejection of outgroups and intolerance of ambiguity are now concepts which are freely applied in psychological description. These studies have affected the way in which the phenomenon of adolescence is regarded, in that it is seen as a marginal phase of development during which the individual stands between two cultures, those of childhood and maturity. It is an ambiguous position arising from his own demands for autonomy in the spheres where his parents are most reluctant to grant it. In contradistinction to this is an adult expectation that he will be responsible and controlled and so abandon the carefree behaviours which curtail parental freedom. Among the former types of behaviour valued by the adolescent are freedom to stay out late at night, use of the family amenities such as the car or guest accommodation, and freedom to choose one's friends. The freedoms demanded most frequently by the parents themselves are from the nuisance of noise and untidiness, the teasing of siblings, silliness and shirking of home duties (Hicks and Hayes 1938). There is a wide range of individual differences among parents regarding the ease with which they can relinquish control. Allowing a child to achieve emancipation is usually difficult in proportion as the parent has achieved satisfaction knowingly or not, for his own wants, by loving and controlling his child. If the child is providing gratification and compensation for frustrations arising elsewhere, he will be surrendered reluctantly, surrendered at a cost or not surrendered at all.

In the exercise of moral belief, the period of most marked change has been observed to be thirteen to fifteen years of age (Morris 1958). During this phase, there is a decline in moral dependence on authority and an increase in independence, but it is subject to considerable fluctuation, and inconsistency is seen in the juxtaposition of rationality and objectivity with superstition and subjectivity. For example, no inconsistency was realised by the Nevaho Mountain Indian children in the research of Havighurst and Neugarten (1955) in that they adopted an equitable attitude towards the rules of baseball as taught at school while retaining their belief that the rules of their tribal games were immutable. During adolescence the rationalisation of belief occurs under the impact of expediency. Lying, for example, tends to increase in frequency as adolescence progresses (Havighurst and Taba 1949). This is a technique for evading the rules imposed by adults, and implies a critical attitude towards them. Morris's (1958) research in English schools suggests that between the ages of eleven and fifteen years pupils enlarge their capacity to justify their opinions and beliefs by normative standards, but there is a slower reduction in scepticism as to whether they are likely to be put into practice. The pupils distinguished clearly between should and would, and the evidence suggests that the formulation of ultimate criteria moved in the van of attitudes favourable to their application in practice. This increasing discrepancy with age between knowledge of the ideal and belief in its feasibility was most marked in the progressive boarding school in Morris's research. Here the atmosphere was more permissive and in consequence resistance to social pressure was greater in the attempt of the pupils to become individuals in their own right. This in no way prevented their knowledge of ideal wisdom from increasing in complexity. In referring to the expectations of friends concerning their behaviour, these adolescents revealed in their protocols that they realised friends could be both an asset and a nuisance, hence the necessity for independence in assertion of rights. A dependent and demanding friend simulates too closely the perceived image of the parent at this age, and is therefore a threat to the ego's increasing need for autonomy. This is a first step towards acceptance of the christian ethic, which exhorts its adherents first to be free and then to obey. The individual who puts obedience before freedom at this age is not admired. As Murphy (1947) points out "acceptance among adolescents is more likely to be related to self-sufficiency, the lack of need for approval, than to the effort to be accepted". The peak of this drive for independence tends to occur in the third and fourth years of the secondary school, between the ages of thirteen and fifteen years, when knowledge of duty and actual performance are at their most discrepant. Marks for bad conduct are more frequently given then than at any other age. At this age, too, the greatest discrepancy occurs between daughters' and mothers' ideas on up-bringing, particularly in those areas of behaviour in which conflict is most likely to occur (Hebron and London 1963). Morris suggests that the implication of his findings for the practical guidance of those concerned with the education of adolescent boys and girls is that the helpful adult inculcates value through the means of implementing it, since for them the validity of a value rests on its pragmatic justification.

The development of a child's idea of God, when he is exposed to such teaching, follows much the same trend as his other concepts. Prior to a mental age of thirteen to fourteen years, the concept of man's relation to God consists of trivialities, verbalism and egocentric gross materialism. The twelfth year is regarded, on experimental evidence, as the boundary line between regarding God as a magician, directly intervening in the world and seeing him as exerting influence through the natural happenings of his own laws. By the thirteenth year the adolescent is capable of envisaging God as bound by his own moral laws, since not to be so limited would be a contradiction in his nature (Goldman 1962). In a theistic culture, an informing religion which conveys to the mass of the people that God is in no way capricious is a great stabilising factor contrasting with the ferment of anxiety associated with security seeking ritual in less mature animistic cultures. Belief in 'science' as a cure-all may have less psychological value as an agency of reassurance, because of its lack of relevance for social and personal areas of behaviour.

By the fifteenth year of mental age, it is possible for the adolescent, when suitably nurtured, to accept as ultimate criteria of God's nature an absence of capriciousness and an absolute integrity. This concept could serve to integrate the effects of categorising through the channels of affective congruence, consensus of opinion and observed consistency. As an ultimate criterion it tends to afford systematic coherence to the individual's thinking and a mode of approach to problems met with in experience.

II. MOTIVATIONAL DEVELOPMENTS

1 *Control of anxiety*

The rapid growth of categorisation during adolescence confers order, control and predictability upon the way the environment is perceived. This was true also of concrete operations in the middle years of childhood. The main difference wrought by adolescent structuring lies in the increased remoteness of the goals that he is capable of contemplating. His critical powers in future oriented behaviour are extended by his ability to use words to reflect on other words and images at second- and third-order levels. Ultimate criteria are relatively succinct because subserved beneath them may be the criteria of affect, sociality and consistency. This conveys a general impression of the desirability of a goal hypothetically entertained. Moreover, goals tend to become more clearly delineated as related concepts are validated empirically. Such revision may result in the total abandonment of some goals during adolescence, but these blind alleys of search leave residues of experience which may constitute aids to entering future situations.

This increase in the value of thought as a predictor of outcomes progressively reduces the amount of insecurity and anxiety in daily living. The adolescent may report himself as carrying a load of anxiety symptoms in his twelfth year when answering a questionnaire such as the Children's Manifest Anxiety Scale (Castenada et al. 1956), but such symptoms are no longer a detriment to social adjustment as they were at earlier ages. The ability to manipulate situations symbolically both in terms of hindsight and foresight, is an expediting factor in establishing ego-identity, and this may be one source of difference between socio-economic groups in anxiety control and direction. Hallworth's (1961) findings suggest that less intelligent children from predominantly working-class homes tend to be slower to substitute socialised anxiety for more primary forms than are children of greater intelligence from middle-class homes. The adaptive socialised form of anxiety termed self blame was more developed in her grammar school sample in the first half of adolescence. It is probable that the superiority of Hallworth's more intelligent girls derives more from the adequacy of models than from their more advanced maturation. When intelligence is held constant such traits emerge as a class difference rather than as a function of intelligence (Margary and Eichorn 1961). In Freudian terms, ego-strength might be defined as the capacity to deal with anxiety on a reality basis rather than as the extent to which the personality experiences anxiety. This capacity to resolve anxiety is developed best in families which are consistent and trusting and which present models of friendliness and spontaneity. Such family characteristics are of prime importance before six years, and result by about the age of ten years in a pattern of conscience and independence which remains recognisably a distinguishing mark of the individual (Peck and Havighurst 1960). As was emphasised in the discussion of the middle years of childhood, the pattern of facilitation and inhibition of impulse termed 'will-control' is closely related to firmness of parental control during these years. The phenomenon of will, however, has another major connotation, namely the whole self in action (Cardno 1962). This was extensively investigated in the researches of the Louvain school of psychology (Aveling 1931) where it was shown that the individual initiated a will-act with a sense of ego-involvement as well as self instruction regarding the goal to be reached and the means of reaching it. Once this set or determining tendency had been effected, action followed automatically towards the desired end. This capacity for decisive action tends to be exercised with increasing frequency as maturity is approached, partly because new technical competencies make independent action more feasible, and partly because planning and review of action sharpen perception of the self. This latter aspect of self activity is regarded by Cattell (1950) as the most important source of its unity. The ability to perceive or contemplate the physical and social self, whereby the satisfaction of any desire becomes subsidiated, in part, to a sentiment for the welfare of the whole self, is a major source of integration. Self perception thus passes from concreteness to abstraction in which generalised properties of the 'proprium' are amenable to rehearsal and review. Categories having such systematic status for the individual provide an information processing device with a large storage capacity that holds among other things complex strategies (or programs) that may be evoked by stimuli. The content of these strategies is already largely determined by the previous experience of the system (Newell et al. 1958). This cybernetic expression of how stimuli become cues is particularly relevant for a study of adolescence. During this phase there occurs the maturation of the storage system subserving the symbolic process, to a level which renders it capable of acting independently of the primary sensori-motor systems for long sequences of behaviour. When this system of secondary signalisation breaks down because of the non-availability of stored categories, the organism tends to adopt a questing attitude which may be expressed by a mild intensification of attention, not only to the external stimuli but also to the imagery and sensations arising within the primary system. This questing attitude arises from an 'intolerance of ambiguity' or a tendency to feel uncomfortable when uncertain.

There are big individual differences in the extent to which persons can tolerate uncertainty. Such differences may reflect degrees of adequacy in the information processing system. This adequacy, however, appears to depend on environmental structuring of an appropriate kind at crucial stages in development.

2 *Cultural determinants*

Such learning contingencies have been discussed in previous chapters, but their effects on adolescent development might be further considered here through the Fels longitudinal study (Kagan and Moss 1962). Some of these findings throw light on how information processing is affected by cultural trends in the three most conflictful motivation areas of sex, dependency and aggression. For example, the young women of this study tended to have higher perceptual thresholds than men for aggression, while men had higher thresholds for dependency. An a-normally high perceptual threshold was regarded by Freud as a sign of unconscious guilt about the object or situation, and in one sense this would seem to be supported by the Fels findings. Women are permitted more frequently than men to be dependent while men are expected to be satisfactorily aggressive. There would thus be less likelihood of guilt in each sex for the areas showing lowered thresholds. It would seem, however, that frequency of experience or extent of learning would also automatically result in lowered thresholds and in consequent rapidity in processing information tachistoscopically exposed. This is to be expected regardless of the amount of praise or blame lavished by caretakers on account of the dependency or aggression. There may be, then, independent antecedents to guilt on the one hand and raised thresholds on the other. Kagan and Moss conclude that delayed recognition of scenes depicting aggression, dependency, sexuality and physical harm showed the highest correlations in the groups for whom repression of relevant content might be assumed to be strong. These were groups in which such behaviour had not been fostered. Thus repression in this context could mean not a dynamic UCS process but rather an attenuation of neural structures for perceptual response to those classes of stimuli through lack of practice. Since speed of perception is the criterion of threshold level, it is clear that habituation could be a sufficient explanation of slowness in some subjects. Such a thesis is also congruent with their finding that an absence of autonomic discharge to stimuli is a more sensitive index of repression than its presence. This too would be the case where habituation was poor. Furthermore, autonomic discharge seemed to be correlated most with the interest value of the stimulus which also suggests that habituation level was high. The delayed recall scores of the scenes exposed tachistoscopically were on the whole lower where there had been rapid perception and higher where the perceptual threshold was high. The authors assume that delayed recall is facilitated by conflict. There is the possibility, however, that pictures were better remembered where there were more exposures (i.e. where thresholds were higher). Such a learning theory approach to high thresholds is not incompatible with that of Freud if a distinction is maintained between the phenomenon and its genesis. The expression 'conflictful areas of behaviour' can refer either to the conflict between child and environment during the structuring process, or to conflicting impulses experienced by the subject when exposed subsequently to such stimuli. Kagan and Moss apparently mean the latter since they define conflict as a simultaneous arousal of incompatible or mutually exclusive goal strivings. Where, however, behaviour forbidden early in life is not exercised, disuse leads to extinction and to a lowered probability of occurrence in most cases. It is unlikely that a simple tachistoscopic stimulus would re-evoke the primary conflict between caretaker and child, and the extinction theory would seem to be more tenable.

Surveys of adolescent reports on their emergent primary sexual characteristics suggest that this experience is traumatic in only a few cases. The onset of the menarche and pubescence is hailed by most children as something to be taken for granted. In a survey of 475 girls, 51 per cent declared themselves to be indifferent, 12 per cent as interested or delighted, a further 12 per cent as rather annoyed and only 1 per cent as terrified, the last category presumably as a result of uninformed naïvety (Conklin 1933). Nocturnal emissions with, on occasion, erotic dreams have been reported by 83 per cent of males in another survey (Kinsey et al. 1953). Boys discuss these experiences among themselves more freely than girls, and are on the whole less worried about their implications.

Presumably in Western culture this sex difference in attitude would be considerably reduced were it not so necessary to protect the girl against premature pregnancy. The halcyon early adolescence of the Samoan girl was attributed by Benedict (1936) to the fact that the adolescent in that culture is not required to inhibit sexual expression. There it is regarded as a time of considerable happiness, for with biological maturation the adult sex role is immediately assumed. There is no period apart from those devoted to brief initiation ceremonies in which the adolescent has a marginal status. Indeed, it would be interesting to know whether Freud's castration complex existed in such a culture where there was no pressure to compel genital inhibition. In the older countries of the Western world and indeed in all technological societies, this marginal period is prolonged at the cost of enforced inhibition of natural sexual proclivities. The christian cult has perforce given support to this economic requirement, but the secular and religious demands for inhibition of the sexual impulse outside of marriage have different roots. The religious ban may derive historically from the need to condemn the heathen practice of fertility rites, which was a powerful rival of the doctrine of personal resurrection. These considerations are a reminder that although somatic changes in adolescence are not among the least important of motivational variables, they are to be distinguished as such from the significance society ascribes to them.

The development of new bodily structures and functions proceeding as it does differentially in the sexes causes reorganisation of the body-image to which cultural attributes attach. Cultural influences are probably responsible to a large extent for some differences in rate of maturation between the sexes. For example, it is commonly observed that strength of hand grip and shoulder thrust and most of the motor functions are more precocious in girls (Jones 1944). This could be accounted for by family expectations that girls should help more with housework than boys and indeed with the care of younger siblings. Boys are expected to help more frequently with the heavier manual labour performed by the father in home and garden, and for this assistance the parents must wait until the boy is strong enough. Since exercise of function rather than muscle size is the main determinant of strength, it is to be expected that girls will be precocious, since they can perform their ancillary functions within the family at an earlier age, but by the age of sixteen years the boys' average handgrip of 50 Kgr. exceeds that of girls by 20 Kgr. (Jones 1944). These expectations have far-reaching effects on value judgments and self regard. While the boy goes freely to his larger enterprises outside the home the girl is restrained at the same age to preoccupy herself with the dull trivia of daily chores. She thus comes to regard her special skills as of no import, and tends not to take the same pride in them as a boy does in the higher skills he acquires at a later age. The boy's skills are more often constructional in nature and the girl's concerned with maintenance of tidiness and cleanliness. Hallworth and Waite (1963) in their study of value judgments among adolescent girls have shown cleanliness to be the most heavily weighted characteristic on their dimension interpreted as 'attitude to virtues, and personalities associated with the maintenance of such virtues'. It is doubtful whether cleanliness would emerge with such prominence in the values of a sample of adolescent boys. It is more likely that potency and activity would emerge strongly as more valued characteristics.

3 *Cognitive growth and motivation*

In both sexes there is a catalytic impetus to physical growth during adolescence, and a consequent change and adjustment in self perception. It would appear that the only somatic and psychological aspects of the self which remain relatively unaffected by these rapid changes are the small muscles and the intellect. The growth in the long bones do not affect to any marked degree the finer motor reactions involved in mechanical skills, for these are dependent largely on the muscles of the wrist and to a lesser extent on those of elbow and shoulder. Manual dexterity thus pursues its own growth, independently of the biceps which are affected by the rapid increase in the distance between their terminal points. This growth in mechanical ability is less than that of intelligence and terminates earlier (Ausubel 1954), but for many adolescents specific skills which are dependent on fine motor abilities become strong motivating propensities at this age. This is particularly so in those adolescents (usually boys) who have been persistently devalued throughout their earlier school life, because of their failure to achieve success in the more verbal skills despite a satisfactory level of spatial intelligence. A new-found confidence emerges with their success in acquiring the manual skills which are future oriented in their usefulness. Early adolescence, round about the age of thirteen years, appears to be a period favourable to the development of manual skills, and it is at this age that individual differences in this type of ability emerge to constitute a normally distributed trait largely independent of verbal intelligence (Burt 1943).

In all probability, however, the effects of intellectual growth on personality are more important than the change they induce in cognitive organisation per se. The development of a capacity to think in generalities results in acquaintance with many abstract terms although clear insight into their significance may be lacking. The semantic differential study of Hallworth and Waite (1963) suggest that while the assimilation of such terms as cleanliness, trust, pleasure, ambition, future and freedom is accomplished by the age of fifteen, others such as honesty, kindness and success are understood best in terms of 'avoidance concepts' such as disappointment, fear, pain, shame, failure, mischief, lies, enemy. This developmental sequence in the assimilation of abstract terms would seem to be analogous to the recognition of 'what-it-is-not', first present in the twelve-month-old child who sobers in the presence of people seen as strangers. Now, as then, such negative awareness constitute first exercises in the acquisition of positive and generalised assimilation. Thus enhanced intellectual powers during adolescence contribute hierarchical depth to the extensive and basic comprehension acquired earlier at a practical level. To the affective levels of early childhood and the sense of practical implication acquired in the middle years, are added self-conscious habits and ideals, which serve as directive and symbolic key points for superordinate control. This generalising factor derives from the second system of signalisation integrated with its functional and affective predecessors in the primary system.

Such constructs are important motivational factors for they provide a new type of orientation for entry into situations. Each person characteristically evolves for his convenience in anticipating events a construction system embracing ordinal relationships between constructs. This is a motivator of preference and choice. Such personal constructs (Kelly 1955) categorise and convey criterial value. The sentiments of MacDougall (1909) and his superordinate self-regarding sentiment was such a system of hierarchical personal constructs. During adolescence, personal constructs are apparent not only in the way the individual perceives himself but also in his perception of how he is regarded by others. Such constructs include a capacity to estimate past, present and future aspects of the self, not only from his own point of view but also from that of others. It is clear that satisfactory personality adjustment is correlated with adequacy of personal constructs, for their predictive function makes possible a greater tolerance of threat. Kasper (1962) found that well-adjusted adolescents were able to tolerate higher levels of threat because of the adequacy of their constructs. They tended not to lose their self esteem, in spite of an awareness of the need to change their constructs. Presumably, the challenge of situations which found them unprepared and inadequate was lessened by the relative adequacy of current personal constructs, compared with those of less well-adjusted individuals. The fact that such threats to self esteem stem from familial situations is suggested in Kasper's finding that the parent appeared as a threatening agent less frequently among the well-adjusted adolescent than among the maladjusted. In their case, defensiveness and pessimism about the future suggested a smaller degree of tolerance of threat. It would seem that the individual's resources for meeting uncertainty will depend on his previous experiential structuring rather than on the difficulties inherent in the situation. Such an insufficiency of categorised criteria results in perceptual rigidity concerning it, and there tends to be a lack of flexibility in exploring its implications. It may be that a physiological predisposition to lack of neural flexibility accentuates environmentally induced rigidity in the neurotic and maladjusted, for in such patients the number of changes when fixating reversible perspective have been found to be significantly smaller than in normal population (Eysenck 1947). Biological deficiency in these extreme cases may augment the effects of inadequate criterial structuring due to privation of experience. So-called denial of reality regarded from this viewpoint would seem to result from an appraisal of too few cues rather than from a purposive evasion of some. If ambiguity is resolved by denying reality it may be because the concepts have not developed beyond the level of a negative awareness that the situation is not what it should be. This could of course be regarded as an unconscious evasion of fact but it arises from ignorance and half knowledge, and also from an emotional disposition to evade what is not fully understood. This is implied in Hamilton's (1957) definition of avoidance of ambiguity which he regards as "a form of cognitive control in the presence of a high degree of total anxiety within a personality, where the principal defence mechanism is repression. By avoiding uncertainty further anxiety is avoided." Repression in this definition is an act of seeking a solution by cognising cues other than the relevant ones about which there is ignorance – a turning away from the ambiguous and seeking relevance irrelevantly in the familiar. This phenomenon has been demonstrated by Luchins (1950) in his work on rigidity of set in problem solution and Woodworth and Sells (1935) on atmosphere effect in verbal reasoning. They have shown a general and normal tendency to a prejudiced appraisal of cues along stereotyped lines. Thus where an adolescent shows a tendency towards black and white solutions employing an oversimplified dichotomy, or an unqualified either/or in their effort after meaning, it may be explained in terms of learning theory. For this reason the judgments made by the average adolescent in situations not yet well assimilated are of this order – ill-considered, prejudiced and out of touch with reality when assessed by adult standards.

4 *Aggression*

These characteristics apply particularly to the stereotypes of aggression. These stem largely from sex role more than from any other source (Buss 1961). For the male, emphasis is on active, assertive, dominant, physical aggression, while girls are constrained to resort mostly to verbal forms, especially to the more indirect types of attack such as tattling and spiteful rejection. The cultural countenancing of male aggression ensures a stability co-efficient for this trait in males between the ages of fourteen and thirty-three as high as 0·91 (Tuddenham 1959).

Sub-cultural group differences in the psycho-genetics of aggression are reported by Davis (1943). The aggressive styles of parents tend to be perpetuated in those of their offspring. Working-class parents tended to punish corporally with greater frequency than middle-class parents and to lose control of themselves when angry. These differences tended to be reflected in the respective aggressive styles of their adolescent sons and daughters. Children in the higher socio-economic group employed more oblique tactics in their aggression against authority. Kohn (1959) too reported on class differences in the punishment of children at the outset of adolescence. He concluded the amounts and types of punishment were more similar in the two groups than the reasons for punishing. Working-class parents tended to modify the severity of their attitude to accord with the consequences of the bad behaviour, while middle-class parents calibrated their punitive intensity to accord with their perception of the child's intention. This suggests that the average middle-class parent's intervention aimed at reform of sentiment and the adjustment of the personal constructs of the offender, while that of the working-class parent tended to operate at the level of decremental conditioning in their tactics. The former would tend to make for generalised change and the latter for specific changes in responses to particular situations. This gives the middle-class child an advantage in generalised orienting to situations and thus makes for greater flexibility and adaptability in solving similar problems to those which were punished. It must be remembered, however, that there are greater differences within groups than between groups, and that a tendency means no more than a slight difference in average scores.

The habitually aggressive adolescent is the most difficult to reform. In schools the ultimate sanction of corporal punishment, though the most effective deterrent with such children, as with all children, succeeds less frequently in the case of this group compared with others (Highfield and Pinsent 1951). This intransigence may be due to a double reinforcement where aggression is successful in removing obstacles. On the one hand it reduces tension by removing frustration and on the other it rewards through the achievement of the desired end. A more submissive attitude in the same situation would involve a single reinforcement, that of reducing the discomfort of mounting tension. The double reward of aggression during childhood would tend to result in the firmer institution of the offending techniques in the adolescent which could not be abandoned easily by those temperamentally predisposed to self assertion. Morris et al. (1956) followed 66 aggressive children from the age of four years up to fifteen years and beyond. Each had at least four of the following symptoms: truancy, dishonesty, cruelty, defiance, distractibility, destructiveness and temper. As maturity was approached only fourteen did well. This represented a 23 per cent amelioration compared with the expected 60 per cent. The prognoses for aggressive girls were worse than those for boys. This can be explained by the fact that a girl must maintain her aggressive symptoms against the pressure of cultural expectation. For her to withstand this influence suggests that her condition was severely detrimental to adjustment at the outset.

Perhaps the simplest and most direct cause of antisocial aggression is tolerance of it by parents. When Bandura and Walters (1959) investigated the methods used to control aggression they found their experimental group had mothers over-permissive of aggression towards themselves. The area in which the enquiry was made was a respectable one, however, and this brought social pressure to bear on the parents to prevent their boys being aggressive towards adults outside the family. This suggests that those permissive of aggression against themselves were compelled to punish their offspring more frequently for extra familial aggression than those who decrementally conditioned theirs within the family circle. A similar cause among girls is reported by Kagan and Moss (1962). They found that those with well-educated parents were more verbally aggressive with peers and less conforming with adults during the ages of ten to fourteen years than girls from poorly educated families. They attribute this to the greater tolerance by the well-educated mothers of deviations from sex role standards. This is a further example of normal aggression structured in a culturally deviant manner. A determinant of this tolerance of female aggression on the part of well-educated mothers may be a personality construct related to prestige. The educated woman is more likely to adopt the values ascribed mostly to the masculine image and associated with work, study, reward and books (Hallworth and Waite 1963). This predisposes her to interpret her daughter's aggression against herself as a quality of drive and firmness to be respected. In the Fels study women who were competitive in their adult years tended to come from well-educated families. Among the adult men in this sample, competitiveness was not a function of social class but one of general masculine import.

5 *Learning in early childhood and adolescence compared*

It would seem that there is an analogy to be drawn between learning in early childhood and in adolescence, in that both conditioning and learning from models may occur as intensively. There is a verbal inadequacy at both ages which makes possible the specificity of conditioning. At the earlier age it arises from general verbal ignorance, while during adolescence it results from ignorance of the practical implications of words representing the generalised abstractions with which adults convey their expectations and demands. Another similarity between the two phases of development arises from the weighting accorded to the two main continua of parental behaviour, namely – the love-hostility dimension and that of autonomy-control. Because of the adolescent's increased power and competence in striving for autonomy the love-hostility dimension once more assumes prior importance as it did in the years of incompetence and dependency before the age of six years. Ideally, increased sensitivity and understanding are necessary in the parents if they are to abandon their own vantage point of autonomy in family control, out of regard for the child's need for independence. Such reorientation on the part of parents makes for positive rather than decremental conditioning during the years when an adolescent viewpoint is in the making. With regards to the renewed need for models, the latter period differs from the earlier in that they tend to be sought on a wider front outside the family circle more than within it. At both periods, however, such love-objects with which to identify, and appreciative supporters who enhance a sense of prestige and self-regard, are a necessity for successful development. In the absence of such models the young person is at a loss to verbally direct his behaviour and he is more exposed to the effects of conditioning through specific deterrents and rewards arising from the consequences of his activities. The gifted adolescent is more precocious in development, and his awareness of his situation tends to be more complex. For this reason, discussion of the gifted adolescent is reserved for the next chapter.

CHAPTER VII

Motivation and learning in the gifted adolescent

I. COGNITIVE ASPECTS

1 *The antecedents of individual differences in intelligence*

Although mental growth appears to decelerate or even terminate at the age of sixteen years for most people, gains in I.Q. between the ages of sixteen and twenty-one years were reported in the University of California growth study (Bayley 1936, 1955). This longitudinal study extending over twenty-five years from one month of age revealed much irregularity in mental growth. Scores appeared to be affected by such conditions as emotional climate, cultural milieu, environmental deprivation and by developmental changes in the nature and composition of the behaviours tested. Something akin to 'g', however, appeared after the second or third year when correlations between test scores at successive ages were in evidence. Moreover, after the fifth and sixth years children can be reliably classified into broad categories of normal, defective and bright. In eighteen factor analyses carried out at yearly intervals it was clear that 'g' was manifested in different behaviours according to developmental areas. In these, a general factor of sensorimotor alertness dominates the first two years, one of persistence is most pervasive in the third and fourth, while after the age of four a factor for the manipulation of symbols accounts for almost the entire variance. Bayley regards these changes as environmentally caused by the complete break between the kinds of functions measured by tests for infants and for school-age children. In early adolescence there is an increase in variability due perhaps to the fact that the very able and the very dull exhibit different patterns of change from the average. This could very well be due to an accelerated use of the abstract symbol which contributes to an exceptional extent to the development of the able, and underlines the degree of retardation among the less than average. This is supported by the fact that intelligence measured by verbal concepts and abstractions continues to grow when populations composed primarily of superior adults are retested. Terman's (1947) retesting at intervals of twelve years, using concept mastery tests with his gifted population, found an increase in scores of +0·5 sigma at each testing. It seems that the growth curve of verbal intelligence rises steeply till the age of twenty and thereon continues to rise gently. This growth is not confined to the bright. It appeared also in the less favoured subjects of the Berkley growth study who were still improving their scores at twenty-five years of age. Much seems to depend on continued exposure to stimuli supportive of abstraction. This kind of experience enters each home more continuously now through mass media of communication than it did when these studies were inaugurated. Hence changing evidence is to be expected concerning the terminal point of mental growth. It was noted first that superior adolescents who were educated in college continued to exhibit mental growth. The cause of this is now operative over all sections of the community since the population generally is exposed continually to verbal stimuli which evoke abstract reasoning and concept formation. Studies in decline of I.Q. convey the same impression. It is greatest among manual workers, who give up pencil and paper and reading activities. The most obvious explanation, however, is a change in exercise of function. All the evidence suggests that, within innately determined limits, changes in I.Q. arise from long-term practice effects, habitual mental alertness and conceptual growth. In the case of the gifted adolescent, a fillip to mental efficiency is given by an increase in the number and complexity of the concepts he can manipulate and it may be this more than any other aspect of mental functioning which lends power to his thinking.

2 *Levels of concept formation*

By the age of sixteen years the gifted adolescent is capable not only of analysing concrete reality with the help of concepts, but has already surpassed the less gifted in his capacity to analyse concepts themselves. This may be illustrated by selected items from the 1938 revision of the Stanford Binet Scale. The ability to use concepts selectively is exemplified in a test item for fourteen and a half years in which the difference between similar abstract terms such as laziness and idleness, poverty and misery, character and reputation is required. At a later stage of maturity, that of seventeen years, three abstract words are given which are required to be grouped into one sentence. These are 'benefactor, institution, contribution' and 'civility, requirement, employee'. A sentence combining all three in a meaningful statement reveals a capacity to synthesise and analyse such broader concepts as public charity and employment-relations with the help of other subordinate concepts. In stating that 'civility is a requirement in an employee' or 'The benefactor gave a contribution to the institution' the testee reveals in all probability an ability to think about reality in terms of general principles. This is the highest level of conceptual analysis (Vigotsky 1962) and is attained as a stable skill by those having an I.Q. of approximately 116 or better. Such levels of abstraction make possible the verbal or symbolic expression of the directional properties of thought. For example, if 'institution, benefactor, contribution' are regarded as related to the superordinate term charity, this term could become directive of the 'set' or direction of a train of thought leading to the inclusion of all three in one sentence. Such a trend could be maintained while a whole paragraph or more was composed on this theme. This directional property of the abstract concept rises into consciousness with higher level skills and can be formulated by the thinker himself not only as he performs (Bartlett 1958) but also retrospectively. Thus the steps in composition are reached through its terminal point, and a title or précis of the paragraph would represent a succinct minimal expression of the essential aspects of the terminal point. This ability to assimilate general principles and propositions has its neural-correlate in complex schemata which facilitate recall of relevant data. Bruner (1960) regards this organisation of facts into general ideas from which they may be deduced as the only known way of reducing the quick rate of loss of human memory. The gifted adolescent contrasts notably with the average among his peers, in his wealth of potential recall, which in more manifest form is recognised as his store of general information. His level of a generalisation may be assessed, in one of its dimensions, by the number of constellations of facts subserved under it. Some insightful general statements imply a considerable hierarchical depth in such constellations. For example, in the study of the Bible, a chronological age of approximately sixteen and a half years and a mental age of nineteen years is generally needed before the concept of Israel as the future cradle of Christianity is assimilated (Goldman 1962). A similar maturity of concept in the sphere of the physical sciences is evident among the gifted. General principles may be attained with such precision by the gifted during adolescence, that their most fruitful use in research is during the third decade of life. Lehman (1953) cites such findings to stress the importance of acceleration in teaching, so that gifted American students will have maximum freedom from the chores of assimilation at the optimal period for productive thinking in early manhood.

3 *Experience and intellectual growth*

Guilford's (1956) work on the structure of the intellect dichotomises it into thirty-eight thinking factors on the one hand and seven memory factors on the other. This differentiation in the thought complex he attributes to transfer of learning from one type of situation to another, which creates complexes of skills with which to meet externally presented problems. Thus growth in complexity must inevitably depend on length and variety of experience, as well as degree of insight. Where the individual has tended to avoid the direct solution of problems in a particular field, such as the mechanical or the verbal or the numerical, it is impossible for him to be 'intelligent' when using these media in thinking. This does not imply that he cannot under any circumstances be intelligent in this area of thought. If motivated to direct his attention belatedly to such activities, the results frequently show there was much latent capacity which had failed to emerge as an ability, because of aversion to the operations required for its growth. Such differentials in amount of application, together with the differential of innate capacity for assimilation, lead to the normal distribution of traits in the population at large and also to their independence. These distinguishable dimensions increase directly with the length of time that the subjects have been exposed to a common experiential front, and one by one Guilford's forty-five known factors emerge as normally distributed traits largely independent of a general capacity to profit from experience (Thurstone 1941, Burt 1943). Since high prestige value attaches to success, it is to be expected that children and adolescents from about the age of ten years onwards will tend to concentrate most spontaneously on those areas of cognitive skill where they are likely to err least. Where, however, they are equally adept over the whole field of commonly acquired knowledge, they are usually compelled on grounds of expediency to abandon one sub-area to concentrate on another in required depth. The current standards of attainment in the discipline he opts for make very specific demands on available attentional powers, and too wide a range of interests may place him among the under-achievers. He is thus constrained to become a specialist with a relatively narrow band of factors on whose distributions he has a favoured position. For example, in the field of mathematics there will be a few individuals who can do no more than count, while at the other extreme will be a tiny bunch of senior wranglers and their equals. The average person will be incapable of learning algebra to any level useful in application but can learn to compute with rapidity. It is clear that those at the positive end of the continuum must not only be well endowed in the capacity to learn but must also be highly motivated to do so.

Guilford in his analysis distinguishes between productive and discovery factors. His productive cognitive factors imply originality in mental output. Something new is thought up, though suggested in the first place by ordinary stimuli. His discovery factors have reference to the picking up of facts in the course of experience, facts recognised as such in textbooks and other forms of instruction. A person's general knowledge or fund of information is arrived at through the operation of discovery factors, discovery of whatever facts happen to be available. Productive factors operate in terms of inference and invention, the former being precise and constrained and the latter more tangential to the starting point. Guilford described these two ways of thinking productively as convergent and divergent respectively. Divergent trends of thought result in novelty and originality of output, convergent in an exclusive and unique product which is consistent with accepted fact. Convergent thinking is exercised in multiple choice answers, in numerical operations, in analogies, and in picture arrangement to accord with a likely sequence of events. In divergent thinking, there may be much searching and going off in various directions, and it is most clearly seen in the thinker when there is no unique solution inherent in the data. It is operative in word fluency, associational fluency, inventing titles for plots and inventing consequences given a particular series of events. It seems to be a factor associated with spontaneous flexibility and a disposition to avoid repeating oneself.

Ancillary to these two major trends in thinking is a third class which Guilford has termed evaluative. These underlie the capacity to make decisions concerning the goodness, suitability, or effectiveness of the results of thinking. The best established of these evaluative factors is logical appraisal, which is the ability to judge the soundness of conclusions where logical consistency is the criterion. Evaluation also is closely allied to the aesthetic factor, in that good taste has among its major criteria decorum and functional efficiency. It is also seen in a more tentatively identified evaluative factor, which Guilford termed 'judgment' and which is best represented in procedure calling for a choice between several alternative solutions. In common terminology, this is called wisdom or common sense. The fact that it appears weakly in the factorial table suggests that this skill is exercised after other criteria such as the logical and aesthetic have been applied. But such processes are largely analytic and this judgment factor may depend on a capacity to retain an overall synthetic view leading to the choice of the best alternative, all things considered. In all probability wisdom is distinguished from cleverness by this element of judgment, and it may be that with experience held constant personality factors concerned with a capacity for delayed response, will power and conscientiousness are likely to be crucial. Burt (1962*b*) stresses the need for thinking to be socially and relevantly related to situations. "Useful creativity must involve the ability to deal not only inventively but also rationally with the material supplied." He points out that in divergent thinking only part of the stimulus sets off the train of associations, and they are not such as to mirror the whole. This is more characteristic of early adolescence when fluency and receptivity in perception of new problems is evident, but at later ages divergent association becomes allied to intuitive synthesis, or insight, or sagacity. He stresses the psycho-genetic interdependence of temperament and fluency, but regards divergent tendencies to arise from habitual modes of entering situations. The discussion so far might be summed up by saying some adolescents are more innately disposed to the fluency and flexibility required in creative thinking, but that wise innovations are dependent upon the intellectual integration of experience into easily apprehended units or concepts or abstract generalisations. These confer a breadth of judgment in accordance with the number of subordinate categories covered by the generalised propositions. The gifted adolescent is likely to be capable of this breadth and complexity and so can exercise eventually responsible judgment in high places where such comprehensive insight is necessary.

4 *The antecedents of creative thought*

Mednick's (1962) steep and flat associative hierarchies are another description of such thought patterns. His steep associative hierarchies subserve logical thinking within the bounds of general propositions. For example, thinking, which is consistent with general truths concerning the law, is exercised by judges when they try to fit evidence into such schemata. Precedence and statute thus constitute excellent examples of steep associative hierarchies, and the good judge must operate with precision within this framework. In contrast, the learned counsel for the defence may successfully appeal to the jury by exercising his flat hierarchical structures through associations which have no replicas in the law books. His skill in taking the prosecution by surprise and in gaining the ear of the jury will depend on his adopting a line of explanation different from the obvious and expected. Such great advocates as Marshall and Birkett were well furnished not only with steep legal associative hierarchies (knowledge of the law) but also with a capacity to side-step from such a system into another steep hierarchical concept of the way ordinary men and women perceive situations. The associative passage from one to the other is made by virtue of an existing flat associative hierarchy in the counsel's neural schemata. Thus the connecting of two well-developed steep associative hierarchies is made by a mediating flat hierarchy. The genius of the defence frequently lies in a capacity for such unusual associative links between areas of well-structured knowledge. It has been suggested that orthodox or unoriginal thinkers tend to lack these flat connecting hierarchies between steep systems. A fuller realisation of what Mednick means by a flat associative hierarchy is afforded by the Remote Associations Test (RAT). In this, stimulus elements from mutually remote associative clusters are presented and the subject subsumes them under one heading. For example, the stimulus elements 'wheel; electric; high' may be combined by the mediating link of 'chair'. Houston and Mednick (1963) claim to have demonstrated that high RAT scorers have a 'need for' uncommon associations. They found that high RAT scorers could be conditioned to a preference for nouns when unusual associations were presented with the nouns. After experiencing many pairings of unusual associations with nouns, and usual ones with other parts of speech, the high RAT scorers as distinct from the low RAT scorers showed a distinct preference for nouns and indifference to other parts of speech. It was concluded on this evidence that high RAT scorers had a 'need for novelty' and were thus more easily conditioned to a positive acceptance of the nouns. This would seem to imply that high RAT scorers preferred stimuli of a rousing nature, to those which were ordinary and often encountered. This is an extraverted characteristic and may be explained by the balance of cortical excitation – inhibition. Since the tilt is towards inhibition in the extravert, he appreciates strong stimuli which bring about excitation more effectively (Eysenck 1957, 1964). This hypothesis of preference for the unusual may be associated with that of arousal through cognitive dissonance at the unusual associations.

Remote associations can lead, of course, to either silly originality or creative relevance, dependent perhaps on the associative integrity of the steep hierarchies. Thus silliness in the young adolescent may or may not be predictive of adult creativity. At each stage in developmental history it is to be supposed that there is a relative depth and breadth in experiential patterning from the primal body image strata upwards, each stratum laying a foundation of steep and flat hierarchies for the next. Presumably the pattern of pervasive flat hierarchies must be preserved while more specific patterns relating to this or that area of experience are being developed in depth or 'steepness'. This implies the need for a general education in breadth for as long as it is possible to avoid specialisation. Early specialisation could result in a too narrowly flung system of flat hierarchies and a tendency for specific skills to be unrelated to general problems. When this occurs, it is possible that steepness of structure comes to prevail as a directing force in the mental operations of the gifted uncreative person. If this has occurred from the earliest years onwards thought tends to be grounded in greater sensori-motor and affective specificity. Such structuring is not without its cultural significance, for every society needs such minds to carry out administration at all levels. The precision of a mind which is not likely to go off at a tangent makes for the good organiser. For creative policy-making, however, the flat hierarchy system contributes a fluent and imaginative element. This permits of a broad intuitive synthesis, which includes not only the pattern of factual organisation but also the organiser's assessment of how far the plans will further ethical, social and other cultural ends.

Flat hierarchies are unlikely to be pervasive in their effects if experience within the family has been markedly restrictive. Restriction, however, does not necessarily arise when parents are strict. Such parents may merely impress upon their children a clear idea of what their standards are while at the same time affording latitude for the type of self expression which comes naturally. Strictness in such a case could encourage a need to achieve without detriment to the creative urge. As Wilson (1958) remarks, there is pretty general agreement that the facilitating conditions for creative thinking are encouragement of independent thought and permissiveness to new ideas, while conditions which produce fear of criticism are likely to inhibit the individual's expression of his original ideas. Such a long-standing emotional climate of fear of criticism during the crucial years of fantasy prior to the age of six years could set up what Cardno called an 'unkissed imagination'. He typifies such a person as an anxious executive, wrestling with business problems in too obsessional a manner, and unsupported by a feeling of reassurance that he is doing the right thing. This reassurance after decisions have been made is in all probability not rational but aesthetic, stemming from the 'flat' earlier systems. It is a comprehensive evaluation of the goodness or rightness of the decisions taken. A well-developed evaluative skill of this kind enables some people more than others to bear responsibility with equanimity and poise, and to be able to detach themselves for recreative purposes. According to Herbert Spencer (1855) one characteristic of aesthetic feelings is that they are separated from the functions requisite to sustain life, and that they cannot function if insecurity and danger is felt. He identifies the aesthetic sentiments of maturity with the play impulse of childhood. This nineteenth-century expression of the relationship between the autonomic and central nervous systems has relevance when considering the problem of accuracy and novelty in thinking. In young children's play, novelty stems from tangential association, while in their conforming behaviour an expected pattern is followed. Where the child is insecure there is too great a sustained tension in the emergency and vegetative functions, and energy is less diverted into fantasy and play. Cortical vigilance is concerned too early in life with the evasion of punitive consequences. In a permissive atmosphere facile intercommunication between the primary schemata is more frequent because there is less inhibition of behaviour where conflict is likely to occur, that is in matters of cleanliness, aggression, dependency and sex. In children a relaxed and ready appraisal of problems in these areas facilitate integrative action.

Such considerations illuminate the importance of a sense of humour for success in adult life. Getzels and Jackson (1960) in their study of adolescents with high I.Q.s but relatively low scores for creative thinking and those with high creative scores and relatively low I.Q.s asked the two groups to rank eight personality characteristics according to their importance for success in life. The two composite rankings were as follows:

High I.Q. (convergent thinkers)	*High Creative* (divergent thinkers)
1. character	1. emotive stability
2. emotive stability	2. sense of humour
3. goal directedness	3. character
4. creativity	4. wide range of interests
5. wide range of interests	5. goal directedness
6. high marks	6. creativity
7. I.Q.	7. high marks
8. sense of humour	8. I.Q.

It is of interest that the divergent thinkers cite first the very traits which research has shown to be associated with creativity, while the convergent have ascribed more importance to directional aspects of behaviour as in goal directedness and character. It would appear that for the divergent thinker creating is not something to be striven for but incidental to what is enjoyable. Such contrasting attitudinal complexes will tend to affect classroom behaviour and learning styles, in both the attainment and formation of concepts. Most concepts are both 'formed' and 'attained' in the sense that the spontaneous activities of early and middle childhood 'form' the groundwork by virtue of which 'attainment' through later instruction is rendered possible. Teachers of adolescent pupils are concerned for the most part with pupils' attainment of concepts, which they transmit symbolically through talk, chalk and textbook. Heuristic methods are too circuitous and involve an uneconomic use of time, and are for the most part unnecessary to the end to be achieved in cultural transmission. Accordingly, it is not surprising that the teachers' ratings for desirability as a student favoured the convergent pattern rather than the divergent in spite of both groups being of equal attainment and significantly superior to the general population of the school. Moreover, the divergent thinkers recognised their classroom styles of behaviour as somewhat contrary to what they deemed to be acceptable to their teachers ($r = -0{\cdot}25$) in contrast to the convergent thinkers who largely agreed with what they believed to be an acceptable style for teachers ($r = +0{\cdot}67$). This impression of contra-suggestibility on the part of the creative group is also conveyed by low correlation ($+0{\cdot}10$) between traits preferred for themselves and those they believed to be predictive of adult success. The convergent (High I.Q.) group showed high agreement between the two rankings ($+0{\cdot}81$). This is reflected too in the trends of their occupational choices. More than 50 per cent of creative adolescents expressed preferences for unusual professions such as adventurer, inventor and writer, while less than a quarter of the convergent thinkers did so. They chose instead conventional occupations such as lawyer, doctor and professor.

It would seem then that the two groups found pleasure in the formation of different types of mental schemata. Where the convergent thinker 'latches on' to a stimulus, the divergent uses it as a 'take-off' point. The convergent kind of thinking might be regarded as relatively stimulus bound and the divergent stimulus free. If, however, such associational buoyancy is to produce novelty which has social value and significance and satisfies reality criteria, it must be checked against the stimulus-bound essentials of the situation. The capacity to take-off from a stimulus is most evident in the normal fantasies of early childhood, but even when the technical skills of literacy are established, it is frequently manifest in early adolescence, especially where the family atmosphere is one of trust and acceptance. For this reason 'silliness' is one of the adolescent traits which creates discomfort for parents. Such behaviour, however, though that of the unformed personality, is probably the germinal process of the novel and productive as distinct from the reproductive and conventional in human behaviour. The subjects of Getzels and Jackson's research were about thirteen years of age and this perhaps accounts for the fact that many of their associations were original rather than realistic. At a later stage of maturity the relevance and utility element in their originality should be increased. A follow-up study to ascertain under what conditions early originality matures into creativity would seem to be called for. As Houston and Mednick (1963) observe, however, any ability which serves to bring otherwise remote ideas into contiguity will facilitate a creative solution; any ability which serves to keep remote ideas from contiguous evocation will inhibit the creative solution. In their account of the introspections of eminent creative people this is well supported. This divergent style of processing data peculiar to any field of observation makes for creativity in that discipline. This is exemplified by serendipity in sciences such as geology where contiguous environmental appearance is important; by perceiving similarity of associative elements in poetry and the visual arts and music; by mediation where the use of symbols is mandatory as in mathematics, chemistry and in any discipline having its special terminology. The 'brain storming' techniques which have been used in some American schools with a view to facilitating the 'take off' attitude towards stimuli are based on the theory that it is at this point that creativity is annulled. Whether such belated exercises in free association would radically reorganise neural structure is doubtful, for it is clear that it is the interaction between divergent and convergent processes which produces the new idea or the novel solution. It is more probable that contact with original minds 'speaking as they think' will induce an orientation which has the right balance between stimulus-free and stimulus-bound content, for in this case a model of the whole integrated process will be presented. Such a model would exemplify a creative set in the face of problematic ambiguous situations, which maintains an attitude poised between the usual, expected, defensive, safe, acquisitive and conforming on the one hand, and on the other the novel, speculative, open, growth producing and inventive. The I.Q. test does not allow of novelty, but represents a skill in recognising that which is usually considered appropriate and correct. By virtue of its usual multiple choice structure it is stimulus bound. The open-ended question is essential in a test of creative intelligence, but this, of course, vitiates its reliability so much as to render it useless for comparing one individual with another in a standardised way.

II. MOTIVATIONAL ASPECTS

1 *Purposive behaviour*

General cognitive style and general motivational structure are inextricably related and can be separated only for analytical purposes. Such concepts as 'set', 'atmosphere effect', 'determining tendency', 'einstellung', 'level of aspiration' and 'orienting response' have been employed to designate the motivated cognitive act. Perhaps the common meaning of these terms is that all imply a process which initiates and sustains a behavioural sequence in its course. In much earlier research, such phenomena were studied as will-acts, and the greater variety of terms used now arises from the differentiation brought about within the generic concept of 'will'. Some of these terms have more reference to the initiating phase and others to the prolongation and maintenance of the course of the behaviour. They are concerned not so much with the content of thought but with its intensity, endurance and flexibility. Perceptual set, for example, may be defined as readiness to perceive the environment in a certain way. Under experimental conditions this would be predetermined by instructions given to the subjects concerning what they were to look for. Postman and Bruner (1949), working with older gifted adolescents, studied the effect of single set, compared with multiple set, on clarity of attention. The perceptual data to which the instructions referred were pairs of words printed crosswise on cards and exposed tachistoscopically for a fraction of a second. One word was a food or colour word and the other a neutral word. During single set exposure they were instructed to look for words which had reference to food (or colour); during multiple set exposures they were instructed to identify either a food or a colour word. Sharpness of tuning of set was measured by the extent to which the first guess was congruent with the instructions. This is tantamount to expecting that the subjects would tend to recognise a food word if well set to do so, since set may vary in intensity ranging from a vague, unverbalised readiness to an intense and explicit expectation. Such variety could be present in any one subject during the course of the experiment.

The instructions which structured the set of the subjects ran thus: "Your task is to see the colour word as fast as you can. Sometimes the colour word will be in the slanting-up position, sometimes in the down position. Keep your eyes on the red dot. The words will appear there. Ready!"

The multiple set tuning led to an increase in incongruent hypotheses as to what the word might be. With simple set 72·6 per cent of first guesses were congruent, under multiple set 64·8. The authors concluded that sharpness of tuning varies along a continuum having vigilance at the positive pole and at the negative one a state of mind which might be termed anoetic, i.e. passively receptive of what is presented, without conscious organisation. They also noted big individual differences in reaction to a change in set. Some subjects found it more difficult than others to revert to single set after a period of multiple set. This implies that the type of selectivity which ignores as well as notices is important. In exploring and scanning situations outside the laboratory, both selective noticing and selective ignoring are usually involved. Simple and multiple set are also operative, now searching for cues on a multiple front, then deciding to ignore some which do not appear to be relevant. Anyone who has learned to drive a car knows how difficult it is at first to ignore cues selectively. Change of set tends to raise perceptual thresholds in some people to a marked extent, inducing a decrease in perceptual sensitivity and thereby weakening any mental operations, including relevant recall, which follow in its train. Difficulties of this kind in the potentially gifted may account for much failure to fulfil promise indicated by I.Q. test prediction. Terman's (1947) 50 per cent of gifted children who fail to reach college will be accounted for to some extent by the bad study habits to which these characteristics may give rise.

Razran's (1961) study of the relationship between orienting response and habit has relevance here. He was concerned with autonomic aspects of the alerting process as measured by vascular changes in forehead and fingers. These were modified in such a way as to suggest habituation with a second application of the stimulus, but the original vigilance response tended to be restored, if the same stimulus were presented in a novel setting. He concludes that when habit sets in, orienting responses disappear. At the first application of the stimulus, vascular dilation in the forehead coincided with restriction in the fingers, suggesting cortical vigilance with inhibition of motor-response. At the second application both sets of blood vessels dilated, as though the organism was now prepared to react to the stimulus immediately. Razran also studied the occulo-motor chart which results when no instruction is given, and when a general or specific instruction is given. In the absence of instruction he found that the orienting responses had an investigatory character. When instruction is given they are vigilant in type. After examining the three patterns of response he concluded that orienting responses may be of these two types and that they are not consummatory but pre-reactive, preparatory and pre-adaptive. The importance of these responses for the organisation of behaviour is suggested by the fact that they are absent in the initial stages of response in schizophrenic and brain-damaged patients. These are notoriously incapable of sustained purposive action, in all probability for this very reason. The relationship between orienting response and set might be sought in Postman and Bruner's dimension of sharpness of tuning. When a person first 'sets' himself to do something orienting responses provide the sharpness of tuning at the vigilance end of their continuum. With habituation orienting responses die out and tuning is at the anoetic end – a state which is more conserving of neural energy. Stimuli, however, are seldom presented in identical situations, which ensures that reactions are seldom completely habitual, and this maintains the orienting vigilance of the organism without which he appears to disintegrate. Such constant tuning is necessary for his psychological comfort as is seen in the discomfort of boredom and the agony of prolonged sensory deprivation. It is perhaps true to say that the orienting response is the pivot on which all re-structuring of mind and brain depends, for strong orienting responses imply investigatory vigilance.

Weak orienting responses may be associated with what Woodworth and Sells (1935) have called atmosphere effect in verbal thinking. This is a global approach to cues which leads to erroneous impressions. Weak orienting responses are also present when mechanisation through repetition in problem solution sets in, and also when reasoning is insufficiently analytic. Woodworth and Sells studied atmosphere effect among college students and found it to result in invalid conclusions when the relationships inherent in the premises were not clearly seen. It is admirably illustrated in the question, 'Polk is pronounced poke, the L is silent, and Folk is pronounced foke also with a silent L, and the white of an egg is pronounced – ?' It is the rare subject that responds 'Albumen'. Sells (1936) regards this as an illustration of the fact that verbal habits can operate as a substitute for thought. Deficiency in orientation and set is one strong reason for inadequate vigilance and exploration of the implications of verbal data, and in consequence the habitual 'feel' of the premises is acted upon. Given also an affective atmosphere, arising from projection of hostile feelings, and the stage is set for such phenomena as prejudice. If the rationalisation of such judgments is analysed down into syllogistic form, the premises and conclusion would read something like this

'All enemies are unpredictable
Jones is unpredictable
Therefore Jones is an enemy'

or more generally the simple converse is tacitly held to be true, 'All enemies are unpredictable, therefore all unpredictable people are enemies.' Except for the fact that the attitude is expressed verbally, it is not far from that achieved by the child of twelve months of age when sobering at strangers. The simple converse of the universal affirmative is regarded as valid because of its 'feel'. From this phenomenon and the findings of Woodworth and Sells it can be deduced that sharpness of tuning or adequate orienting responses are essential for realistic and valid thinking.

Mechanisation in problem solution is of the same order and was studied by Luchins (1942, 1950). After solving a number of problems using an identical procedure manipulating two vessels of known capacity for obtaining a third amount, their subjects were given problems which could be solved by a simpler and more direct procedure. Almost all continued to use the circuitous method, and Luchins concluded that an individual tends to persist in the use of a stereotyped mode of response, until some dramatic occurrence causes him to start searching for new methods. This was found to be true even in a group selected for mathematical skill and intelligence. Such vague warnings as 'Don't be blind' had little ameliorating effect, and only with older adolescents were more specific warnings concerning a different procedure effective. No consistent change with age and educational level was apparent, but Luchins (1942) did find that the group most immune from mechanisation was bright, and aged ten to fourteen years. In these, then, it is to be concluded that questing orienting responses more frequently brought about a change of set. Such questing and vigilance in orientation can become a habit in itself, where the variety of stimuli in the environment frequently arouse them. A readiness to orient afresh is thereby established and the person is regarded as being especially responsive to his environment. It is in all probability for this reason that Luchins found less evidence of einstellung or mechanisation in thinking in so-called progressive schools. These findings concerning mechanisation in problem solution may be generalised under three headings. Firstly, vigilant propensities in symbolic learning are most easily engendered during early adolescence in the gifted; secondly, in later adolescence, a multiple set can interfere with habitual response if instruction to this end is given; and thirdly, a varied environment with opportunity for active participation can reduce the amount of mental inertia which is usually associated with problem solution.

2 *Adaptability*

The concept of einstellung is related to the dimension of rigidity – flexibility in mental functioning, and this in turn has relevance for a study of concrete and abstract levels in thought content. For Goldstein and Scheerer (1941) abstract and concrete attitudes are capacity levels of the total personality. Concreteness in thinking is a normal phenomenon during the middle years of childhood, but as a predominant form it should give place to abstraction as maturity is approached. The concrete attitude differs from the abstract in its specificity, for thought and action are directed by the immediate claims of one particular aspect of the cognised object. The abstract attitude has differing qualities in that it transcends the immediately given situation and so is not of necessity ego-involved; it tends to have an element of mental set which is easily verbalised; it questingly hovers between analysis and synthesis and is conceptually hierarchic. It thus facilitates forward planning and hypothesis making. It is clear from these characteristics that the abstract attitude can be assumed towards concrete material and that this is necessary for success in performance tests of intelligence such as Kohs Block Design. Luchins (1951) investigated the relationship between rigidity or einstellung in problem solution and the concrete-abstract dimension of Goldstein and Scheerer. He used twelve pairs of words from the similarities test of the Wechsler-Bellvue scale, and four groups of subjects characterised by distinguishable degrees of rigidity or mechanisation in problem solution. A few significant differences were found between the most and least rigid of the four groups. These were for the pairs of words egg – seed, poem – statue and eye – ear. In describing the similarity of egg and seed, and poem and statue, 24 per cent of the least rigid group gave functional or concrete reasons as against 50 per cent of such replies in the most rigid group. For the eye – ear item 44 per cent of the least rigid gave abstract responses as against 14 per cent in the most rigid. A similar contrast of 60 per cent as against

32 per cent was found for poem – statue. It would seem, then, since nine of the twelve pairs of similar words yielded no group differences on the concrete-abstract dimension, that it manifests itself only under certain conditions. One of these may be the need for the material to be marginal in difficulty between the individuals present and future levels of maturation. Where this is so a lapse into concreteness may tend to take place in those with relatively weak abstract attitudes. Two items which showed this were among the more difficult. The other condition is exemplified by the eye – ear item. This pair suggests of itself a functional definition, since both serve the individual in his functioning, but in spite of this more of the flexible subjects gave abstract similarities than was the case in the rigid group. Thus the flexible group may have a greater tendency to accelerate the growth of its capacity for abstraction and a more stable abstract attitude when stimuli suggest functional concreteness. It is assumed that this trait is independent of intelligence but that it is significant for level of maturity in personality development. The concrete attitude would seem to imply weak verbal orientation and perhaps a lack of the flexibility which facilitates breadth of scansion. Flexibility in this context could arise from the degree of arousal during the orienting phase.

3 *The need to achieve*

In Western society there is much preoccupation with the problem of self realisation. The individual is looked upon as a potential which is more likely than not to remain unrealised to some extent. Concern with social self realisation is implicit in studies of the authoritarian personality and leadership; with intellectual fulfilment in studies of creativity, the need to achieve, and levels of aspiration. Longitudinal and correlational studies have examined the familial and socio-economic antecedents of these trends. Adorno (1950), Buss (1955), Beloff (1958) and Allport (1960) are all agreed that the authoritarian personality is too acquiescent towards people in authority, that he feels comfortable when supporting stereotyped and conventional norms, and likes his perceptual and cognitive fields to be well structured. Among the student population he tends to be obedient rather than creative. This conformity suggests an underlying insecurity and anxiety for which obedience is an unconscious defence. Its antecedents may be seen perhaps in maternal protection of sons between the ages of six and ten in the Fels study (Kagan and Moss 1962). This is associated with an expectation of rejection during the next four years and later with social anxiety. This may be related to Adorno's postulation of the latent hostility of the authoritarian personality, which could be projected in the form of an expectation of rejection. According to the findings of the Fels study these middle years of childhood are also significant for N-ach when the child is expedited in his learning by the impetus of parental expectation. This is the reverse of over-protection. Thus both socially, and in self achievement, the over-protected child is privated of an essential learning contingency stemming from spontaneous and free endeavour in the social and academic fields. For this attitude to become pathological, maternal over-protection would need perhaps to reflect her own insecurity. In this case her concern for the child would be subordinate to her own needs and he would tend to perceive her actions as inconsistent and incongruent with his own desires. Her capriciousness would also cause him to be conflicted about feeling secure in her acceptance on the one hand and obeying his ego-impulses thereby incurring her rejection on the other. Over-protection of sons, however, could conceivably arise from apprehension for him which was consistent and objectively oriented though culturally a-normal. In this case protection would be less likely to leave unconscious residues of hostility and insecurity and merely result in attenuated experiential structuring. Within these narrowed limits he could conceivably be creative because not too insecure and anxious. This anxiety concerning social contacts and practical enterprises could be enhanced by the mother's social withdrawal. Her own timidity would prevent her from presenting a good model for her son in social behaviour.

Rogers' (1959) delineation of the characteristics of the potentially creative person are in direct contrast, in that self standards are more important than externally provided ones and that there is pleasure in resolving ambiguity which arises in the course of spontaneous exploration. The activity and enjoyment may spring from temperamental sources but as Jones and Morris concluded in their study of temperament and values, receptivity, self control and self sufficiency are acquired traits. Rogers' creative person is more concerned with expression than communication. This is a somewhat ambiguous statement, but it in all probability refers to the fact that communication is a secondary motive and incidental rather than essential to expression. The antecedents of this type of character have been suggestively investigated by the retrospective assessments of the home backgrounds of creative adolescents by Getzels and Jackson (1962). Parents of original, divergent thinkers liked their children's friends to have a sense of values, keen interests and frankness. The parents of intelligent children who were uncreative valued their children's friends according to whether they were of good family, good manners and studious. It is not difficult to form the opinion that these two sets of preferences in the parents should be correlated with their expectations regarding their children's behaviour. Both appeared to be equally stimulating concerning school achievement since scores of the high creative and high I.Q. groups did not differ. Parents of original children, however, stimulated N-ach by different techniques. Since the styles of both parental expectation and children's preferences are so consistently patterned, it is possible that the traits measured were largely affected by constitutional factors. The two samples were highly selected for intellectual capacity and by techniques which would throw into relief introvert-extravert characteristics. They thus appear to be type extremes in which both caretaking styles and cognitive processes may be influenced markedly by genetic factors.

In less selected samples, where genetic factors are randomised, or held constant, the effects of caretaking should appear more clearly. Ausubel (1954) summarises the traits of the successful student as having better study habits, more compensatory than defence mechanisms and more realistic levels of aspiration. They are deemed to excel in such personality traits as dependability, self reliance, ambition, investigativeness and persistence. These qualities were predictive of performance in adult vocational spheres. Without exception they appear to be acquired rather than stemming from temperament. This psychological profile implies consistent training, and it is not surprising that McClelland (1953) found a positive correlation between high N-ach and a felt lack of love or perceived severity of upbringing. He also noted a resistance to group conformity in his N-ach group. This latter element is attributed by him to internalisation of the consistency of the parent. This independence is perhaps related to the self sufficiency noted by Rosen and Andrade (1959). This they regarded as incorporated from the paternal model in boys, while achievement motivation appeared to be due to maternal influence. In girls N-ach appears to be best fostered by maternal criticism and some conditional acceptance during the first three years (Kagan and Moss 1962), and this too supports McClelland's correlation between perceived severity and high N-ach. These findings suggest that any failure to achieve in high N-ach subjects would be accompanied by considerable anxiety, which in the well-adjusted would be compensated for by renewed effort rather than defensive self excuse. Where there is uncertainty about the self, Gruen (1945) found a tendency to be uncertain about whether goals would be achieved, though they tended to be set high. A pessimistic self image was associated with low goal setting. Normally levels of aspiration are adaptively functional in that they tend to keep goals consistent with perceived reality. Where, however, uncertainty is expressed in high goal setting, it may be concluded that a high level of aspiration was reinforced and subsequent failure excused. Low levels of aspiration in the pessimists could result if failure had been punished by blame or rejection. Starbuck (1963) has pointed out that from day to day levels of aspiration are highly dependent upon recent or similar experience, but that their general character is determined by cultural background, long-run achievement history and social forces. This generalised level of aspiration provides the latent element which emerges in short-run goals as they contribute to long-range projects. In other words, exercise of aspiration and its reinforcement structures a capacity for set and orientation. Such capacities tend to be highly developed in the gifted adolescent after sixteen years of age, because long-run goals are more clearly conceived in abstract terms and thus permeate minor motivational complexes.

The review of experimental evidence on the exceptional child, by Margary and Eichorn (1961), suggests that the adolescent with high N-ach who is successful has a much reduced chance of popularity among peers. His only hope of general social acceptance resides in his athletic prowess provided he is not also regarded as too given to bookish pursuits. Such a social force could conceivably delay or destroy the emergence of N-ach in persons where it had weak antecedent reinforcement. In a cultural matrix which is achievement oriented, such conflicts are certain to arise because of rejective envy. Such cultural pressures also tend to increase a sense of under-achievement in those who are intelligent but who have poor self concepts. These adolescents tend to feel that the gap between perception of present status and their aspirations is too great to bridge. They tend also to see their parents as dominating and as having poor morale. Since this could account for their pessimism and self devaluation, they are probably correct in their assessments. They often defend themselves from despair by resorting to wishful thinking, that chance may suddenly make things right. This portrait, culled from the evidence on under-achievers by Margary and Eichorn, contrasts with that of Strodtbeck (1958) concerning the conditions which foster strong achievement motivation. These are summarised as being present in democratic families with a relatively powerful mother. This facilitates a son's ability to move to new loyalties in larger systems outside the family, without rupturing family controls. A permissive rather than a dominant caretaking style would inevitably afford opportunity to experience more widely throughout childhood. Ambition too appears to have little to do with socio-economic class membership as such, but to be closely related to the attitude of the family towards its occupational status. For example, among lower middle-class boys of high intellectual ability, Kahl (1953) found the son was less apt to consider going to college where the family was content to maintain their present standards of living. Among those who wished to better themselves, a college education was seen as a means to that end within the family.

These findings have considerable relevance for the education of girls. Where an educated father respects competence and independence in a daughter she is thereby reinforced in these attitudes and is likely to respect them in her children. Moreover, an educated mother produces in her son a respect for competence in women and a willingness to depend on that of his wife (Kagan and Moss 1962). Education of both parents therefore perpetuates the democratic atmosphere from generation to generation, which fosters rising I.Q.s and good N-ach. For a boy, identification with the father is important for his assumption of masculine roles. It is to be expected, however, that the earlier identification with the mother should affect the transition to that with the father, and this would depend largely on the extent to which husband and wife were harmoniously related. Kimball's (1953) intensive case studies of brilliant under-achievers and intelligent boys who were achieving normally suggest that this dual pattern of identification was not present. In the case of the under-achievers there tended to be identification only with the mother, with a failure of the father image.

Freudian theory is undoubtedly responsible for this concentration on the child's perception of the parent, and all the evidence suggests that early models stem from a parental source, but Nason's (1958) study of circumstance in relation to achievement suggests that the etiology is more complex. He holds that the number of motivators missing constitute a general circumstance of under-achievement. His pattern of circumstance includes (1) personality adjustment, (2) pupil's and parent's level of academic aspiration, (3) pupil's and parent's choice of future vocation, (4) pupil's inspiration or choice of encouragement. All of these factors appear to be contributive but none more than any other. If all these circumstances are favourable, the gifted adolescent is assured of membership in the top quartile for achievement. Contrary to common assumption, low scores on the personality test if accompanied by high scores on the other factors did not militate against high achievement.

4 *Maturity of personality*

A gifted person who is maladjusted in personality may be capable of arriving at a reconciling frame of reference for himself in the universe at large and in his intimate circle through insight. Fromm (1941) stresses the need for such a Weltan-schaung with which to reduce to rational dimensions the contradictions, puzzles, anomalies and incompatibilities of perceived existence. Facility in adding steepness to relatively broad-based conceptual hierarchies during adolescence can result in a comprehensive and articulate viewpoint. This will tend to happen where there is a felt need for such stability, and the individual is exposed to cultural influences which will inculcate symbols for the elaboration of general ideas. All religious and metaphysical systems and inclusive ideologies serve the same fundamental need: to relate man significantly to the universe, to himself and to his fellow-men.

Fromm reverses Freud's opinion that religion is a form of universal neurosis. Instead, he regards neurosis as a private form of religion. With Jung, he regards the desire for a frame of this sort as man's most fundamental and all inclusive need. He needs as William James pointed out to feel at home in the Universe. Such attitudes and nascent ideologies are provided for the majority of adolescents by their upbringing. In most no profound disillusionment is undergone and they tend to carry on in the same vein (Ausubel 1954). The chief influences which bring about change in religious belief, when it does occur, are those of teachers, peer-groups, literature, ministers of religion, various organisations such as the Y.M.C.A. and exposure to other faiths or creeds. Some are shocked into preoccupation with religious themes by the loss of a close relative or friend, or by an awareness of an injustice done (Douvan and Kaye 1957).

Allport (1951) regards the religious sentiment as having the characteristic of all dominant motivational structures which belong to maturity. It is the out-growth of many successive acts of discrimination. It is differentiated, comprehensive and consistent. It is dynamic and heuristic. It is therefore one of the 'propriate' or ego-involved motivational systems. It is to be distinguished from 'opportunist' patterns of conduct which are linked in complexes geared to earlier biological and psychological motivational patterns, and are thus not harmoniously integrated with the current system of 'propriate' motives. He expresses an individual's maturity in terms of the autonomy of his motivational schemata. By this is meant that at each phase of development there is a comprehensive or integrated modification of the primary system. Thus all that was immature is still present and operative, but subordinated to a schema which tempers it to accord with a mature perception of situations. For example, if mature judgment deems it wise to indulge in a slight temper tantrum, to fend off the unwarranted encroachments of another person, an adaptive selection is made from a repertoire of tantrum reactions to suit the situation. Autonomy of such a trait as that which deals with the encroachments of others would be evident in the aptness of the selection from a repertoire of response, which had been maturing throughout infancy and childhood. It is seldom that elements of less maturity than those of middle childhood are re-evoked in their pristine condition, but even in a well-integrated person some frustrating situations may be seen as calling for a three-year-old stance and emotional expression. A religious sentiment is dominatingly autonomous when all role systems are integrated by its terms of reference. If the religion does not provide a complete coverage of all roles, to that extent it increases the chances that 'opportunist' traits will co-exist with propriate ones, thus leaving interstices for the entry of superstition. In the case of any particular person, it increases the chances of hypocrisy. Organised religion is necessary in any culture to maintain exercise of function, not only in practising members of a church, but in society at large. The same is true of any doctrine or belief and its organised adherents. Exercise of function is a sine qua non of all behavioural continuity.

In their summary of the motivational components uncovered by recent research, Cattell and Horn (1963) describe one component as the desired-ideal-self element in personality. By this is meant the super ego demands which have as yet been unmet by the ego. These yearnings in gifted young people are tested and revised in behaviour which stems at any one moment from a complex composed of personality structure, role, mood and situational characteristics, but of these role is the empirical spearhead of growth. Through role functioning he is able to observe the consequences of his performance, which are processed back into earlier response systems, causing erroneous reactions to be inhibited and others to be reinforced. The structuring of reaction through role is performed, of course, in a verbal context, and in the highly educated and gifted individual a rich vocabulary elucidates implication to the point of generalisation and provides representations of conduct which may become precepts. Example too presented by others may be verbally delineated and exert cultural influence through history and literature and drama. Cultural heritage is, however, translated into social practice only through the medium of role performance. By the age of eighteen years the gifted adolescent is capable of placing the interests of society before his own, in suggesting solutions to hypothetical problems, and tends to be concerned least frequently about family and friends. Generally speaking adolescents at this age tend to be motivated in order of frequency thus: (1) Responsibility to society or country; (2) towards school; (3) towards the desirability of an ideal; and (4) by the practical utility of self interest and prudence. Sympathy or shared feelings with others is least frequently regarded as a desirable motive in solving problems. It tends to be found chiefly among girls at a normative level, and very rarely at both a normative and realistic level (Sumotirto 1962). This suggests that the more able adolescent by the age of eighteen years has acquired a viewpoint suited to the responsibilities he is likely to assume when vocationally prepared, and it is to be expected that the majority of both gifted and less than gifted adolescents will have achieved a stable footing on a career ladder by the age of twenty-five years (Carter 1944). Moreover, matrimony and the founding of a family usually during the third decade brings about further maturation and creates frequently a willingness to abandon agnosticism and youthful cynicism for a guiding hypothetical framework of belief to which he becomes committed (Allport 1951). The maturation process continues and accelerates with every adjustment of role within the family and in society at large, rendering the individual less 'adolescent' than he was. His management of the problems created by his changing circumstance is rendered more stable and consistent by the conceptual generality of his awareness of principles or values. His ability to distinguish between expediency and what accords with the national mores is perhaps the crucial aspect of his social awareness, which distinguishes him from the majority of people. Moreover, it is highly probable that he will be articulate concerning these distinctions and so be able to exert a catalytic effect on current social attitudes. In order to perform this role, however, he must care about society in general. Such a concern stems from an emotive structure activating his insight and response tendencies. It is designed and reinforced by social appraisal of independence in action and judgment throughout his infancy, childhood and adolescence.

CHAPTER VIII

Learning and motivation in maturity

The concept of maturity can be defined along several lines, but for the purpose of the present discussion a three-fold approach will be made, namely: biological, psychological and social. Biological maturity will determine a person's general physiological fitness to cope with responsibility, his rate of ageing and his expectation of life. Psychological maturity is a measure of his adaptive capacity and self awareness. Social maturity will be indicated by the effectiveness of his habits or manners and the roles he assumes. Since maturity is regarded as a relatively short peak condition between growth and decline, these three categories can serve also to designate areas of growth and ageing. It is generally accepted that biological factors are the most fundamental pace-makers of the organism's development and decline, but it is becoming increasingly recognised that experience is an essential aspect of growth, and exercise of function a defence against the premature onset of senescence. This may be the reason why individual differences in behavioural capacities widen among successive age groups after the age of thirty. This increase in heterogeneity may imply that cultural expectations are more uniform while the organism is growing and more diverse after this age. As age advances, in democratic societies, an institutionalized imposition of norms gives way to more autonomous motives, and it is a matter of common observation that people go their own ways as they get older. This autonomous selectivity increases the range of individual differences in so far as they arise from circumstantial variation.

I. BIOLOGICAL MATURITY

1 *Physiological changes*

Genetic indications of maturity occur between the ages of thirty and thirty-five in most people. This is the age at which the pituitary gland, the master gland among the endocrines, reaches maximum size and weight, to remain stable at this level throughout life. At the same age the maximum level of muscular strength throughout the body is attained by most people. After thirty there is a decline in muscle strength although the skeletal muscles increase in bulk and density until fifty (Fisher and Birren 1947). Correlated with muscular strength is speed of sensori-motor reaction. For example, foot movements such as those used in accelerator-brake changes reach their peak reaction times in the twenties (de Silva 1936). Thereafter, providing the skill is frequently exercised, there is a slow decline in speed. This slowing up of reaction could arise from either a sensory source, i.e. the appraisal of cues in perception, or from a reduction in the speed of neural transmission. The writer leans towards the former explanation because of the increased difficulty with age in reacting to complex as distinct from simple stimuli, and because there is no perceptible change in the conduction velocity of nerves until round about sixty (Wagman and Lesse 1952). Further discussion of the differential reactions to complex stimuli is included later in the chapter in the section on psychological maturity, and this will clarify the present hypothesis.

2 *The central nervous system*

The evidence suggests then that the middle years of life witness a decline in the capacity to deal quickly and efficiently with complex environmental problems but there are also physiological areas of motor response about which little is known and which may affect, through feed-back, perception of situations. For example, the function of the cerebellum is a co-ordinating one on the response side of behaviour. This organ was not included in the first chapter as one associated with motivation and learning, but it deserves mention in connection with the process of unlearning. In graphic representations of the CNS, it is easily recognised as situated posterior and inferior to the main spheres, and like them as having two convoluted lobes (Fig. 1). Little has been learned about the cerebellum since Bell, in 1826, described it as receiving a heavy input from the voluntary muscles involved in the control of movement. Its receptor or sensory side then is in no way directly in contact with the environment and it does not subserve consciousness. It appears to operate more as a servo-mechanistic refiner of movements made under conscious direction. Thus its function is regulatory in a general sense and structures no specific movement. The organisation of the movement itself is programmed in the cortical sensori-motor areas. This may mean that the cerebellum is a sort of computer which can compare the true in-put from the operative muscle, with the auditory or visual representation of the goal and the proprioceptive indication of the limb's position. The fact that such structured behaviour is not dependent in a primary sense on the cerebellum is indicated when its ablation leaves the pattern of movement intact. What is affected however by cerebellar assault is the timing of the components of a movement (Ruch 1952).

Deterioration of the cellular structure of the cerebellum with age has been studied by Ellis (1920), who set the norm for more rapid decline at the approximate age of forty-five years. His sixty-three subjects ranged from twelve to ninety-two years and his cell count indicated an acceleration of loss during the fourth decade, till by about forty-five years it was reduced by a third. There is a loss from within cells of the large granules first noticed by Nissl in 1892, and sometimes referred to as 'Nissl substance'. Such cellular structures are not confined to the cerebellum and a similar loss is evident in other parts of the CNS. This deterioration would appear to rise from three sources which interact differentially. Firstly it is an inevitable process, genetically determined; secondly it is the result of failure to maintain functioning in relation to these tissues; thirdly it is the result of covert pathological assault. The genetic factor is perhaps paramount in the increased impetus of senescence after fifty, and the relative stability of more refined co-ordination between twenty and fifty. Exercise of function as a maintainer of youthfulness in the mature may be exemplified in the slower rate of decline in speed of finger movements compared with foot reaction times. That the CNS is prematurely aged by pathological assault is apparent in the effects of alcoholic excess. Korsakoff's syndrome might be regarded as the premature onset of senility in cortical mediation of attention and immediate recall. The interaction of the three determinants gives rise to a change in normative levels with age. For example, in reacting to a constantly changing stimulus with accuracy, e.g. the pursuit rotor, seventy-five per cent of elderly people occur below the average level of young people in their prime (Miles 1931). It is, however, relevant for the mental hygiene of the elderly to remember that 1 in 4 retain their capacities for co-ordinated movement at the level enjoyed by the average person of thirty or better. These favoured ones may have been those who were among the best of their age group when young.

II. PSYCHOLOGICAL MATURITY

The period of life round about thirty may be regarded as a peak period for the type of motivation stemming from know-how. This tendency of liking to do what can be done well first achieves motivational primacy in middle childhood. In middle-age it operates in a reverse direction.

Instead of new activities being made possible by growth, established activities are engaged in because potentiality for them is still present. This is particularly noticeable in the games of maturity. Skill in ball games requiring stamina, strength and speed tends to reach its peak in the twenties, in car racing in the thirties and in slow deliberate ball games such as golf and billiards after thirty and before forty (Lehman 1953). In this succession, speed, strength and impulse give way to deliberation, strategy and judgment. It is not difficult to align these manifestations with the physiological changes adumbrated above.

1. *Increase in individual differences*

Since psychological maturation is brought about by organism-environment interaction, it is to be expected that physiology will affect rate of learning and environmental opportunity its extent. But at all ages rate of learning is itself a limiting factor on extent, for restructuring of behaviour is proportional to what has been learned already. This means that the slow learner at any one time in his growth has received less imprint from what he has been exposed to than a quick learner similarly exposed. He cannot, therefore, move to the same new stage of skill as his contemporaries. Moreover, by the age of thirty he exhibits a relative general backwardness which can never be remedied except to some extent by special effort in certain areas. An example of this was the remedial work carried out with illiterate recruits in the last war. But wherever this was successful, it is safe to deduce that this learning could have taken place prior to maturity had motivation been suitably stimulated. For most people, cultural pressures at school and work hold motivation to learn constant until maturity is reached.

Thus between the ages of thirty and thirty-five individual differences among the population at large are in all probability least widespread. By this is meant that on the whole the slower learners have been educated to their maximum capacity and the average person encouraged to develop potentiality as near that of the able section of the community as possible. Institutionalised scholastic and industrial pressures are certain to create such a trend when they are comprehensively applied. This is reflected in Western society, in the size of correlations between psychological traits at various age levels. All the evidence suggests that they are relatively low at the peak of maturity but higher among younger and older people. For example, Balinsky (1941) found correlations of 0·43 between the sub-tests of the Wechsler-Bellvue sub-tests at the ages of eight years and fifty years, but one of only 0·18 at twenty-nine. He attributes this to a gradual differentiation of abilities followed by reorganisation and restriction. This is tantamount to saying that learning is paced more and more by educational influences as maturity is approached, bringing about a reduction of the differences between people, considerable as these may seem. At the same time educational influences become more and more specialised. Balinsky would regard individual choice in specialisation as giving rise to the lower correlation at twenty-nine. The Wechsler-Bellvue sub-tests, however, are not based on specialised areas of knowledge, and it is therefore unlikely that any special influences could produce differentiation in such general skills. Vocabulary, memory span, information, comprehension, arranging pictures in a story sequence and so on are skills which a person exercises under normal conditions in everyday life. An additional cause may be a reduction in variance, owing to gradual increase in the homeogeneity of the population brought about by the common features of everyday experience. If this is so, a similar explanation in reverse must be found for the increase in heterogeneity after the age of thirty-five years. Perhaps the biggest single explanation of this is lack of exercise of some functions. If there are certain kinds of activities which tend to be abandoned because they require speed or close attention, it is to be expected that the tail of ability will lengthen in these unpractised skills. Thus the heterogeneity arises from loss of skill rather than from increase in the spread of ability at the positive end. The well-exercised areas are indicated by the norms of the sub-tests of the Wechsler-Bellvue scale which do, or do not, hold up with age. The analyses of Wechsler and others (Hunt 1949) suggest that there is least loss in the information and comprehension sub-tests which are to all intent tests of general knowledge. There appears, however, to be some inconsistency in the findings concerning the effect of age on ability, and the explanation of this is to be found perhaps in the sampling of both tests and population. Where the test employed is suitable because the testees are constrained in everyday life to exercise the functions implied in its items, there will be less deterioration with age. For example, manual workers asked to do a pencil and paper test will produce lower mean scores with age than clerical workers because they are less accustomed to use reading and writing skills. Thus the new general factor which emerges after thirty is determined perhaps by differences among occupational classes in the exercise of the skills involved in the testing. The manual worker may find himself less able to afford time for reading as family chores in house and garden are added to his working hours, even though as a younger man he enjoyed a good detective novel. Moreover, if personal responsibilities call for more money, overtime working tends to reduce his opportunities for exercise in reading and writing still further. If to this is added the mental passivity which accompanies physical fatigue, it is clear that the general vocational patterns of society could operate to increase individual differences. This would be particularly true of skills subserving the higher cognitive processes which were largely involved in the process of occupational selection at an earlier age. Thus, although evidence from twin studies suggest that the senescent potential is inborn (Birren 1964) the environmental factor after thirty is perhaps of greater importance for mental testing than before that age.

2 *Deterioration in the cognitive processes*

In view of this hypothesis it is interesting to examine those aspects of mental functioning which decline with age. Perhaps the most crucial of these is capacity for multiple set. Set is an instruction to the self to do something when a particular stimulus occurs. If the instruction concerns only one kind of stimulus, the set is regarded as single, when several, multiple. The effect of ageing on multiple set is more in evidence than on single set. Naturally set is involved in the learning of new tasks and a number of researches suggest that orientation to new situations differs in style and efficiency as people get older. For example, a research by Uhlmann and Saltz (1965) on maintenance of set against the suggestion of contrary stimuli in adults is remarkably similar to the experiments of Martsinovskaya reported in Chapter IV above. The subjects of the adult study were skilled men between the ages of twenty-five and sixty-four. They were selected in two groups of fifty according to whether they were adept or weak in retention of self instruction, in two tasks which were confusingly similar. In the first task they were shown the words red, green, yellow and blue, each printed in one of the other three colours. These colour names were exposed one at a time in a long series, and the men were asked to react as quickly as possible by saying the first letter of the word. They were then shown the same words, but asked this time to say as quickly as possible the first letter of the name of the colour in which the word was printed. They had thus to selectively ignore a colour name in order to name a colour at speed. The fifty men who could do this best were termed high differentiators and the fifty who were more frequently confused were termed low differentiators. These two groups were then given a test of mental abilities used in business and industrial situations and also of memory for an account of a building explosion which was read to them. Group differences in the results were found for the memory test but not for the test of business and industrial skills. The high differentiators remembered more detail of the less dramatic kind in the story than the low differentiators. This appertained for those over the mean age of forty-seven years as much as for those younger. When, however, the mean recall score for the high differentiators among the older men was compared with those for the two younger groups, they were found to be equal to the poorer younger group. Thus, older men who had the better control of their attention and hence of their retention, compared unfavourably with their counterparts at younger ages. Their memories, however, and powers of attending were as efficient as those of the fifty per cent of the younger men within the same ability range. Thus the best older men were not as efficient as the best younger men but they were as good as the average younger men. This finding occurs constantly in the literature.

It would seem that deterioration of attentional powers with age is more obvious in complex than in simple sensori-motor tasks. Welford (1951) has demonstrated the slower, more deliberate and accurate performance of older men in such simple activities as grid matching and target throwing, but where mental manipulation is required, as when the cues are mirrored, there is a falling off in both time and accuracy with age.

3 *Verbal compensations in sensori-motor tasks*

Similar trends are implied in another of Welford's experiments in problem solution, but in this differences in strategy were observed. The task required that sequences among ten morse keys should be learned in order to produce correlated light patterns among an array of ten electric bulbs. The results indicated that the problem was solved with approximately equal facility over the three decades between twenty and forty-nine years, the peak age for learning being thirty to thirty-nine years. These men in their fourth decade appeared to combine the flexibility of the younger groups with the circumspection of the older. They attempted to arrive at some strategic principle of operation by careful observation of the apparatus and by asking questions about it. This appeared to be a sophisticated attempt to establish a multiple set or a self-instructive orientation towards the task. Errors were lower in this age group than in any other. The younger men committed most errors, but as they worked more quickly using a trial-and-error strategy they arrived at the solution as soon. The subjects in their fifties and sixties showed the widest individual differences, which ranged from the optimum performance of the thirties and forties to a difficulty in understanding what the task required. It would seem from these results that the effects of ageing on speed may be minimised where the task can be verbally explored and controlled. The younger subjects arrive at their generalisations inductively and empirically, the older ones by attempting to fit the new schema into an older one. The younger men displayed the basic strategy necessary for any learning. For this as Mace (1950) has suggested, three ingredients are necessary: (1) intention to produce some required effect; (2) executive action; (3) perceptual guidance. To this the older men seemed to add two other factors which Mace regards as being necessary when the task is complex. These were situational information and general knowledge. This they endeavoured to clarify before beginning the task. There was no doubt that the task involved the higher cognitive functions and it is probable that these were in covert operation in the younger men. Their overt expression in the older men may represent a change in style of learning which for them leads to easier assimilation. This would appear to depend on the simultaneous arousal of not only the speech ideation centres but also of their sensori-motor counterparts used in speaking aloud. These might be regarded as the rather laboured establishment of a verbal orientation to the task, associated with all three of Mace's ingredients. The younger men relied on perceptual guidance or the feed-back of results, for the establishment of their generalisations which they doubtlessly verbalised covertly after their discovery.

The value of verbal aids in learning among older men was also evident in an experiment by Balbin and Shimmin (1964) on training the middle-aged in inspection work. They observed the efficacy of three methods. The first was the traditional method of merely conveying information. In this, a display chart was used and all possible types of fault were demonstrated. The second so-called 'lead-in' method consisted of sorting faulty items into designated bins. The items were labelled with the name of the fault, and a blue spot to left, middle or right indicated the correct receptacle. The third method was termed the discrimination method because it called for more active participation by the learner than the second. This included three stages. The display chart was used as in the traditional method, but the types of fault were discussed and explained orally. At the second stage the lead-in method was used but this time particular faults were confined in batches and each type of fault to be expected was explained. There was thus greater homogeneity and definition among the practice items. This time the bins were labelled with the type of fault, rather than having the item directed to the correct bin by a blue spot. In the final stage of the discrimination method, the faulty items were presented randomly, and whenever they were placed in the wrong bins there was an immediate feed-back of information regarding error. Items which showed repeated error were given additional practice. By this discrimination method a small older group of four men and four women aged fifty to fifty-six years surpassed all younger ages taught by the other two methods. Unfortunately, the experiment with this small sample appears to have been almost an afterthought, and there is no adequate comparison of results obtained by the same method with younger people. The first two methods, however, did suggest the desirability of the discrimination method, because the younger subjects under thirty-five years and with a mean age of twenty-two years benefited most by the lead-in method, while the older group with a mean age of forty-six years had better results in the traditional method. The older workers lost ground in the lead-in method at the point where transfer from labelled to unlabelled items occurred in the last ten minutes of a seventy-five-minute learning session. This again would seem to stem from a weakness in empirical generalisation which seems more facile in men under thirty-five years. It is encouraging, however, that this decline in inductive reasoning with age is largely annulled by verbal supplementation of sensori-motor behaviour. This is due perhaps to the evocation of increased neural schemata by using verbal stimuli as well as perceptual ones. The technique is justified by the same psychological laws as were demonstrated by Razran (1961) in two-year-olds when they learned the names of things more quickly if they were allowed to handle them while hearing the names (see Chapter III above). In elderly people, however, the reverse process is apparent. The name reinforces the learning of the objects. It would seem that after the third decade the inductive approach to concept formation is supported spontaneously by an already acquired symbolic skill. After that age there is better success if both the sensory stimuli and their verbal counterparts are built into the learning situation and presented simultaneously. It would be interesting to know the reason for this. The inductive facility of younger people may arise from greater synaptic flexibility in neural organisation. This would facilitate the process of questing scansion in the presence of the ambiguous. Loss of this power among the middle-aged could be exacerbated by routine work, low motivational levels and excessive fatigue.

4 *Resistance to change*

The nervous strain involved in change of set is implied in van Beek's (1964) study of assembly-line organisation. Where assembly lines are too long, much waiting is incurred and the rhythm of action is disrupted. The introduction of buffer stocks ensuring a relatively unbroken flow of materials to be processed reduced waiting time by 45 per cent. It was estimated that as a result of this greater continuity, morale was improved 200 per cent and efficiency 400 per cent. Moreover, when the number of waiting hours was correlated with absenteeism the coefficient was as high as 0·56 which suggests rhythmic anticipation is an important aspect of industrial hygiene. As one of the workers reported, "Carrying on regularly is best. When you have stopped, beginning again is not nice. The working is much more irregular. Once you have got hold of the rhythm it goes on automatically."

The facility afforded by rhythmic expectation suggests the relative ease with which 'set' can be maintained when the intervals between presentation of stimuli are short. It also implies that more nervous energy is consumed by the inauguration of set than by its maintenance. Botwinnick's (1959) survey of the data in this field indicates that older subjects do best when the stimulus occurs at regular intervals following a warning signal. The organism in its middle years becomes less keyed-up perhaps because of reduced stimulus input. This reduced capacity for set appears to be independent of the speed factor but its nature is not yet known.

Stultification of the process of habitual scanning on entering new situations could arise from a cause secondary to that of routine and fatigue. The autonomous adult attends to his environment in a very selective way in accordance with his needs and the established techniques whereby he satisfies them. During his younger years, social pressures constrained him to attend to many more classes of situations than he would have done had he been free to choose. This increase in selective ignoring of stimuli which are not ego-involved was high-lighted in a report on an educational campaign to acquaint people with the United Nations Organisation (Star and Hughes 1950). In spite of propaganda through hundreds of films, broadcasts, newspaper articles, pamphlets and speakers, over a period of six months, the 7 per cent of people who understood how the power of veto was exercised did not change at all. The proportion of people (34 per cent) who had heard of the veto at the outset was increased by only 3 per cent. It is clear from this failure that the mass of the people of Cincinnati did not view U.N.O. with any degree of ego-involvement.

Such conservatism is usually present even where a person's economic interests are involved providing they are not in jeopardy. A study by Rogers and Beal (1958) of the adoption of new farming practices led to the postulation of four stages of assimilation. The first was one of awareness at the initial exposure during which no details were taken in. This mass media stage appears to have been both the initial and final stage in the U.N.O. campaign. At the second stage information is secured, and at the third the innovation is tried out. For these two stages interpersonal influence was of paramount importance. The final stage was represented by a decision to adopt the technique or to reject it. Where this stage was prolonged interpersonal influence was often effective. From this it would seem that ego-involvement is as essential an aspect of learning in maturity as in youth, and that it is best encompassed in face-to-face communication. Thus social legitimation precedes its validation by results. The hidden persuasion of the commercial advertisement stems more frequently from covert social communication than from the merits of the commodity and appeals to a narrow range of values most likely to evoke personal interest and commitment. The concept of ego-involvement as a very real determinant of economic trends was fully appreciated by Keynes (1936) for he accorded human expectations a central place in his system. He was certain that "the power of vested interests is vastly exaggerated compared with the encroachment of ideas". Thus the adventure of business-life resides in the interval between incurring costs in producing an article and consumer validation. In this system, advertisement pays off because it renders more certain the ego-involvement which will cause the reciprocal expectations of consumer and entrepreneur to be fulfilled. This is made possible by reference points for the ascription of status in the structure of society. Particularly powerful status symbols used by the advertiser are in the areas of sex, achievement and popularity. Without these ancillary motivators each point of transition in a line of communication is a point of resistance (Mace 1953*a*).

5 *The need to achieve*

Since society is achievement oriented it is to be expected that this factor will appear as the most important motivational area of occupational stratification. Centers' (1948) study suggests that people are most satisfied with their jobs when they offer satisfactory avenues to promotion. The chance to enjoy life was equated with this chance of advancement. When the writer ran rank order correlations between the ratings of Centers' seven occupational groups for vocational opportunity and chances of happiness, a coefficient of 0·89 was found. Satisfaction with the job itself and with its economic reward were less closely related to chances to enjoy life, yielding rank order correlations of 0·65 and 0·67 respectively. It would seem, then, that a chance to 'get on' in life is even more essential to human happiness than economic security in an achievement-oriented society.

N-ach is, of course, dependent on a necessary modicum of conditional acceptance and reward in childhood. It is therefore to be expected that among those who have been reinforced negatively rather than positively, i.e. through rejection on account of failure rather than acceptance on account of success, there will be many who experience in their adult years a sense of personal inadequacy. Men suffer from this more than women because their role is regarded as more achievement oriented in a competitive sense, and this pressure of expectation begins to arouse greater anxiety in the male from the age of eleven years onwards (Zubek and Solberg 1954). It is present also in unmarried career women, particularly among those highly motivated enough to make a particular success of their jobs. Ellis's (1952) successful group of women seemed to lack the capacity for making friends, they were less attached to their parents and had a sense of rejection by both parents and community. This suggests that they were motivated to achieve by a fear of rejection on account of failure, rather than a desire to achieve with a view to enjoying greater warmth of acceptance. They would, of course, experience true rejection in adult years in proportion to the degree of competition present in their vocational context, and any refined study of the social consequences of N-ach should control this factor. An ambitious woman in a small retail shop will naturally incur less envy than one in a large firm with a number of competitors on the ladder for promotion. Such motivational patterns as those which are associated with N-ach are important for differentiation of mental aptitude. Any mental ability which causes a favourable mirror image of the self to be reflected from parental sources will tend to be exercised more intensively than others. In maturity, too, the self image is reflected back in face-to-face encounters. It is doubtful whether the ideas underlying Mozart's juvenile compositions, or Verdi's operas (written after he was eighty), would have been realised without the support of a doting public beyond the fringe of the family. As Bartlett demonstrated, the interest setting of life will affect not only what is learned but also how the learning will take place – its intensity and direction. Each composer enjoyed what Smith (1959) concluded to be the essential aspects of the climate of creativity, namely: adequate reward and recognition, sensible communication and an organisation which does not frustrate. This is the climate of creativity and self differentiation, not only for artists and scientists, but for all persons.

III. SOCIAL LEARNING AND MOTIVATION

1 *Social skill and self acceptance*

In routine productivity it is perhaps true to say that the social skills are the only ones which have not been reduced in level by automation. Fragmentation of productive processes has reduced the level of complexity of working operations and these are viewed as a complex whole only by the few. As a consequence, the complexities of economic life have become for the most part social in nature. As Mace (1950) has pointed out, the need for rare complex physical skills has been replaced by the need for social skills which may be rarer still. He regards social skills as involving similar processes as physical and intellectual skills, but requiring in addition a primary function of direction and a secondary function of maintaining appropriate motives. This is tantamount to saying a person must be attracted to other people and must subsequently find the experience satisfying. Such satisfactions imply that a person has found an appropriate function in a group or role situation. Sarbin's (1954) definition of role would appear to be apposite in the present discussion. For him a role is a patterned sequence of learned actions performed by a person in an interaction situation. This facilitates the reciprocal naming or locating of the position of the other. But such placement is not always clearly recognised. Its clarity may be measured on a continuum from deliberate to automatic, from witting to unwitting. Such reciprocal judgments underlie the social learning which will occur whenever self perception is modified under the influence of role change. The reactions of others in the role situation mirror back the discrepancies between his current self knowledge and how he appears to them.

When an individual becomes affiliated to a group, there ensues a reciprocity of projective guessing between himself and the other members. Gradually the ambiguity of the situation will be clarified and guesses validated in role experience. This greater certainty permits a more confident use of social habit. Should the individual find the group does not confirm and assent to his social habits, they become extinguished rather than reinforced and a process of withdrawal begins. This social phenomenon was elaborately investigated by Tuckman (1964) who showed that habitual styles of group co-operation cannot be predicted during the developmental and de-developmental phases of group membership. His subjects displayed their personal preferences for autocratic or democratic styles during the middle six of his experimental sessions.

It would seem that the most important general asset an individual can have in entering new social situations is self acceptance. This is likely to be a measure of the extent to which he has an expectation of acceptance by others. It affords an initial advantage, though disillusionment and revision of the self image may ensue. Miyamoto and Dornbusch (1956) obtained self ratings and alter ratings after their subjects had made one another's acquaintance in groups of twenty. Those who rated themselves highly were also rated most highly by others, but self ratings tended to be higher than alter ratings. Moreover, when the subjects were asked to rate themselves as they thought other members of the group perceived them, the high self raters tended to overestimate their standing in the regard of the others. In other words, he estimated them to be perceiving him as he knows himself to be. Social relationships thus get off to a good start where individuals are self accepting because of the good will reciprocally engendered. Similar reciprocal structuring is implied in the fact that those who retire at sixty tend to describe themselves as elderly, while those who continue working and thus maintain their social contacts unbroken tend to regard themselves as middle-aged (Blau 1956). Thus the social learning of maturity is concerned with changes in self perception as each role suggests to the adult that there are discrepancies between his self image and the perception of his self by others. His sense of personal security rests on the smoothness and gradualness of decoding and encoding such information. In fact, it might be said that the crisis points of life are when this process is disrupted through uncertainty about role. Such crises are major ones when one absorbing and comprehensive way of life is left for another which may be contrary in many respects. Marriage, parenthood, widowhood and retirement represent for many adults periods of stressful uncertainty regarding role. They find their self perception is suddenly inadequate, because they do not perceive themselves as others do, when such situations come upon them. In addition to this cognitive element, there is a change in self value. The married woman deprived of her admiring colleagues, or a widow of her appreciative husband, suffers a loss of positive self perception because it is no longer reinforced. While she is seeking new criteria for self valuation others perceive her as less positively responsive to them and so come to devalue her too.

2 *The marital role*

Marriage and a job are the first sudden changes of role encountered in maturity, and for twenty years or so these two roles are related and primary motivators. A man's role in marriage is defined more rigidly and inflexibly than a woman's by his function of being the economic provider. The woman's traditional role as the domestic provider leaves her more freedom to accept various roles in addition to her prime function. Thus normally in the small family characteristic of relatively affluent cultures, she operates within a secure context regulated by her husband's earning capacity. The role strain experienced by the husband arises from a less stable set of expectations in his work and home situations. For him, these may not be congruent with those of his colleagues nor with the status expectations prevalent in his family. In either of these events there is continuous interference on the part of some occupants of one position with the goal achievements of those occupying other positions.

For a marriage to be successful there must be a balanced reciprocity between role playing and role taking. Imbalance in this respect was studied by Jacobson (1952) using a questionnaire designed to elicit opinions concerning male dominance versus equality for women. The averages for divorced and married couples indicated that the divorced male tended to favour male dominance most, and the divorced female least. The mean attitudes of the married couples occurred between these two extremes. The difference between the average scores for the divorced samples of men and women was four times greater than between the mean scores of the married pairs. Every divorced woman favoured equality for women more than her former husband, but among those still married 25 per cent favoured equality less than their husbands. How far the extreme attitudes of the divorced couples were exacerbated by role strain is unclear, but their disagreements in matrimony had brought about neither the change in self perception nor the revision of role structure, which it is the function of lovers' quarrels to perform. Presumably, these should lead to a role structure in which one partner played a submissive role when the other took up a dominant one.

3 *Similarity and complementarity in dyadic relationships*

Considerable interest exists at present in the aspects of dyadic relationships, both in marriage and in friendship, which stem either from similarity or from the complementary function of satisfying one another's needs. Complementarity implies that the expectations of one partner are specifically directed at the other in the form of covert demand. In intimate relationships there are few reserves, and friction arises when such demands are not met. Moreover, the less they are consciously realised, the more irrational the expressions of annoyance appear to be. Such interference with the autonomy of the partner against whom the aggression or reproach is levelled arouses counter resentment. Winch (1958) observed, in twenty-five couples whose marriage had failed, four types of complementarity. These were suggestive of the following kinds of relationship: (i) mother – son; (ii) father – daughter; (iii) master – servant; (iv) mistress – servant. Statistical support for these four types of relationship was no more than suggestive. This is not surprising, for these four forms of complementarity are experienced by all people who have been brought up in a normal family and they constitute the know-how which makes possible a fairly smooth passage into matrimony. Any psychogenetic study of marriage could not ignore the model presented by the parents to the children and experience of the mutual service which maintains a family in being. The mutual gratification of need is culturally built in to the structure of the matrimonial role and this patterning is therefore socially rather than psychologically engendered. It is not surprising therefore that evidence of personal need complementarity as a motive in dyadic relationships is preponderantly negative at present (Secord and Backman 1964*b*). If the stability of a marriage rests on a revision of self image, to accord with that reflected back by the partner, it is the initial similarity between the husband and wife which facilitates matrimonial integration. Unusual forms of relationship, however, which are frequently the themes of musical hall jokes may indicate the presence of complementarity of idiosyncratic kinds. This is seen whenever one of Winch's four types of complementarity is predominant. In some stable marriages, the husband is hen-pecked, the wife is bullied or is an old man's darling, or the husband is spoiled and cosseted as a child substitute. Such partnerships are frequently enduring and satisfying, and it is clear that each partner is complementary to the other. But behind such expectancies there is in all probability a stable parent-child relationship such as that of Doctor Johnson and his middle-aged mother. He learned in his early childhood the nuances of an intimate relationship with a wife twenty years his senior. The mutual satisfaction of need in such unusual marital relationships is a-normal rather than abnormal, for it ensues upon normal learning. Moreover, providing such future spouses arrive at maturity and marriage with a well-integrated set of expectations, their problem in mating is a normal one – to find a partner with congruently reciprocal expectations. Since identification occurs with both parents, especially in the case of the boy, similarity should underlie some of the congruency. This will enable a man to feel like his wife as well as to perceive her as complementary to himself. This recognition reduces the extent to which she appears as ambiguous at the first meetings and creates the atmosphere in which romantic love can develop. The re-evoking of the feelings associated with the long-forgotten parent-self identification enables the partner to see once more an unconditionally accepted self in the expressive behaviour of the other person. Romantic love then is a special form of interpersonal congruency in which a person perceives another person as behaving in a way which confirms his self concept. But this applies to all forms of dyadic friendship. For the relationship to develop, it is probably necessary for each member to see the other as behaving in a manner congruent with his self concept.

In an attempt to explore related hypotheses, Secord and Backman (1964*a*) asked 152 people to answer a questionnaire on both their own needs and those of their best friend of the same sex. Thus they were able to compare one partner's perception of both complementary and similar needs in self and friend. Several points in this research are illuminating. For example, all the largest correlations are associated either positively or negatively with the need for autonomy, aggression and achievement. Deference, succourance (needing help) and affiliation were less closely integrated needs, perhaps because they are less externalised than the former set. It would seem from this that the most salient needs in friendship are in relation to the first three.

One of the larger positive correlations was between self need to nurture and friend need to be succoured. This was an example of congruence, i.e. complementarity. A somewhat different finding which the authors found difficult to explain was a highly significant positive correlation between a self need for dominance and the friend's need for autonomy. This is perhaps a matching pair of needs and indicates similarity. During the earlier discussions of adolescent growth it was shown that autonomy rather than dependence was preferred in a friend if they were not to prove a limitation on one's freedom. The autonomous individual is more likely to allow a friend to exercise his need for dominating without sacrificing any of his freedom, and the relationship remains unimpaired by the impact. The same implication can be made regarding the positive correlation found between achievement and aggression. High N-ach in a person causes him to seek assertive persons as friends and vice versa. There was an even more pronounced tendency for those needing to achieve, to avoid friendship with people who who were neither desirous of helping nor of being helped. The absence of these needs suggests a withdrawn social attitude. In fact, the general findings suggest that positive driving people seek in their friends overt evidence of attitude, whether it is as a receiver or as a contributor of the benefits of friendship. This reduces the ambiguous element in the relationship and lessens any sense of insecurity. Backman and Secord conclude that perceived similarity of need pattern between self and friend is an important source of attraction between friends and that it is independent of the factor of interpersonal congruency. They also make the important observation that whereas a questionnaire method is adequate for measuring perceived similarity, the best estimate of interpersonal congruency is to be obtained in direct observation of dyadic interaction. It is possible the similarity is important for decoding, i.e. perceiving information in intimate communication, while the results of past congruent and incongruent interaction facilitate an encoding of response. The friendship should therefore endure to the extent that interpersonal congruency is validated through active participation. The well-integrated person can tolerate any threat to his self constructs that may arise, and bring a revised self image to the next evocation of incongruent needs. Presumably this constant reinforcement should produce a greater similarity in the partners because of the imitation of habits and techniques for dealing with shared situations.

4 *The stabilising factor in marriage*

According to Kelly's (1955) findings in an eighteen-year follow-up study of 215 couples, husbands and wives do not become alike as a result of co-habitation in so far as mental and personality characteristics are concerned. Stability of marriage then did not stem from an increase in similarity in these respects. A more probable source was suggested by the relative stability of values and vocational interests. It is conceivable that a firm set of values and vocational commitment, because of their ethical and economic superordinacy in motivation, would be the major factors in a stable marriage.

The same conclusions may be drawn from a research by Levinger (1964) in his study of sixty comfortably-off middle-class couples. There was an amusing discrepancy between the perception of the self's and of the spouse's task performance. For example, in the item 'repairs things around the house' the husband's estimate of his wife's contribution correlated —·046 with the wife's view of her own efforts. That this is based on prejudice is suggested by a near perfect correlation of —0·91 between the husband's estimates of his own and of his wife's contribution. The husband's viewpoint is more likely to be a rationalization for he is not at home all day. This failure to understand the extent of role performance is a traditional source of folklore and humour. Even the osculatory activity of the spouses is differentially perceived although it is an activity shared on every occasion. The wives saw themselves as very like their husbands in the frequency of kissing on leaving for work or on returning, with a correlation of 0·91, but the estimates of husbands and wives of each other's frequency of kissing on such occasions was only 0·48. Thus the wives perceived a similarity which was not perceived by the husbands so consistently. The wives are more likely to have rationalised in this item. The relevance of these empirical findings for the present discussion resides in the high consistency of the ratings when carried out by the one partner of self and alter performance of role. In the two items above, repairs and kissing, the first is seen as highly complementary by the husband and the second as very similar by the wife. The correlations between the independent opinions of husbands and wives suggest these viewpoints are true but exaggerated.

The perception of the spouses in the minutiae of daily life is to a large extent guided by their realisation of the goals of marriage. In ranking these in order of priority there was little difference between husbands and wives (rho = 0·83). Their combined rankings were: (1) affection; (2) companionship; (3) happy children; (4) personal development; (5) living according to religious principles; (6) economic security; (7) an attractive home; (8) wise financial planning; (9) a place in the community. The only rank order discrepancy of more than one place between husbands and wives was for affection, which wives placed first and husbands third, and for companionship which husbands placed first and wives third. Both ranked happy children second in order of importance. It appears then that a superordinate sense of values directs in a broad sense the practical details of living and causes the spouses to perceive their actions as congruent with these principles and thus as confirming the self concept. The extent to which these couples had departed from stereotypical understanding to one rooted in the realities of role functioning was also measured. They were asked to rate independently, from the conventional point of view, the need for autonomy, nurturance and succourance as experienced by men and women. They were then asked to do the same thing for their own needs of these kinds. There was a significant shift towards lower scores for n-autonomy and a marked rise in those for n-nurturance and n-succourance when the estimating was related to their personal marital context. Whereas the stereotypical estimates showed strong sex differences, those that were judged from actual situations showed no sex differences in mean scores. But where normal role functioning is frequently disrupted by chronic alcoholism in the husband, women continued to use conventional stereotypes for perception of marital role. Kogan and Jackson (1963) using a check-list of conventional sex roles concluded that wives of alcoholics saw themselves as more feminine than normally situated wives presumably because interaction in role had not increased differentiation to include elements of a masculine viewpoint. This privation of experience would inevitably operate after their marriage, even if the same ultra feminine trends had to some extent influenced mate selection. Role strain caused by the husband's alcoholic deviations from marital goal expectancies would deprive the wife of stable reference points for a revision of self image to accord with a masculine viewpoint. Moreover, it is unlikely that among alcoholic husbands the marital goal of companionship would rank first. Thus in marriage the structure of marital roles affects fundamentally the personality structure of the spouses. Values held in common are a generalised homeostatic influence when conflict occurs. This is so because in the long term values exercise three functions: (i) the determination of personal needs; (ii) the modification of tastes and habits; and (iii) the resolution of conflict between needs by mutual adjustment (Mace 1953*b*). This process of restructuring occurs in both partners as common goals are sought.

5 *Success in marriage*

Surveys purporting to indicate the auspiciousness of varying lengths of courtship and the danger points as matrimony runs its course suggest that a happy pre-nuptial confluence of maturity and mutual knowledge are the best predictors of marital happiness. The continuance of harmony, however, is endangered by any radical change of role within the married state.

Burgess and Cottrell (1939) found there was least risk of failure when the couple married between the ages of twenty-eight and thirty. Before and after this age prediction is less favourable. The ideal period of acquaintance prior to marriage was five years or more. This length of time reduced the chance of failure to 15 per cent, while the chance of happiness was as great as 55 per cent. In a courtship of under six months chances of the same outcomes were 45 per cent and 20 per cent respectively.

Terman's (1938) survey of degree of happiness among 800 married couples revealed that on the whole it is greatest during the first two years of matrimony, and least at six to eight years. The greatest number of divorces occur at this point. Terman's graph indicates that each period of minimal happiness is succeeded by a rise in happiness level, suggesting that some new structuring, a more adaptive form of co-operation, had emerged to lessen role strain. It is clear that any change in family structure, or any change in an extrafamilial role which has repercussions on the family, will occasion role strain. Such changes in circumstance demand an adaptation of learned actions to accord with the reorganised role. Each partner must learn afresh how the new role is valued by the other. For example, the nadir of happiness after six to eight years of marriage coincides for many couples with the most exacting stage of producing a family. After the ninth year at which a peak of happiness occurs, the parents are accustomed to their role, the children are less dependent, and present an interesting ego-involved sphere of observation for the liberated parents. The decrease in happiness after fifteen to seventeen years of marriage coincides perhaps with the peak of their family's adolescent conflicts during which parents and children may not agree about deportment and conduct. The relative autonomy and maturity of the children at this age enable them to be a disruptive influence, especially if the parents do not agree on the amount and kind of independence which should be permitted. The final peak of happiness noted by Terman is twenty-one to twenty-three years after marriage. This would appear to coincide, for many, with the ending of family responsibility and the realisation of vocational ambition. It is perhaps of significance that this period of married life coincides with the final peak of job turn-over (Kitson 1925), and that it is at this age that administrative powers earn the recognition of promotion (Lehman and Heidler 1949).

6 *The self and the group*

Becker (1964), in an endeavour to arrive at the essentials of personality change in adult life, recognised two overriding factors. The first is that of situational adjustment which he regards as the wedge of change. The second is the process of commitment which he regards as the source of stability. Commitment in any area of living implies that when motives are in conflict a solution is likely to be reached which supports an activity necessary to the attainment of an end. The major areas of commitment are culturally determined for most people and have their institutionalised forms of expression supported by folklore and rite. The stability of any society depends on this structure. It operates covertly more than overtly and is present in the thought of the most radical of men. Where an outcome is uncertain, a side-bet is made concerning the expediency of a strategy for reaching the valued goal. Thus a consistent line of activity occurs in a sequence of varied situations. This could account for Kelly's (1955) finding of a mere 8 per cent of stability in attitudes over eighteen years of married life. It implies that values are continually and incrementally reinforced, while attitudes tend to extinguish with change of circumstance, because they are more specifically geared to expediency and less associated with self esteem. Thus, a sense of security and an avoidance of threat to self constructs appear to reside more in the implementation of value than in the expression of attitude, for an attitude implies a pattern of response, and a value a perceptual criterion of worth. Thus the attitudinal factor changes with the perception of its usefulness in maintaining self esteem.

These considerations are relevant to a discussion of group cohesion among adults where there is exercise of autonomy concerning affiliation or withdrawal. Most studies support the view that leaders who have high status conform closely to the values of the group (Secord and Backman 1964*b*). For example, Whyte's (1955) study of an informal street corner gang in a slum area suggested that the two men who emerged as leaders were depended on by the others. Experience of their ideas showed that they were right in the perception of the group. Thus the members of the group were conditioned to accept further ideas from them. They became recognised as rewarding stimuli. A leader then must be active in implementing the common values of the group, in order to suggest lines of action which are supportive of its expectations. In unstructured face-to-face situations this is likely to be a person with the same values as most of the group, but who is more active in manipulating problem situations than the other members. Because of his involvement he knows much about the members of the group, and usually holds a key position in the group's communication structure. Such active participants relay communications consonant with group values and filter out those which are dissonant. A group of such leaders forming a committee has a normative function in that it sets standards and enforces conduct and belief.

In loosely cohering social structures, such as those of social class, reference groups serve a comparative purpose. In America, for instance, the upwardly mobile Negro has absorbed the reference criteria of his macro-society. The four questions asked about the aspirant to higher social status among Negroes are: (1) What has been his education? (2) Has he professional or semi-professional status? (3) Are his manners, language and dress polished? (4) Is he black? The answer to the last question must be no (Marks 1943). The same phenomena are present in the upwardly mobile individuals in English society, but there are less clearly defined criterial stereotypes. The class differences of which English people are conscious appear to be dependent on experience of prestige and power in daily life (Bott 1954). The minority situation of Negroes in America intensifies their ego-involvement concerning class, and thus sharpens their perception of the status criteria manifested by reference groups.

In so-called inverted snobbery, negative reference groups provide stimuli by virtue of their opposite characteristics. Such a pattern of reference is normal and common in adolescence and can persist into maturity where a positive affiliation with the group has not been established. In such an event the individual behaves in a contrary fashion to that advocated by the group. The non-conformity implies that reinforcement of values by the group has been decremental rather than incremental. For this reason, a familiar tactic of the sophisticated group leader is to draw the defecting person into the group by regarding his contrary values with respect, thus disarming criticism by incremental reinforcement of his self esteem. Where, however, such an individual is already committed to another group, his personal status in his own perception will stem from his appraisal of its reference points, and he is less likely to be amenable to persuasion.

These are the processes underlying the political maturity of a democratic culture. Voting preferences are strongly influenced by a person's reference groups. For example, the threat of Nazism before 1939 was directed at values and self esteem more than at physical survival. This caused many people to affiliate to the Left Book Club because it reflected their values more than the right wing leadership of the day. This movement exemplified the principles underlying opinion leadership. It was specialised and confined to a particular content area; it expressed the values of the group; it was competent and had a strategic social location (Secord and Backman 1964*b*). The enormous success which the Left Book Club enjoyed arose from just these factors, and in consequence it changed fundamentally the face of English politics among the intelligentsia for some decades to come. The promoters provided an acceptable frame of reference for both self evaluation and attitude formation. Their success depended on the second of these aspects in that they suggested viable ways of implementing values in the bewilderingly ambiguous international crisis which threatened people's self constructs. Normally, voting preferences are less dramatically structured by reference groups. The individual who early in an election campaign favours a candidate not preferred by his family or by his close associates frequently casts his final vote for their candidate, not his. That this shift is due to actual pressures from the group is suggested by the fact that most of a voter's discussion of politics takes place with his friends, co-workers and family (Berelson et al. 1954). The opinion leaders among these primary reference groups should, according to the above principles, convince others by their common sense alignment of value and its practical implementation, thus changing the attitudes of the group members towards this or that candidate on account of his election promises.

7 *The system versus social service*

Vocational interests have been shown to stem largely from a liking for organising on the one hand, and on the other from a desire to render social service (Crites 1963). Where there is a passion for system, human freedom is likely to be sacrificed to it. Where there is a strong love of humanity, it is difficult to be systematic while being consistently kind to individuals. Cultures, too, may differ concerning the relative importance placed on these two aspects of civic and industrial organisation. Naturally, where economic organisation is weak, efficiency is a valued commodity. In India, for example, among supervisory staff, the functions assumed to be important were production oriented, and there was less emphasis on human relations. The characteristics of the good supervisor were deemed to be high intelligence and dependability; ability to please others was accorded a low rating (Bhatt and Pathak 1962). On the American scene a similar study described successful foremen as less production oriented, better communicators and as giving general rather than detailed supervision (Kay et al. 1962). In this latter study, there is clearly a shift of emphasis towards the social aspects of industrial efficiency.

In England, the social aspect of shift work was studied from a different point of view by Shimmin and de la Mare (1964*a* and 1964*b*). They observed the motives of telegraph operators, aged thirty to thirty-nine, and found that increases in the amount of overtime worked was associated with family responsibilities as measured by income tax coding. In these men, any worries about health were not overt and were subordinate to anxiety concerning their liabilities if less overtime were available in the future. They found their main social satisfactions at work and may have been highly motivated generally by social consideration for their families. Low overtime workers tended to be more introverted and unsociable men. The authors concluded that while overtime was at first socially motivated, it became an addiction. This was taken to be an example of Allport's theory of the functional autonomy acquired by personality traits through their exercise. The motive became autonomous in the sense that the work-related stimuli aroused their own set of response attitudes.

These telegraph operators were trained comprehensively to carry out all duties that might be required and in consequence there was no division of labour which might reduce flexibility in the shift system. Any man was able to arrange an exchange of shift and this made possible clearer observation of free choice. Under these conditions there was a tendency to prefer a constant rhythm in work. The most sociable people, as measured by questionnaire (Heron 1956), tended to opt for night-work and the more unsociable for day-work. A few preferred changing from day to night, because of flexible social commitments and active financial programmes. The night-workers perceived the scene as more relaxed and friendly because of the absence of interruption from administrative sources. Working conditions thus became less production oriented and more sociable. These observations are a reminder that a major aspect of a man's social education is work-related, and that a friendly flow of communication in industrial social situations is an important aspect of social hygiene.

8 *Successful ageing*

After the peak of physiological maturity is reached, at about the median age of the life-span, the slow process of ageing may be viewed as successful if the optimal balance of engagement and disengagement is observed. If engagement becomes more selective, it leads to an increase in social distance between the individual and certain other classes of individuals. This takes place in the ordinary course of events and results from the fact that values are slowly modified to bring about a change of reference groups and a diminution of the area of affiliation. Thus successful maturing results from an indefinable interaction between physiological capacities and their psychological and sociological motivators, but successful ageing depends most perhaps on the extent to which sociological motivation remains dominant.

CHAPTER IX

Changes in later life

1 *Physiological functions*

Degenerative changes in the bodily tissues are often regarded as symptomatic of ageing but, as was shown in the previous chapter, decline begins at different ages ranging from the taste and smell organs before and soon after birth to degenerative changes in the retina and skeletal muscles in the fifties and sixties. The last outpost of youthfulness is the smooth musculature, which retains its efficiency when all else is decrepit. Likewise the autonomic nervous system by which it is activated continues to differentiate throughout life. The short dendrites of the ANS increase in number (Kuntz 1945). This change in structure suggests an increase in the complexity of the systems of arousal and subsidiation, perhaps on account of interaction with the CNS through the functioning of the psychological mechanisms of self control to which adults are socially conditioned. There is certainly an expectation that people of a certain age should keep arousal and departure from usual ways within reasonable limits. This continued efficiency of the autonomic nervous system and its associated organs may explain why death cannot be encompassed easily in the very aged, for whom life has become a burden.

Hormone treatment in old age may restore several physiological and psychological capacities to varying degrees. The sex glands are particularly important as avenues to rejuvenation. In addition, to their primary products, the sex glands secrete two other classes of hormones, the estrogens in females and the androgens in males. But, in either sex, the adrenal cortex secretes both androgens and estrogens, and before the onset of pubescence the androgens-estrogens ratio is closely similar for both sexes. Even in maturity, clinical evidence suggests that the adrenal cortex may contribute two thirds of the steroidal hormones, the remainder being of gonadal origin (Dempsey 1951). It is of interest to note, in relation to this, that the adrenal gland, like the gonads, develops from the embryonic genital ridge.

The steroid hormones produce a feeling of well-being, and too great a decrease in secretion induces involutional depression. This is particularly so in woman after the menopause, because by the age of sixty her output is reduced, on an average, to a sixth of the amount she secreted at forty. At the height of her sexual potency, between the ages of seventeen and thirty-nine, her output as measured by urinary excretion is 300 per cent that of the male. In him, there is no similar reduction in estrogens in middle age. From secreting only 35 per cent as much as the female at forty, he enjoys 127 per cent of her output at fifty and 187 per cent at sixty (Kirk 1951). Androgens output drops steeply in both sexes after thirty and begins to level out after sixty. From these considerations it would seem that output of estrogens is the more important sex variable, especially after middle age and that although women have a slightly longer expectation of life, they are not so advantageously constituted to enjoy it.

Sex hormone treatment would seem to be the answer to this problem. The literature on this theme was surveyed by Kirk (1951) who concluded that atrophic changes can be made good to a large extent and function re-established. In this, however, the uneven restoration of function may endanger the general condition, and the pituitary master gland ceases to exert its erstwhile regulatory function. It is thus a piecemeal problem for the biochemist and neurologist. The pituitary gland itself appears to be remarkably stable well into old age. These degenerative changes vary greatly in time of onset and rate of advance within any group of people. The most simple and overt evidence of biological age is provided by the rate of healing. For example, a skin wound of 40 sq. cm. in a young person of twenty years of age heals completely in forty days; in a forty-year-old eighty days are necessary. At eighty years healing takes five times as long as in a ten-year-old child (Carlson 1949). It would seem therefore that the change which occurs with age is a slowing up of process. This is supported by the effect of age on behavioural processes.

2 *Decline in functional efficiency*

Most sensory, motor and intellectual functions decline slightly between the ages of thirty and fifty but exhibit pronounced changes later especially after the sixtieth year. This acceleration may be due to an environmental factor as much as from any biological cause, for it is the age after which many people retire from their usual avocations. This cessation of function will naturally lead to atrophy among the disused tissues. Further suggestive evidence in support of this is provided by studies of test performance at successive ages and various levels of intelligence.

These indicate that in vocabulary (Berkowitz and Green 1953), synonyms (Sward 1945) and reasoning ability (Raven 1948) there is no decline with age among the top 5 per cent for intelligence, as measured by I.Q. tests. Among those of average intelligence there is some decline in these abilities, but among the least able 25 per cent there is marked decline with age. These findings suggest that although growth is genetically paced, decline could very well arise from the extent of disuse in each group. It is possible that only those of accelerated maturation acquire sufficient facility in these symbolic skills for their frequent use in everyday life.

This atrophy of function is reflected in changes in brain tissue. Recent research has revealed a brain shrinkage caused by a decrease in the size of the cells of the frontal and occipital lobes, i.e. those used in association and vision. The frontal lobes are very much involved in reasoning, and the higher intellectual processes and the visual area of the occipital lobe in reading and the finer manipulative skills. Degenerative changes in the eye structure would cause vision to be less used and hence lead to atrophy of the retina and the visual cortex. Where, however, symbolic habits of reading and speaking and thinking were highly developed the likelihood of their continued use is greatly increased, for they would be touched off by the minimal amount of receptor sensitivity and sustained by a greater complexity of associative potential. In this case it would seem that an old person's functional efficiency will be proportional to the level to which his capacities were developed before the age of thirty. It is of considerable interest with regards to this function-structure hypothesis that Vogt (1951) reports counter reactions produced by the nerve cells in those aged people who led active lives. In his examination of the brains of active nonagenarians he found a larger nucleus and more nissl substance in the cell bodies, and concluded that the continued use of the cells had delayed degenerative processes. All the evidence suggests that the activity which preserves the cell potential is prior in maintaining its functional efficiency. Since loss of cerebral neurones begins from birth onwards, it is reasonable to suppose that atrophy through disuse begins even at the outset of life and that the main difference between the senium and childhood resides in the proportion of the particular areas which fall into disuse in old age and the non-availability of areas for new learning. But new learning and its retention is paced by the general efficiency of brain activation, and the old person with areas of the brain atrophied through lack of exercise of function may be analogous to Lashley's rats when relearning after various degrees of cortical extirpation. In his experiments they assimilated at a rate proportional to the amount of cortex which remained (Lashley 1929).

Thorndike and his colleagues (1928) studied learning efficiency in age-groups ranging from twenty-two to sixty years. His experimental data ranged from skills having little or no dependence on past learning, such as learning a letter code, to book learning of the type pursued at University. They found the oldest group (thirty-five to sixty years) was equally as efficient as the youngest (twenty-two to twenty-four years) at book learning, but 39 per cent inferior in learning the letter code. They concluded that learning efficiency in respect of sheer modifiability of behaviour deteriorated between the ages of twenty-two and forty-two years at the rate of 1 per cent per year, while learning, which utilised established skills remained at a constant level. Welford's (1951) study of learning sequences in key pressing to given signals, mentioned in the previous chapter, is comparable to Thorndike's letter code experiment in that there is little transfer from past experience. His experimental design included a control of the subject's interest and background and groups representing the five decades between twenty and sixty-nine years. He found there was little change during the first three decades, but after forty-nine, time and errors mounted steeply. His sixty-year-old subjects were twice as slow and three and a half times as erroneous. These decrements in learning were matched by weaker retention of what had been learned. This failure to retain new learning was corroborated by Halstead (1943) and Gilbert (1941). Where the task was simple, such as visual memory span for digits, there was only an 8·5 per cent loss, but in a more complex and varied task with strange symbols, that of learning an English-Turkish vocabulary, the loss was 60·4 per cent. Gilbert's brightest elderly subjects evidenced less deterioration both absolutely and relatively. When compared with young people of similar intelligence they showed a mean loss of 20 per cent as against 36 per cent for the whole elderly group. Raven (1948) and Foulds (1949), using the Matrices test on 8,000 subjects between six and sixty years of age, found that the mean loss after the age of twenty years, in the top 5 per cent of ability, was 10 items in contrast to the loss of 22 in the bottom 25 per cent. This kind of deterioration is more in evidence when the intelligence test is a speed-power test than when it is one which allows the subject to operate at his own pace. Using two such speed-power tests, The Army Alpha and Otis S–A, Lorge (1936) found that there was greater decline in score with age. Goldfarb (1941) also found speed scores to be negatively correlated with age. In untimed tests he found no difference among the age-groups. Goldfarb's samples for age were small, a mere 168 subjects spread over an age range of forty-seven years, but they were well matched for intelligence and educational opportunity. His lack of variation with age may have been due to the fact that the untimed tests included vocabulary and synonyms. It should be remembered, however, that this lessening of speed is a normal phenomenon at any age when intensive exercise of function is relinquished. Athletes and sportsmen lose speed long before the specific skills of their prowess show any deterioration, and the same is true of any combination of intellectual and sensori-motor activity which calls for speed.

To summarise this physiological and psychological evidence on the effects of ageing, it might be said that deterioration with age is paced by both physiological changes and the extent to which function is exercised. With regard to physiological changes the least ambiguous, which seems largely independent of function, is that of estrogens secretion in women. For the rest, where facility in function has been reached before the age of thirty and where exercise of function has been maintained at a satisfactory level, deterioration is less in evidence. There is, however, a loss of speed with age, even under optimal conditions and this may be due to changes in such dynamic activators of the organism as androgens. Certainly decrease in both sexes in these secretions begins and continues in line with decrease in speed of function.

3 *Sex role and ageing*

Sex differences would seem to be sharpened by family roles and social pressures and expectations. Men, more frequently than women, are required to change their main roles after the age of sixty and are at a greater disadvantage for achieving significant alternative avenues to self realisation. Men differ most from women in attitude and interests at the age of eighteen. Thereafter, when exposed to the influences of courtship and marriage, there is a regression towards the feminine mean which is most proximate at sixty (Terman and Miles 1936). Since it is a long continuous process, it is unnecessary to attribute it to any causes other than environmental. It seems highly improbable that it is due at all to changes in the estrogens-androgens ratio in elderly males (Zubek and Solberg 1954). In these, after sixty M–F scores are still much more masculine than those of their wives. Women, however, remain throughout at a constant feminine level, except for a brief masculine trend at eighteen among college sophomores. It is the male who makes the adjustment to the extent of sacrificing 72 of his adolescent marks for masculinity of interests. This indicates an enormous adjustment even in norms spread over 170 marks.

Some changes in the philosophy of life of both sexes may be guessed at from studies of religious attitudes and beliefs. Several enquiries during the first half of the century (Starbuck 1900, Cavan et al. 1949) indicate that there is an intensification in religious belief and practice in old age. But a change in motives is apparent soon after marriage. In an enquiry into reasons for church attendance (Pressey et al. 1939) it was clear that motives changed after incurring family responsibilities. Search for friends, entertainment and for a philosophy of life declined sharply as major motivators and were replaced by such responsible reasons as 'To keep alive the spirit of Christ' and 'To encourage family attendance'. This suggests a more mature attitude towards cultural stability and the caretaking of children. Concern about immortality was present in a very small percentage before fifty, but by sixty years of age (Cavan et al. 1949) 75 per cent of old people expressed their certainty of an after-life. It appeared to be more prevalent among those enjoying longevity. Increase in concern about the problem of immortality round about the age of fifty could conceivably arise from first experiences of the death of those to whom they were particularly attached, such as parents. Close identification with the deceased persons would tend to evoke an ego-involved response which is likely to be even greater when the marital partner dies. There is very little interest in the problems of the soul and its immortality between the ages of twenty-five and fifty, but after that age interest is at about the same level as in adolescence, increasing rapidly as the senium is approached. At this age, however, interest in religion appears to be socialised, and a matter of choice and decision rather than superstition. These remarks apply to both sexes but more preponderantly to women. This may be because the Christian faith extols the feminine virtues as is evidenced by the fact that those fulfilling the role of the clergy have the lowest M–F scores of all the masculine vocations (Terman and Miles 1936). Their mean score anticipates that of men generally at the age of sixty, and is situated near the mid-point of the scale, implying no bias either way. It would seem then that men tend to change the direction of their interests with age while women are more conservative.

4 *The problems of men and women in old age*

It is perhaps true to say that in Western industrialised society the male is required to endure greater stress in terms of role. This is evidenced by the suicide rate in men which increases from adolescence onwards, but remains comparatively rare in women. As it is well established that suicide rates are correlated with economic trends (Jones and Caplan 1945) the increase among men is to be explained by the stress encountered as the economic provider of the family. Such strains may also account for the male loss of a few years in expectation of life when compared with the female norm. The first cultural pressure which he does not share with his sister is that of changing his parent identification in early childhood. This is an experience accompanied by evidence of anxiety and conflict in many boys. In maturity, his role as father is geared mainly to economic provision. This has less chance of being as intrinsically satisfying as a more direct role of child care. Moreover, the problem of family economy has no absolute solution, but is constantly changing to accord with variation in the needs and aspirations of the individual members of the family. This unpredictability tends to occasion strain in those responsible for making the provision. Finally, when released from such responsibilities, the mainspring of his self regard as the economic provider of the family is removed.

Such loss, however, is somewhat mitigated if his circumstances include financial security, a late retirement, good living arrangements, close family ties and friendships, a positive attitude to religion expressed in church attendance, extent and variety of interests, and good health (Pressey and Simcoe 1950, Havighurst and Shanas 1950). Well-adjusted elderly people are distinguished from the less happily adjusted by these kinds of circumstance. It is probable that the first three circumstances are the most crucial in freeing old people from psychological insecurity and in maintaining their customary contacts and interests.

For the female there appear to be two major problems. The first is to release herself from the stultifying effect of the domestic role. The second derives from her tendency to hormonal deficit after middle age. These problems would seem to be simple, in the sense that their solution depends not so much on her own efforts as on technical and scientific advance. They call for practical measures and are not deeply entrenched in cultural tradition. A third type of problem, that of combining the roles of wife and mother with that of a career occurs frequently in an expanding economy. The social changes induced by such economic demands for labour increase the complexity of women's reference groups and enable them to experience autonomy within a wider social context. In so doing, however, women come to share with men the stress which arises when ego-oriented drives conflict with social expectations. Incidental to this, there should be a lessening of strain in fathers and husbands, when wives and mothers share their erstwhile masculine role.

Under such economic conditions, it is to be expected that every decade will witness a change in the social pattern of ageing in men and women and this in its turn should call for a flexible organisation of social services to meet their needs. The social relevance of geriatric studies may become comparable to that which is accorded to the study of child development, for the senium is now almost as prolonged a period of disengagement as childhood is of increase in social involvement. In fact, it may be that the wheel will turn full circle – the processes of ageing being seen as a reflection in reverse of the processes of growth. In this event the norms for growth and ageing should come to rest on criteria common to both.

Bibliography

ADORNO, T. W., FRENKEL-BRUNSWIK, E., LEVINSON, D. J. AND SANFORD, R. N., *The Authoritarian Personality*, Harper Bros, N.Y., 1950.

ALEXANDER, I. E. AND ADLERSTEIN, A. M., 'Studies in the Psychology of Death', *Perspectives in Personality Research*, eds. David, H. P. and Brengelmann, J. C., Crosbie, Lockwood and Son Ltd, London, 1960.

ALLEN, E. P. AND SMITH, P., *The value of vocational tests as aids to choice of employment*, City of Birmingham Education Committee, 1932.

ALLPORT, G. W., *The individual and his religion*, Constable, 1951.

ALLPORT, G. W., 'Uniqueness in Students', *The goals of higher education*, ed. Weatherford, W. D., Harvard University Press, 1960.

ALLPORT, G. W., 'Pattern and Growth in Personality', *Annual Review of Psychology*, Annual Reviews Inc., U.S.A., 1962.

ALLPORT, G. W. AND VERNON, P. E., *Studies in Expressive Movement*, Macmillan, 1933.

AMBROSE, J. A., 'The Development of the Smiling Response in Early Infancy', *Determinants of Infant Behaviour*, ed. Foss, B., Methuen, 1962.

AMBROSE, J. A., 'The concept of a critical period for the development of social responsiveness in early infancy', *Determinants of Infant Behaviour*, II, ed. Foss, B., Methuen, 1963.

AMOS, W. E., *A study of self-concept: delinquent boys' accuracy in selected self-evaluations*, Genet. Psychol. Monog. 67, 1963.

ANDERSON, H. H. AND BREWER, J. F., *Studies of teachers' classroom personalities*, II. Appl. Psychol. Monogr. of A.P.A., No. 8, 1946.

ANTHONY, S., *The child's discovery of death*, Harcourt, N.Y., 1940.

ATKINSON, J. W., ed., *Motives in fantasy, action and society*, Van Nostrand, Princeton, 1958.

AUSUBEL, H., *Theory and Problems of Adolescent Development*, Grune and Stratton, N.Y., 1954.

AVELING, F. A. P., *Personality and Will*, Nisbet, London, 1931.

BALBIN, E. AND SHIMMIN, S., 'Training the middle aged for inspection tasks', *Occup. Psychol.* **38**, 2, 1964.

BALDWIN, A. L., KALHORN, J. AND BREESE, F. H., *Patterns of Parent Behaviour*, Psychol. Monog. 58, 1945.

BALINSKY, B., *An analysis of mental factors of various age groups from 9–60*, Genet. Psychol. Monog. 23, 1941.

BANDURA, A. AND WALTERS, R. H., *Adolescent Aggression*, Ronald Press, N.Y., 1959.

BARTLETT, F. C., *Thinking. An experimental and social study*, Allen and Unwin, 1958.

BASS, B. M., 'Authoritarianism and acquiescence', *J. abnor. soc. Psychol.* **51**, 1955.

BAYLEY, N., *California Scale of Motor Development*, University of California, Syllabus Series 259, 1936.

BAYLEY, N., 'On the growth of intelligence', *Am. Psychologist* **10**, 12, 1955.

BAYLEY, N. AND SCHAEFER, E. S., 'Maternal Behaviour and Personality Data', from the Berkley Growth Study, unpublished paper reported by Allport, G. W. in *Annual Review of Psychology* 1962, Annual Reviews Inc., U.S.A., 1960.

BECKER, H. S., 'Personal change in adult life', *Sociometry* **27**, 1, 1964.

BELOFF, H., 'Two forms of social conformity: acquiescence and conventionality', *J. abnor. soc. Psychol.* LVI, 1958.

BENDER, L., 'The treatment of aggression: III Aggression in Childhood', *Amer. J. Orthopsychiat.* **13**, 1943.

BENEDICT, R., *Patterns of culture*, Routledge and Kegan Paul, 1936.

BENNETT, C. C., *An enquiry into the genesis of poor reading*, Teachers' College Contributions to Education, No. 755, N.Y. Teachers' College, Columbia University, 1938.

BENTLEY, M., *The New Field of Psychology*, Appleton Century, 1934.

BERELSON, B. R., LAZARFIELD, P. F. AND MCPHIE, W. N., *Voting: a study of opinion formation in a presidential election*, Univ. Chicago Press, 1954.

BERKOWITZ, B. AND GREEN, R. F., 'Changes in Intellect with age', *J. genet. Psychol.* **103**, 1953.

BERLYNE, D. E., *Conflict, Arousal and curiosity*, McGraw-Hill, N.Y., 1960.

BHATT, L. J. AND PATHAK, N. S., 'A study of functions of supervisory staff and the characteristics essential for success as viewed by a group of supervisors', *Manas* 9, reported in *Psychol. Abstracts* **38**, 3, 4778, 1964.

BIRREN, J. E., *The psychology of aging*, Prentice-Hall, 1964.

BLAU, Z. S., 'Changes in status and age identification', *Am. Soc. Rev.* 17, 1956.

BLAUVELT, H. AND MCKENNA, J., 'Mother - Neonate Interaction: Capacity of the Human Newborn for Orientation', *Determinants of Infant Behaviour*, ed. Foss, B., Methuen, 1962.

BOEHM, L., 'The development of independence: a comparative study', *Child Development* **28**, 1957.

BOTT, E., 'The concept of class as a reference group', *Hum. Relat.* VII, 1954.

BOTWINICK, J., 'Drives, expectancies and emotions', *Handbook of aging and the individual*, ed. Birren, J. E., Univ. Chicago Press, 1959.

BOWLBY, J., 'The Nature of the Child's Tie to his Mother', *International J. of Psa.* **39**, 1958.

BRENGELMANN, J. C., 'Complex perceptual processes', *Perceptual processes and mental illness*, ed. Eysenck, H. J., Maudsley Monog. 2, Chapman and Hall, 1957.

BRENNAN, W. K., 'The relation of Social Adaption, Emotional Adjustment and Moral Judgment to Intelligence in Primary School Children', *Brit. J. Educ. Psychol.* XXXII, 2, 1962.

BRUNER, J. S., *The process of education*, Harvard Univ. Press, 1960.

BRUNER, J. S., GOODNOW, J. J. AND AUSTIN, G. A., *A study of thinking*, Wiley, N.Y., 1956.

BULL, M., 'Science in Secondary Modern Schools', *Studies in Educ.*, Univ. Hull, II, 5, 1957.

BURGESS, E. W. AND COTTRELL, L. S., *Predicting success or failure in marriage*, Prentice-Hall, N.Y., 1939.

BURT, C. L., 'Factorial analysis of emotional traits', *Char. and Person.* 7, 1939.

BURT, C. L., 'The education of the young adolescent: the psychological implications of the Norwood Report', *Brit. J. Educ. Psychol.* XIII, 3, 1943.

BURT, C. L., Critical notice: 'The psychology of creative ability', *Brit. J. Educ. Psychol.* XXXII, 3, 1962.

BUSS, A. H., *The psychology of aggression*, Wiley, N.Y., 1961.

BUSWELL, G. T., *Fundamental reading habits: a study of their development*, Supplementary Education Monog. Univ. of Chicago No. 21, 1922.

BUTCHER, H. J., AINSWORTH, M. AND NESBITT, J. E., 'Personality factors and school achievement', *Brit. J. Educ. Psychol.* XXXIII, 3, 1963.

CARDNO, J. A., 'Will in the dictionaries', *Australian J. Psychol.* **14**, 3, 1962.

CARLSON, A. J., 'Physiologic changes of normal ageing', *Geriatric Medicine*, ed. Steiglitz, E. J., Saunders, Philadelphia, 1949.

CARTER, H. D., 'The development of interest in vocations', *Adolescence*, 43rd year book N.S.S.E. Part 1, Univ. of Chicago Press, Chicago, 1944.

CASTENADA, A., BOYD, R., McCANDLESS, B. R. AND PALERMO, D. S., 'Anxiety in children and social status', *Child Development* **27**, 3, 1956.

CASTENADA, A., BOYD, R., McCANDLESS, B. R. AND PALERMO, D. S., 'The Children's Form of the manifest anxiety scale', *Child Development* **27**, 3, 1956.

CATTELL, R. B., *Description and Measurement of Personality*, Harrap, London, 1946.

CATTELL, R. B., *Personality: a systematic, theoretical and factual study*, McGraw-Hill, N.Y., 1950.

CATTELL, R. B., 'Personality, Role, Mood and Situation-perception', *Psychol. Review* **70**, 1, 1963.

CATTELL, R. B., BLEWETT, D. B. AND BELOFF, J. R., 'The inheritance of personality', *Am. J. Genet.* **7**, 1955.

CATTELL, R. B. AND COAN, R. W., 'Personality Factors in middle childhood as revealed in parents' ratings', *Child Development* **28**, 4, 1957.

CATTELL, R. B. AND HORN, J., *An integrating study of the factor structure of adult attitude-interests*, Genet. Psychol. Monog. 67, 1963.

CATTELL, R. B., HORN, J. AND BUTCHER, H. J., 'The Dynamic Structure of Attitudes in Adults: A description of some established factors and of their measurement by the motivational analysis test', *Brit. J. Psychol.* **53**, 1, 1962.

CAVAN, R. S., BURGESS, E. W., HAVIGHURST, R. J. AND GOLDHAMER, H., *Personal adjustment in old age*, Science Research Associates, Chicago, 1949.

CENTERS, R., 'Motivational aspects of occupational stratification', *J. Soc. Psychol.* **28**, 1948.

CHANG, H-D., 'Electrical Activity of Dendrites': in XXVIIth Annual Conference of Millbank Memorial Fund, *The Biology of Mental Health and Disease*, Cassell and Co. Ltd, 1952.

CHILD, I. C., 'The relation of somatotype to self ratings on Sheldon's temperamental traits', *J. Pers.* **18**, 1950.

CHOWN, S. M., 'Rigidity – a flexible concept', *Psychol. Bull.* **56**, 3, 1959.

CLARAPEDE, E., 'Recognition and me-ness', Rapaport, D., *Organisation and pathology of thought*, Columbia Univ. Press, N.Y., 1911.

CLARKE, A. D. B., 'Problems in assessing the later effects of early experience', *Foundations of child psychiatry*, ed. Miller, E., Pergamon Press, 1965.

COHEN, J., DEARNLEY, E. J. AND HANSEL, C. E. M., 'A quantitative study of meaning', *Brit. J. Educ. Psychol.* XXVIII, 2, 1958.

COLE, L. W., *Human behaviour*, World Book Co., N.Y., 1953.

CONKLIN, E., *Principles of adolescent psychology*, Holt, N.Y., 1933.

CONRAD, H. S., FREEMAN, F. N. AND JONES, H. E., 'Differential Mental Growth', *Adolescence*, 43rd book, N.S.S.E. Part I, Univ. of Chicago Press, Chicago, 1944.

CRANE, A. R., Symposium: 'The development of moral values in children IV – Preadolescent gangs and the moral development of children', *Brit. J. Educ. Psychol.* XXVIII, 2, 1958.

CRITES, J. O., 'Vocational interest in relation to vocational motivation', *Brit. J. Educ. Psychol.* LIV, 5, 1963.

DAVIS, A., 'Child rearing and social class', *Child Behaviour and Development*, eds. Barker, R. C. et al., McGraw-Hill, N.Y., 1943.

DAVIS, K., 'Final note on a case of extreme isolation', *Am. J. Soc.* **52**, 1947.

DEMPSEY, E. W., 'Homeostasis', *Handbook of Experimental Psychology*, Ed. Stevens, C. S., Wiley, N.Y., 1951.

DE SILVA, H. R., 'On an investigation of driving skill', *Hum. Fact.* **10**, 8, 1936.

DEUTSCHE, J. M., *The Development of Children's Concepts of Causal Relations*, Univ. of Minnesota Press, 1937.

DITCHBURN, R. W., *Research* **9**, 466, London, 1956.

DOLLARD, J. AND MILLER, N. E., *Personality and psychotherapy: an analysis in terms of learning, thinking and culture*, McGraw-Hill, N.Y., 1950.

DOUVAN, E. A. AND KAYE, C., *Adolescent girls*, Ann Arbor, Michigan, 1957.

DYKMAN, R. A., REESE, W. C., GALBRECHT, C. R. AND THOMASSON, P. J., 'Psychophysiological reactions to novel stimuli: measurement, adaptation and relationship of psychological and physiological variables in the normal human', *Ann. N.Y. Acad. Sci.* **79**, 1959.

EISENSTADT, S. N., *From generation to generation*, Routledge and Kegan Paul, London, 1956.

ELLIS, E., 'Social and psychological correlates of upward social mobility among unmarried career women', *Am. Soc. Rev.* **17**, 1952.

ELLIS, R. S., 'Norms for some structural changes in the human cerebellum from birth to old age', *J. compar. neurol.* **3**, 2, 1920.

ESCALONA, S. AND HEIDER, G. M., *Prediction and Outcome*, Basic Books Inc., 1959.

EYSENCK, H. J., *Dimensions of personality*, Kegan Paul, 1947.

EYSENCK, H. J., *The Structure of human personality*, Methuen, 1953.

EYSENCK, H. J., *The dynamics of anxiety and hysteria*, Routledge and Kegan Paul, London, 1957.

EYSENCK, H. J., *Eysenck Personality Inventory*, Univ. of London Press, 1959.

EYSENCK, H. J. ed., *Experiments with drugs*, Pergamon Press, 1963.

EYSENCK, H. J., 'Principles and Methods of personality description, classification and diagnosis', *Brit. J. Psychol.* **55**, 3, 1964*a*.

EYSENCK, H. J. ed., *Experiments in motivation*, Pergamon Press, 1964*b*.

FELDMAN, M. P., 'Motivation and task performance', in Eysenck, H. J. ed., 1964*b* above.

FESTINGER, L., *A theory of cognitive dissonance*, Row, Peterson, 1957.

FISCHER, J. A. AND A., 'The New Englanders of Orchard Town U.S.A.', *Six cultures*, ed. Whiting, B. B., Wiley, N.Y., 1963.

FISHER, M. B. AND BIRREN, J. E., 'Age and strength', *J. appl. Psychol.* **31**, 1947.

FLEISHMAN, E. A. AND HEMPEL, W. E., 'Changes in factor structure of a complex psychomotor test as a function of practice', *Psychometrika* **19**, 1954.

FLEISHMAN, E. A. AND HEMPEL, W. E., 'The relation between abilities and improvement with practice in a visual discrimination reaction task', *J. exp. Psychol.* **49**, 1955.

FOULDS, G. A., 'Variations in the intellectual activities of adults', *Am. J. Psychol.* **62**, 1949.

FRAISSE, P. ET VAUTREY, P., 'La perception de l'éspace, de la vitesse, et du temps chez l'enfant de cinq ans', *Enfance*, **1**, 1952.

FREEMAN, G. L. AND KATZOFF, E. T., 'Methodological evaluation of the Galvanic Skin Response, with special reference to the formula for R.Q. (Recovery Quotient)', *J. exp. Psychol.* **30**, 1942.

FREEMAN, G. L. AND SIMPSON, R. M., 'The effects of muscular tension upon palmar skin resistance', *J. gen. Psychol.* **18**, 1938.

FREUD, A. AND DANN, S., 'An experiment in group upbringing', *Psychoanalytic study of the child, no. 6*, International Univ. Press, 1951.

FREUD, S., 'Fifth lecture on psycho-analysis', *Standard edition of the complete psychological works of Sigmund Freud*, XI, Hogarth Press, 1910.

FROLOV, J. P., *Pavlov and his school: The theory of conditioned reflexes*, Oxford Univ. Press, 1937.

FROMM, E., *Escape from freedom*, Rinehart, N.Y., 1941.

GAGNÉ, R., *Factors in acquiring knowledge of a mathematical task*, Psychol. Monogr. 76, 7, 1962.

GAL'PERIN, P. YA. AND TALYZINA, N. F., 'Formation of elementary geometrical concepts and their dependence on directed participation by the pupils', *Recent Soviet Psychology*, ed. O'Connor, 1961.

GESELL, A. et al., *The first five years of life*, Harper Bros., N.Y., 1940.

GETZELS, J. W. AND JACKSON, P. W., 'A study of giftedness: a multidimensional approach', *The goals of higher education*, ed. Weatherford, W. D., Harvard Univ. Press, 1960.

GETZELS, J. W. AND JACKSON, P. W., *Creativity and Intelligence*, Wiley, N.Y., 1962.

GILBERT, J. G., 'Memory loss in senescence', *J. abnor. soc. Psychol.* **36**, 1941.

GOLDFARB, W., *An investigation of reaction time in older adults and its relationship to certain observed mental test patterns*, Columbia Univ. Contributions to education 831, 1941.

GOLDMAN, R. J., *Some aspects of the development of religious thinking in childhood and adolescence*, Research summary, unpublished, Univ. of Reading, 1962.

GOLDSTEIN, K. AND SCHEERER, M., *Abstract and concrete behaviour*, Psychol. Monog. **53**, 2, 1941.

GRANGER, G. W., 'Personality and visual perception: a review', *J. ment. Sci.* **99**, 1953.

GRANGER, G. W., 'Simple perceptual processes', *Perceptual processes and mental illness*, ed. Eysenck, H. J., Maudsley Monog. 2, Chapman and Hall, 1957.

GRUEN, E. W., 'Level of aspiration in relation to personality factors in adolescents', *Child Development* **16**, 1945.

GUILFORD, J. P., 'The structure of intellect', *Psychol. Bull.* **53**, 4, 1956.

HALLWORTH, H. J., 'Anxiety in secondary school children', *Brit. J. Educ. Psychol.* XXXI, 3, 1961.

HALLWORTH, H. J. AND WAITE, G., 'A factorial study of value judgments among adolescent girls', *Brit. J. Stat. Psychol.* XVI, 1, 1963.

HALSTEAD, H., 'A psychometric study of senility', *J. ment. Sci.* **89**, 1943.

HAMILTON, V., 'Perceptual and personality dynamics in reactions to ambiguity', *Brit. J. Psychol.* **48**, 3, 1957.

HAMILTON, V., 'Techniques and methods in psychological assessment', *Bull. Brit. Psychol. Soc.* **17**, 56, 1964.

HARLOW, H. F., 'The development of affectional patterns in infant monkeys', *Determinants of infant behaviour*, I, ed. Foss, B., Methuen, 1962.

HARLOW, H. F., 'Maternal affectional system', *Determinants of infant behaviour*, II, ed. Foss, B., Methuen, 1963.

HARTSHORN, H. AND MAY, M. A., 'Studies in deceit', Part 1 of *Studies in the nature of character*, Columbia Univ., Macmillan, 1930.

HAVIGHURST, R. J. AND NEUGARTEN, B. L., *American Indian and white children*, Univ. of Chicago Press, Chicago, 1955.

HAVIGHURST, R. J. AND SHANAS, E., 'Adjustment to retirement', *Sociol. Soc. Res.* **34**, 1950.

HAVIGHURST, R. J. AND TABA, H., *Adolescent character and personality*, Wiley, N.Y., 1949.

HAYES, K. J., 'Vocalization and speech in chimpanzees', *Amer. psychologist* **5**, 1950.

HEBB, D. O., *A textbook of psychology*, Saunders, 1958.

HEBB, D. O., *Organisation of behaviour*, Wiley, N.Y., Chapman and Hall, London, 1949.

HEBRON, M. E., 'The curriculum of the secondary modern school', *Studies in Educ.*, Univ. Hull, II, **5**, 1957.

HEBRON, M. E., 'A factorial study of learning a new number system and its relation to attainment, intelligence and temperament', *Brit. J. Educ. Psychol.* XXXII, **1**, 1962.

HEBRON, M. E. AND LONDON, W., 'A study of stereotypes in the caretaking of English children', *Brit. J. Educ. Psychol.* **32**, 1, 1963.

HEBRON, M. E. AND DE SAMARDICK, A., 'A comparison of pupils and teachers in national and subcultural groups', *Studies in Educ.*, Univ. Hull, III, **4**, 1960.

HERON, A., 'A two-part personality measure for use as a research criterion', *Brit. J. Psychol.* **47**, 1956.

HICKS, J. A. AND HAYES, M., 'Study of the characteristics of 250 junior high school children', *Child Development* **9**, 1938.

HIGHFIELD, M. E., *The diagnostic significance of the Terman-Merrill Scale*, M.A. thesis, London Univ., 1945.

HIGHFIELD, M. E., *The education of backward children*, 2nd ed., Harrap, 1951.

HIGHFIELD, M. E. AND PINSENT, A., *A survey of rewards and punishments in schools*, Report No. 3, N.F. Ed. Res., Newnes, London, 1952.

HOLLINGSHEAD, A. B., *Elmstown's youth: the impact of social classes on youth*, Wiley, N.Y., 1949.

HOLLINGWORTH, L. S., *Psychology of the adolescent*, Staples Press Ltd, 1930.

HORNEY, K., *Neurotic personality of our time*, Kegan Paul, 1937.

HOUSTON, J. P. AND MEDNICK, S. A., 'Creativity and the need for novelty', *J. abnor. soc. Psychol.* **66**, 2, 1963.

HOVLAND, C. I. AND WEISS, W. I., 'Transmission of information concerning concepts through positive and negative instances', *J. Exp. Psychol.* **45**, 1953.

HUDSON, L., 'The relation of psychological test scores to academic bias', *Brit. J. Educ. Psychol.* XXXIII, 2, 1963.

HULL, C. L., *A behaviour system*, Yale Univ. Press., New Haven, 1952.

HUNT, J. MCV., *Intelligence and experience*, Ronald Press Co., N.Y., 1961.

HUNT, W. L., 'The relative rates of decline of Wechsler-Bellevue "hold" and "don't hold" tests', *J. Consult. Psychol.* **13**, 1949.

INHELDER, B. AND PIAGET, J., *The growth of logical thinking*, Routledge, 1958.

ISAACS, S., *The intellectual growth of young children*, Routledge, 1930.

JACOBSON, A. H., 'Conflict of attitude toward the role of the husband and wife in marriage, *Am. soc. Rev.* **17**, 1952.

JONES, H. E., 'Adolescence', *N.S.S. ed. 43rd year book*, part I, chap. VI, 1944.

JONES, H. E. AND CAPLAN, C. J., 'Psychological aspects of mental disorders in later life', *Mental disorders in later life*, ed. Kadan, O.J., Stanford Univ. Press, 1945.

JONES, L. V. AND MORRIS, C., 'Relations of temperament to the choice of values', *J. abnor. soc. Psychol.* **53**, 1956.

JUNG, C. G., *The integration of the personality*, Kegan Paul, 1940.

KAGAN, J., 'The child's perception of the parent', *J. abnor. soc. Psychol.* **53**, 1956.

KAGAN, J., 'American longtitudinal research on psychological development', *Child Development* **35**, 1, 1964.

KAGAN, J. AND MOSS, H. A., *Birth to maturity*, Wiley, N.Y., 1962.

KAHL, J. A., 'Educational aspirations of "common man" boys', *Harvard Educ. Review* **23**, 1953.

KALUGER, G. AND MARTIN, R., 'The loneliness of the gifted child', *Elementary school journal* **61**, 3, 1960.

KASPER, S., *Measurement of adjustment in adolescents: an extension of personal construct theory and methodology*, Psychol. Monog. **76**, 6, 1962.

KAY, E. et al., 'The development of a job activity questionnaire for production foreman', *Personnel Psychol.* **15**, 4, 1962.

KEATS, J. A., 'Formal and concrete thought processes', *Research Bulletin*, RB-55-17, Educational Testing Service, Princeton, New Jersey, 1955.

KELLOG, W. M. AND KELLOG, L. A., *The ape and the child: A study of environmental influence upon early behaviour*, McGraw-Hill, N.Y., 1933.

KELLY, E. L., 'Consistency of the adult personality', *Am. Psychol.* **10**, 1955.

KELLY, G. A., *The psychology of personal constructs, Theory of personality, I*, Morton, N.Y., 1955.

KEYNES, J. M., *A general theory of employment, interest and money*, Macmillan, London, 1936.

KIMBALL, B., 'Case studies in educational failure during adolescence', *Am. J. Orthopsychiatry* **23**, 1953.

KINSEY, A. C., POMEROY, W. B., MARTIN, C. E. AND GERRARD, P. H., *Sexual behaviour in the human female*, Saunders, Philadelphia, 1953.

KIRK, J. E., 'Steroid hormones and ageing: a review', *J. Geront.* **6**, 1951.

KITSON, H. D., *The psychology of vocational adjustment*, Lippincott, Philadelphia, 1925.

KOCH, H. L., 'The relation in young children between characteristics of their playmates and certain attributes of their siblings', *Child Development* **28**, 1957.

KOGAN, K. L. AND JACKSON, J. K., 'Conventional sex role stereotypes and actual perception', *Psychol. Reports* **13**, 1, 1963.

KOHN, M. L., 'Social class and the exercise of parental authority', *Am. Soc. Rev.* **24**, 1959.

KUHLEN, R. G. AND ARNOLD, M., 'Age differences in religious beliefs and problems during adolescence', *J. gen. Psychol.* **65**, 1944.

KUNTZ, A., *Autonomic nervous system*, Lea and Febiger, Philadelphia, 1945.

KUO, Z. Y., 'Ontogeny of embryonic behaviour in aves: V. The reflex concept in the light of embryonic behaviour in birds', *Psychol. Rev.* **39**, 1932.

LACEY, J. I., 'Consistency of patterns of somatic response to stress', *Am. Psychologist* **4**, 1949.

LARKIN, P., *The Whitsun Weddings*, Faber, 1964.

LASHLEY, K. S., *Brain mechanisms and intelligence*, Univ. Chicago Press, 1929.

LASLETT, P., *Social change in England 1901–1951*, B.B.C. Broadcast, 25 March 1962.

LEHMAN, H. C., *Age and achievement*, Princeton Univ. Press, 1953.

LEHMAN, H. C. AND HEIDLER, J. B., 'Chronological age vs. quality of literary output', *Am. J. Psychol.* **62**, 1949.

LEONTEV, A. N., 'Learning as a problem in psychology', *Recent Soviet Psychology*, ed. O'Connor, 1961.

LEVIN, H., 'The influence of classroom control on kindergarten children's fantasy aggression', *Elem. School J.* **55**, 1955.

LEVINGER, G., 'Task and social behaviour in marriage', *Sociom.* **27**, 4, 1964.

LEWIN, K., *A Dynamic Theory of Personality*, McGraw-Hill, N.Y., London, 1935.

LEWIN, K., *Field theory in social science*, Tavistock Publications, 1952.

LEWIS, M. M., *Infant speech: A study of the beginnings of Language*, Kegan Paul, 1936.

LINDSLEY, D. B., 'Emotion', *Handbook of Experimental Psychology*, ed. Stevens, S. S., Wiley, N.Y., 1951.

LINDSLEY, D. B., 'The reticular activating system and perceptual integration', *Electrical stimulation of the brain*, ed. Sheer, D. E., Univ. of Texas Press, 1961.

LORGE, S. A., 'The influence of the test upon the nature of mental decline as a function of age', *J. Educ. Psychol.* **27**, 1936.

LOVELL, K. AND OGILVIE, E., 'A study of the conservation of weight in the junior school child', *Brit. J. Educ. Psychol.* XXXI, 2, 1961.

LOUTTIT, C. M., *Clinical Psychology*, Harper, N.Y., 1936.

LUCAS, W. P., PRYOR, H. B., BEST, C. AND POPE, S. T., 'Growth problems: II Basal metabolic rate variations in relation to body build, adolescence and allergy in children', *J. Pediat.* **3**, 1933.

LUCHINS, A. S., *Mechanisation in problem solving: the effect of einstellung*, Psychol. Monog. 54, 6, 1942.
LUCHINS, A. S., 'The Einstellung test of rigidity: its relation to concreteness of thinking', *J. Consult. Psychol.* **15**, 1951.
LUCHINS, A. S. AND E. H., 'New experimental attempts at preventing mechanisation in problem solving', *J. of Genet. Psychol.* **42**, 1950.
LURIA, A. R., 'The nature of human conflicts: or emotion, conflict and will, an objective study of disorganisation and control of human behaviour', *Trans.* Gantt, W. H., Liveright, N.Y., 1932.
LURIA, A. R., 'The role of rhythmic patterns in childhood', *Am. J. Psychiat.* **105**, 1949.
LURIA, A. R., 'Experimental analysis of the development of Voluntary Action in children', *Perspectives in Personality Research*, eds. David, H. P., Brengelmann, J. C., Crosby Lockwood and Son Ltd, London, 1960.
LURIA, A. R., 'Genesis of voluntary movement', *Recent Soviet Psychology*, ed. O'Connor, Pergamon Press, 1961.
LURIA, A. R. AND YUDOVICH, F. I., *Speech and the development of Mental Processes in the child*, Staples Press, 1959.
MACCURDY, J. T., *Common principles in psychology and physiology*, Harvard Univ. Press, Cambridge, 1928.
MACE, C. A., 'Satisfaction in work', *Occup. Psychol.* **22**, 5, 1946.
MACE, C. A., 'The analysis of human skills', *Occup. Psychol.* **24**, 1950.
MACE, C. A., 'Resistance to change', *Occup. Psychol.* **27**, 1953*a*.
MACE, C. A., 'Homeostasis, needs and values', *Brit. J. Psychol.* **44**, 1953*b*.
MACKAY, G. W. AND VERNON, P. E., 'The measurement of learning ability', *Brit. J. Educ. Psychol.* XXXIII, 2, 1963.
MAGOUN, H. W., 'The ascending reticular system and wakefulness', *Brain mechanisms and consciousness*, ed. De la Fresnaye, J. F. C. Thomas, Springfield, Ill., 1954.
MARGARY, J. F. AND EICHORN, J. R., *The exceptional child*, Holt, Rinehart and Winston, N.Y., 1961.
MARKS, E., 'Skin colour judgments of Negro college students', *J. abnor. soc. Psychol.* **38**, 1943.
MATHEW, G., *Byzantine aesthetics*, Murray, 1963.
MAXWELL, A. E., 'Discrepancies between the patterns of abilities for normal and neurotic children', *J. ment. Sci.* **107**, 1961.
MCCLELLAND, D. C., ATKINSON, J. W., CLARK, R. A. AND LOWELL, E. L., *The Achievement motive*, Appleton-Century-Crofts, N.Y., 1953.

MCDOUGALL, W., *An introduction to social psychology*, Luce, Boston, 1909.

MCGEOCH, J. A., 'Learning', *Introduction to psychology*, eds. Boring, E. G., Langfield, H. S. and Weld, H. P., Wiley, N.Y., 1939.

MEDNICK, S. A., 'The associative basis of the creative process', *Psychol. Rev.* **69**, 3, 1962.

MEIER, N. C. ed., *Studies in the psychology of art*, Psychol. Monog. XLV, vols. I, II, III, 1933.

MILES, W. R., 'Measures of certain human abilities throughout the life span', *Proc. nat. acad. Sci., Washington* **17**, 1951.

MILLER, N. E., 'Implications for Theories of reinforcement', *Electrical stimulation of the brain*, ed. Sheer, D. E., Univ. of Texas Press, 1961.

MIYAMOTO, S. F. AND DORNBUSCH, S., 'A test of interactionist hypotheses of self-conception', *Am. J. Soc.* **51**, 1956.

MOORE, K. C., *The mental development of the child*, Psychol. Rev. Monogr. 1, 3, 1896.

MORGAN, C. T., 'The Psychophysiology of Learning', *Handbook of Experimental Psychology*, ed. Stevens, S. S., Wiley, N.Y., 1951.

MORGOULIS, J. AND TOURNAY, A., 'Poliomyélite et schéma corporel', *Enfance*, Nos. 4–5, 1963.

MORRIS, H. H. (Jr.), ESCOLL, P. J. AND WEXLER, R., 'Aggressive behaviour disorders in childhood: a follow-up study', *Am. J. Psychiat.* **112**, 1956.

MORRIS, J. F., Symposium: 'The development of moral values in children. II – The development of adolescent value-judgments', *Brit. J. Educ. Psychol.* XXVIII, 2, 1958.

MOSS, H. A., 'Standards of conduct for students, teachers and parents', *J. counsel Psychol.* **2**, reported in Mussen, P. H., Conger, J. J. and Kagan, J., *Child Development and Personality*, 2nd. ed., Harper and Row, 1955.

MOWRER, O. H., 'A stimulus-response analysis of anxiety and its role as a reinforcing agent', *Psychol. Rev.* **46**, 1939.

MOWRER, O. H., *Learning theory and the symbolic processes*, Wiley, N.Y., 1960*a*.

MURPHY, G., *Personality: a biosocial approach to origins and structure*, Harper, London and N.Y., 1947.

NASON, L. J., *The Academic achievement of gifted high school students*, Univ. of S. California, Educ. Mon. series, No, 17, 1958.

NAUTA, W. J. H., 'Hypothalmic regulation of sleep in rats: an experimental study', *J. Neurophysiol.* **9**, 1946.

NEFF, W. D., 'Neural mechanisms of auditory discrimination', *Sensory Communication*, ed. Stone, G., Technology Press, Cambridge, Mass., 1962.

NEILSON, P., 'Shirley's babies after fifteen years', *J. Genet. Psychol.* **73**, 1948.

NEWELL, A., SHAW, J. C. AND SIMON, H. A., 'Elements in a human theory of problem solving', *Psychol. Rev.* **65**, 1958.

NIETZSCHE, F., *Beyond good and evil*, 1886.

NUTTIN, J., *Tâche, Réussite et Échec: Théorie de la Conduite Humain*, Publications Universitaires de Louvain, Louvain, 1953.

OSGOOD, C. E., 'Motivational dynamics of language behaviour', *Nebraska Symposium*, ed. Jones, M. R., 1957.

OSGOOD, C. E., TANNENBAUM, P. H. AND SUCI, G. J., *The measurement of meaning*, Univ. of Ill. Press, Urbana, 1958.

OVSIANKINA-RICHERS, M. A., *Rorschach Psychology*, Wiley, N.Y., 1960.

PARNELL, R. W., 'Physique and individual alcohol consumption', *Int. J. Alc. and Alcoholism* **3**, 1955*a*.

PARNELL, R. W., PEIERLS, G. E., STANLEY, C. C. AND WESTTROPP, C. K., 'Physique and the grammar school entrance examination', *Brit. Med. J. i.*, 1955*b*.

PECK, R. F. AND HAVIGHURST, R. J., *The psychology of character development*, Wiley, N.Y., 1960.

PENFIELD, W., 'Studies of the cerebral cortex of man: A review and an interpretation', *Brain mechanisms and consciousness*, ed. Charles, C. T., Springfield, Ill., 1954.

PENFIELD, W. AND JASPER, H., *Epilepsy and the functional anatomy of the human brain*, Little, Brown and Co., Boston, 1954.

PENFIELD, W. AND ROBERTS, L., *Speech and brain-mechanisms*, Princeton Univ. Press, 1959.

PETERSON, D. E. et al., 'Child behaviour problems and parental attitudes', *Child Development* **32**, 1, 1961.

PIAGET, J., *The child's conception of physical causality*, Harcourt, Brace and Co., N.Y., 1930.

PIAGET, J., *The psychology of intelligence*, Routledge, 1950.

PIAGET, J., *Language and thought of the child*, 3rd ed., Routledge, London, 1952.

PIAGET, J. AND INHELDER, B., *Le développement des quantités chez l'enfant*, Delachaux et Nestlé, Neuchatel, 1941.

PIAGET, J. AND INHELDER, B., *La genese de l'idée de hazard chez l'enfant*, Presses Universitaires de France, Paris, 1951.

PIAGET, J. et al., *Les notions de mouvement et de vitesse chez l'enfant*, Presses Universitaires de France, Paris, 1946*a*.

PIAGET, J. et al., *Le développement de la notion de temps chez l'enfant*, Presses Universitaires de France, Paris, 1946*b*.

POSTMAN, L. AND BRUNER, J. S., 'Multiplicity of set as a determinant of perceptual behaviour', *J. exp. Psychol.* **39**, 1949.

PRESSEY, S. L. et al., *Life: a psychological survey*, Harper, N.Y., 1939.

PRESSEY, S. L. AND SIMCOE, E., 'Case study comparison of successful and problem old people', *J. Geront.* 5, 1950.

PRIBRAM, K. H., 'Theory in Physiological Psychology', *Am. Rev. Psychol.* **11**, 1960.

PRIBRAM, K. H., 'The implications for systematic studies of behaviour', *Electrical stimulation of the brain*, ed. Sheer, D. E., Univ. of Texas Press, 1961.

PROVENCE, S. AND LIPTON, R. C., *Infants in institutions*, International Univ. Press, 1962.

RABAN, G., 'Le sens de la symmétrie chez les enfants', *Enfance* **1**, 1952.

RABBAN, M., *Sex-role identification in young children in two diverse social groups*, Genet. Psychol. Monog. 42, 1950.

RABIN, A. I. AND GUERTIN, W. H., 'Research with the Wechsler-Bellevue Test', *Psychol. Bull.* **48**, 3, 1951.

RADKE, M., TRAGER, H. C. AND DAVIS, H., *Social perceptions and attitudes of children*, Genet. Psychol. Monog. 40, 1949.

RANSON, S. W., 'Somnolence caused by hypothalmic lesions in the monkey', *Arch. Neurol. Psychiat.* **41**, 1939.

RAVEN, J. C., 'The comparative assessment of intellectual ability', *Brit. J. Psychol.* **39**, 1948.

RAZRAN, G., 'The observable unconscious and the inferable conscious in current Soviet Psychophysiology', *Psychol. Rev.* **68**, 2, 1961.

REIFF, R. AND SCHEERER, M., *Memory and hypnotic age regression*, International Univ. Press Inc., N.Y., 1959.

RIESS, B. F., 'Genetic changes in semantic conditioning', *J. exp. Psychol.* **36**, 1946.

ROGERS, C. R., *Client centred therapy: its current practice, implications and theory*, Houghton Mifflin and Co., Boston, 1951.

ROGERS, C. R., 'Toward a theory of creativity', *Creativity and its cultivation*, ed. Anderson, H. H., Harper Bros., N.Y., 1959.

ROGERS, E. C. AND BEAL, G. M., 'The importance of personal influence in the adoption of technological changes', reported in Secord, P. F. and Backman, C. W., *Social Psychology*, McGraw-Hill, 1958.

ROSEN, B. C. AND D'ANDRADE, R., 'The Psychological origins of achievement motivation', *Sociometry* **22**, 3, 1959.

RUCH, T. C., 'The motor systems', *Handbook of experimental Psychology*, ed. Stevens, S. S., Wiley, N.Y., 1952.

SARASON, S. B. et al., *Anxiety in Elementary School children*, Wiley, London, 1960.

SARBIN, T. R., 'Role theory', *Handbook of social Psychology* I, ed. Lindzey, G., Addison-Wesley, Reading, Mass., 1954.

SCHAEFER, E. S., 'A circumflex model for maternal behaviour', *J. abnor. soc. psychol.* 59, 1959.

SCHAFFER, H. R., 'Some issues for research in the study of attachment behaviour', *Determinants of infant behaviour* II, ed. Foss, B., Methuen, 1963.

SCHILDER, P., *The image and appearance of the human body*, Int. Univ. Press, N.Y., 1950.

SCHONELL, F. J., *Backwardness in the basic subjects*, Oliver and Boyd, 1946.

SEARS, P. S., *Problems in the investigation of achievement and self esteem motivation*, in Jones, M. R., *Nebraska Symposium*, ed. Jones, M. R., 1957.

SEARS, R. R., 'Experimental analysis of psychoanalytic phenomena', *Personality and behaviour disorders*, ed. Hunt, J. M., Ronald Press, N.Y., 1944.

SEARS, R. R. et al., 'Some child rearing antecedents of aggression and dependency in young children', *Genet. Psychol. Monog.* **47**, 1953.

SEARS, R. R., MACCOBY, E. AND LEVIN, H., *Patterns of child rearing*, Peterson and Co., Illinois, Evanston, 1957.

SECORD, P. F. AND BACKMAN, C. W., 'Interpersonal congruency, perceived similarity and friendship', *Sociom.* **27**, 2, 1954*a*.

SECORD, P. F. AND BACKMAN, C. W., *Social Psychology*, McGraw-Hill, 1964*b*.

SELLS, S. B., 'The atmosphere effect', *Archiv. Psychol. N.Y.* 29, no. 200, 1936.

SHEER, D. E., 'Emotional facilitation in learning situations with sub-cortical stimulation of the brain', in *Electrical stimulation of the brain*, ed. Sheer, D. E., Univ. of Texas Press, 1961.

SHELDON, W. H. AND STEVENS, S. S., *Varieties of temperament*, Harper Bros., 1940.

SHELDON, W. H., HARTLS, E. M. AND MCDERMOTT, E., *Varieties of delinquent youth: an introduction to constitutional psychiatry*, Harper, N.Y., 1949.

SHIMMIN, S. AND DE LA MARE, G., 'Individual differences in overtime working', *Occup. Psychol.* **38**, 1, 1964*a*.

SHIMMIN, S. AND DE LA MARE, G., 'Preferred patterns of duty in a flexible shift-working system', *Occup. Psychol.* **38**, 3, 1964*b*.

SHIRLEY, M. M., *The first two years. A study of 25 babies*, Univ. of Minnesota Press, Minneapolis, 1931.

SMITH, H. T. AND STONE, L. J., 'Development Psychology', *Annual Review of Psychology*, eds. Farnsworth, P. S. et al., 1961.

SMITH, W. R., 'Favourable and unfavourable working conditions reported by scientists at two research centres', *Creativity: progress and potential*, ed. Taylor, C. W., McGraw-Hill, 1964.

SOKOLOV, E. N., 'Neuronal models and the orienting influence', *The central nervous system and behaviour*, ed. Brazier, M. A. B., Josiah Macy Jr. Foundation, N.Y., 1960.

SOLOMON, P. etal., *Sensory deprivation*, Harvard Univ. Press, 1961.

SONTAG, L. W., BAKER, C. T. AND NELSON, V. L., 'Mental growth and personality development: a longitudinal study', Monog. Soc. for Res. in *Child Development XXIII*, **68**, 2, 1958.

SPEARMAN, C., *The abilities of man*, Macmillan, 1927.

SPENCER, HERBERT, *Principles of Physiology*, 2nd ed., Vol. II, 1855.

SPITZ, R. A. AND WOLF, K. M., 'Anaclitic depression: an enquiry into the genesis of psychiatric conditions in early childhood', *P.A. Study of the child* 2, Int. Univ. Press, N.Y., 1946.

STAINES, J. W., Symposium: 'The development of children's values, III. The self picture as a factor in the classroom', *Brit. J. Educ. Psychol.* XXVIII, 2, 1958.

STAR, S. A. AND HUGHES, H. M., 'Report on an educational campaign: the Cincinnati plan for the United Nations', *Am. J. Sociol.* **55**, 1950.

STARBUCK, E. D., *The psychology of religion*, Scribner, N.Y., 1900.

STARBUCK, W. H., 'Level of aspiration', *Psychol. Review* **70**, 1, 1963.

STERN, W., *Psychology of early childhood*, 2nd ed. rev., Allen, London, 1930.

STEVENSON, H. W. AND WEIR, M. W., 'Developmental changes in the effects of reinforcement and non-reinforcement of a single response', *Child Development* **32**, 1961.

STRODTBECK, F. L., 'Family interaction, values and achievement', *Talent and society: New perspectives in the identification of talent*, ed. McClelland, D. C. et al., Van Nostrand, Princeton, 1958.

SUBES, J. et al., 'Preferez-vous être une fille ou un garçon?', *Enfance* 7, 1954.

SULLIVAN, H. S., *The interpersonal theory of Psychiatry*, Norton, N.Y., 1953.

SUMOTIRTO, B. W., 'Social attitudes among high school students in Indonesia', *Brit. J. Educ. Psychol.* **32**, 1962.

SWARD, K., 'Age and mental ability in superior men', *Am. J. Psychol.* **58**, 1945.

TERMAN, L. M., *Psychological factors in marital happiness*, McGraw-Hill, N.Y., 1938.

TERMAN, L. M. AND MILES, C. C., *Sex and personality*, McGraw-Hill, N.Y., 1936.

TERMAN, L. M. et al., 'The gifted child grows up', *Genetic Studies of Genius*, IV, Stamford Univ. Press, 1947.

THOMAS, R. C., *Mother-daughter relationships and social behaviour*, Catholic University of American Press, Washington, D.C., 1955.

THORNDIKE, E. L., BREGMAN, E. O., TILTON, J. W. AND WOODYARD, W., *Adult learning*, Macmillan, N.Y., 1928.

THURSTONE, L. L. AND T. G., *Factorial studies of Intelligence*, Psychometr. Monog. No. 2, 1941.

THURSTONE, L. L. AND T. G., *S.R.A. Primary Mental Abilities*, Science Research Associates, Chicago, 1958.

TING-CHUAN LING, *Les réactions chez les Nouveau-Nés avant et après le Repas*, E. Nauwelaerts, Louvain, 1949.

TOMKINS, S. S., 'Personality Research and Psychopathology: A commentary', *Perspectives in personality research*, eds. David, H. P. and Brengelmann, J. C., Crosby Lockwood and Son Ltd, London, 1960.

TUCKMAN, B. W., 'Personality structure: group composition and group functioning', *Sociom.* **27**, 4, 1964.

TUDDENHAM, R. D., *The constancy of personality ratings over two decades*, Genet. Psychol. Monog. 60, 1959.

UHLMANN, F. W. AND SALTZ, E., 'Retention of anxiety material as a function of cognitive differentiation', *J. Pers. Soc. Psychol.* **1**, 1965.

VAN BEEK, H. G., 'The influence of assembly line organisation on output, quality and morale', *Occup. Psychol.* **38**, 1964.

VAN RIPER, C., *Teaching your child to talk*, Harper Bros., N.Y., 1950.

VERNON, M. D., *Further studies in visual perception*, Cambridge Univ. Press, 1954.

VERNON, P. E., *Personality assessment*, Methuen, 1964.

VOGT, O., 'Study of the ageing of the nerve cells', *J. Geront.* **6**, 1951.

VYGOTSKY, L. S., *Thought and language*, Wiley, N.Y., 1962.

WAGMAN, I. H. AND LESSE, H., 'Maximum conduction velocities of motor fibres of the ulnar nerve in human subjects of various ages and sizes', *J. Neurophysiol.* **15**, 1952.

WALLON, H., *Les origines du Caractère chez l'enfant*, Presses Universitaires de France, 2nd ed., 1949.

WALLON, H., 'Importance du mouvement dans le développement psychologique de l'enfant', *Enfance* **9**, 2, 1956.

WALLON, H. AND LURÇAT, L., 'Espace postural et espace environnant (le schéma corporel)', *Enfance* **5**, 1962.

WECHSLER, D., *The measurement and appraisal of Adult intelligence*, 4th ed., Baillière, Tindall and Cox Ltd, London, 1958.

WECKOWICZ, T. E. AND SOMMER, R., 'Body image and self concept in schizophrenia', *J. ment. Sci.* **106**, 1960.

WELFORD, A. T., *Skill and age: an experimental approach*, Oxford Univ. Press, 1951.

WENGER, M. A., 'The measurement of individual differences in autonomic balance', *Psychosomatic Medicine* III, 4, 1941.

WHITING, B. B. ed., *Six cultures: studies of child rearing*, Wiley, N.Y., 1963.

WHITING, J. W. M. et al., *Child training and personality*, Yale Univ. Press, New Haven, 1953.

WHYTE, W. F., *Street corner society: the social structure of an Italian slum*, 2nd ed., Univ. Chicago Press, 1955.

WILKINS, L. T., *Delinquent generations*, Home Office Research Unit, London Research Report no. 3, H.M.S.O., 1960.

WILSON, R. C., 'Creativity', *N.S.S. ed. 57th Year Book*, Chicago Press, 1958.

WINCH, R. F., *Mate selection: a study of complementary needs*, Harper Bros., N.Y., 1958.

WITTENBORN, J. R., 'Inferring the strength of drive', *Nebraska Symposium*, ed. Jones, E. R., 1957.

WOLFE, D., 'Training', in Stevens, S. S., *Handbook of Experimental Psychology*, ed. Stevens, S. S., Wiley, N.Y., 1951.

WOLFF, D. H., 'Observations on the early development of smiling', *Determinants of Infant Behaviour*, II, ed. Foss, B., Methuen, 1963.

WOODWORTH, R. S. AND SELLS, S. B., 'An atmosphere effect in formal syllogistic reasoning', *J. exp. Psychol.* **18**, 1935.

YOUNG, J. W., *Lectures on fundamental concepts of algebra and geometry*, Macmillan, N.Y., 1911.
YOUNG, K., *Handbook of Social Psychology*, Kegan Paul, Trench, Trubner, 1946.
ZAPOROZHETS, A. V., 'The origin and development of the conscious control of movements in man', *Recent Soviet Psychology*, ed. O'Connor, Pergamon Press, 1961.
ZAZZO, R., 'Une Recherche d'équipe sur la débilité mentale', *Enfance*, Nombre Spécial, December, 1960.
ZUBEK, J. B. AND SOLBERG, P. A., *Human development*, McGraw-Hill, 1954.

Subject Index

Author Index